Art revolution
in the Roussillon

ISBN : 978-2-35073-759-1

Art revolution
in the Roussillon

Jane **Mann** & Brian **Cotton**

Les Presses Littéraires éditions

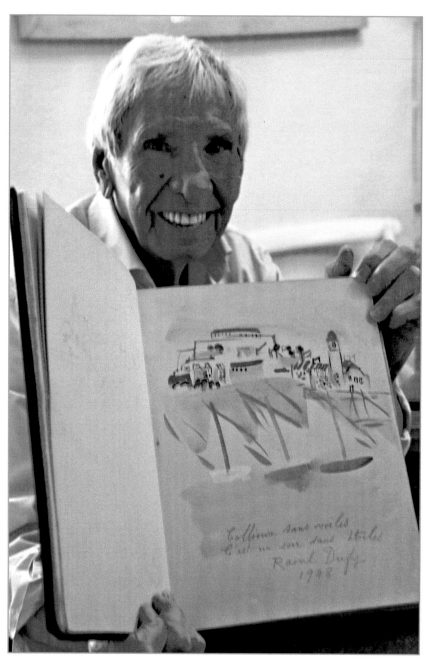

Jojo Pous with the Livre d'Or, Dufy page.

*This work is dedicated to Jojo Pous (1927-2013)
who sadly died as the book was going to press.*

Part I

Table of contents

Part II

Sketch map
of principal locations

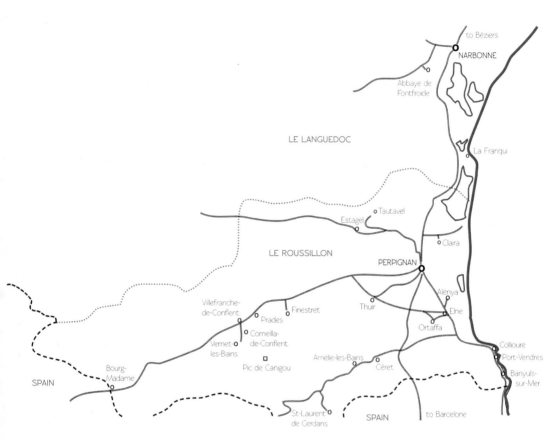

to Béziers

NARBONNE

Abbaye de
Fontfroide

LE LANGUEDOC

La Franqui

Tautavel

Estagel

Claira

LE ROUSSILLON

PERPIGNAN

Alénya

Villefranche-
de-Conflent

Finestret

Thuir

Prades

Elne

Cornella-
de-Conflent

Ortaffa

Vernet-
les-Bains

Collioure

Port-Vendres

Pic de Canigou

Amélie-les-Bains

Bourg-
Madame

Céret

Banyuls-
sur-Mer

SPAIN

St-Laurent
de Cerdans

SPAIN

to Barcelone

Introduction

The Roussillon, at the start of the twentieth century, was a very remote corner of France. Indeed, until the Treaty of the Pyrenees of 1659, it had not been part of France at all but belonged to the Kingdom of Aragon. The language of the region was Catalan, French was seldom spoken or understood, Paris was a very long way away and outsiders from the north were viewed with considerable misgivings. However, for artists wishing to recharge away from the hectic hubbub of the artistic life of the city, its distance from the capital was a distinct plus. Far from the restrictions of Paris academia they could concentrate fully on their art, undistracted by the outside world. Living was inexpensive, the weather was clement, the sun shone and the light was clear and bright.

The Roussillon of 1905 was unsophisticated and provincial. Villages like Collioure were smelly and ramshackle, provincial towns like Céret were small minded and introverted. This did not deter the visiting artists. In common with those who were born and brought up there, they needed the inspiration and interaction provided by Paris with its academies and annual exhibitions and, at the same time, they needed to get away. The northern artists came south to escape and the southern artists went north to benefit from the capital. There was a constant to-ing and fro-ing.

It was in this way that Matisse came to Collioure and Picasso to Céret. Here they painted with great fervour and concentration for relatively short periods of time.

Matisse, inspired by the colours and light of the Mediterranean, was outward looking and gave birth to the bright explosion of Fauvism

Jojo Pous in the Templiers Hotel

Rooftops, Céret

whilst Picasso was introspective looking and relatively uninfluenced by the landscape around him as he developed the angular images of Cubism. Matisse's paintings are full of light and bright colours, flowing lines and simplicity; Picasso's are sombre complex studies with browns and blacks predominating. Both contributed to the revolution that was taking place in the modern art of the twentieth century.

The ten years or so between 1905 and 1914 were a decade of astounding artistic activity in this remote region and this book tells some of the stories of the artists, both the outsiders and the locals, who made this happen.

This story is a tale of their interlocking lives, loves and approaches to art played out against a background of the Roussillon towns and landscape in which they lived and worked. Of course Paris comes into it as well. How could it not when it was so central to the world of art in France just as it still is today? Mainly, however, the Roussillon is the setting and the drama of the artistic revolution takes place against the Roussillon's remote and rugged backdrop.

Collioure view from beach

Prologue

This book was conceived one winter's day, in the upstairs room of the Templiers Hotel in Collioure, watching Jojo Pous turn the pages of the Hotel's visitors' book, *Le Livre d'Or*. Each page prompted a reminiscence, each reminiscence another story to be told. Listening to the stories it was impossible to ignore the artistic riches accumulating in this remote corner of France from the start of the twentieth century...

LES TEMPLiERS

Sign at Les Templiers, Collioure

The Templiers Hotel and Restaurant grew out of the Café des Sports inherited by René and Pauline Pous between the wars. Their son, Jojo, took over in the seventies and continued his father's tradition of welcoming artists, writers and entertainers, most of whom signed the Livre d'Or. In the bar of the Templiers Hotel Jojo Pous is to be found most afternoons, playing a never-ending game of cards with the same old men with whom he went to school as a boy. The bar itself, a carved Catalan boat, mermaid madonna at its prow, dominates the room full of paintings, some given, many bought by the Pous family over the years. His family's

Jojo Pous with the Livre d'Or - Volume II

connection with Collioure is told in the pictures crammed onto every centimetre of wall space. Dedicated to "René", to "Pauline and family", to "Pous, the artist's friend", to "Jojo". The pictures climb the stairs, fill the corridors and the bedrooms. They adorn the walls of the first floor room where we were sitting, where the rugby club meets and private parties are held, the room where Jojo was born.

The story they tell started between the wars when Pauline Frances married René Pous. Collioure, then, was a poor fishing village. The fishermen of anchovies and sardines were also wine growers. There

Bar of Hotel des Templiers, Collioure

François Bernadi page, the Livre d'Or

was no running water, there were open drains and plenty of cats. But it was becoming a centre for artists. Leaning on the bar of his Café des Sports, René Pous, welcomed them. He had been at school with Matisse's children, he enjoyed the company of artists.

One day, in 1927, the year his son Jojo was born, he went to the house of an artist named Leopold Survage to help him repair a lamp. René refused to be paid for his help. Survage gave him one of his canvases, a cubist view of the port. René hung it on the wall in the place of a publicity poster. Soon the walls of the Café des Sports began to fill with paintings. Artists came from far and wide to Collioure to paint and they stopped to drink chez René and Pauline. One of them, Augustin Hanicotte, round glasses and beret on his unruly hair, became part of the village scene after meeting Maillol in Banyuls-sur-Mer in 1915. He lived in Collioure for almost forty years and was one of René Pous's many friends. In 1925, with the collaboration of the local school, he started painting classes. "Les Gosses de Collioure" was the name he gave them. "The Kids of Collioure". He was a good teacher. He took the children out painting all around Collioure. He came up against the authorities and both he and the school had to fight to continue. They succeeded. He arranged exhibitions of the children's work not only in Perpignan but also in Paris, Cannes, Marseilles and Carcassonne. Several of those "gosses", François Bernadi and François Baloffi, to name but two, went on to become well known artists. Hanicotte's huge painting, almost 3 x 5 metres, of the beach of Collioure, full to overflowing with the daily life of the village and its villagers, is, thanks to Joséphine Matamoros, in the archives of Collioure's Peské Museum of Modern Art.

Another artist, Balbino Giner, frequented the Templiers bar and was a close friend of the Pous family. Jojo Pous describes him as a "delicious man and talented artist, so full of fun and life..." Many of his portraits of René, Pauline and Jojo Pous hang on the walls of the bar. His son, also an artist, also called Balbino Giner, lived and worked in Collioure.

On the spine of the first volume of the Livre d'Or of the Templiers is written:

CAFE DES SPORTS
LA COBA
RENÉ POUS ET FILS
COLLIOURE

Spine of the Livre d'Or Volume 1

The visitors book begins in 1948 when the Templiers Hotel and Restaurant was still the village café: the Café des Sports. Jojo Pous smiles as he points out *La Coba*. "My father opened *La Coba* as a night club for me to manage..."

With care and evident pride he opens the package containing the second volume:

LES TEMPLIERS
RENÉ ET JOJO POUS
COLLIOURE

The two volumes span sixty years of famous visitors, all friends of the Pous family, all leaving their mark in the form of paintings, scribbles, poems, good wishes.

As the pages turn, Jojo remembers each painter, journalist, singer, actor, sculptor, writer and poet to have contributed. They are his past, his present too. He grew up with them. From his father he learnt the importance of friendship, his memories are warm with fondness, uncloyed by nostalgia.

"Oh yes," he points to a drawing of a leaf with two faces, a poem and a signature, "this is the first one, Survage..." and he tells again of his father refusing money for some electrical work, taking, instead, a painting...

In fact the first signature, on the flyleaf, is that of the Polish artist, Willy Mucha who introduced Raoul Dufy to Collioure. Jojo, who never says anything against anyone, described him as sometimes "bizarre" but regarded him as a friend.

From the end of the war onwards Collioure became a Catalan version of St Tropez. Tourists started to appear, artists of all descriptions as well. And René Pous was the genial host of all. Edouard Pignon, friend of Picasso, Descossy the director of the Beaux-Arts of Montpellier... The list of illustrious names grew. René and Pauline opened a restaurant. They lodged their guests in a nearby property. In 1955 they opened the *Hotel des Templiers*. Jojo smiles as he recounts failing his *baccalauréat* explaining how there

Camille Descossy page, the Livre d'Or

was scant time for school as all the family had to work in the hotel. For him it never felt like work. It was a way of life.

The artists continued to give their paintings. René had become a patron of the arts. He gave gala evenings: Chevalier, Trenet, Piaf and Tino Rossi all sang in them. Stars, artists, all of them friends of the Pous family, illustrated the *Livre d'Or*. It was the golden age of Collioure.

And still the pages turn. The Dufy page, sold in poster form in every gallery, prompts Jojo to remember how he stood by his side as he painted it... Beneath the bright painting of Catalan boats sailing out of Collioure, the words:

> "Collioure without sails
> is a night without stars":
>
> *Collioure sans voiles*
> *C'est un soir sans étoiles*
>
> Raoul Dufy
> 1948

"...and this is Masse, this one Mucha, Willy Mucha..."

A few pages later and there is a pencil sketch of the cheeky profile of Maurice Chevalier in straw boater, and, beneath it:

"Not Dufy,
not Mucha

but (a swirling signature):

Maurice Chevalier, only possible thanks to René Pous."

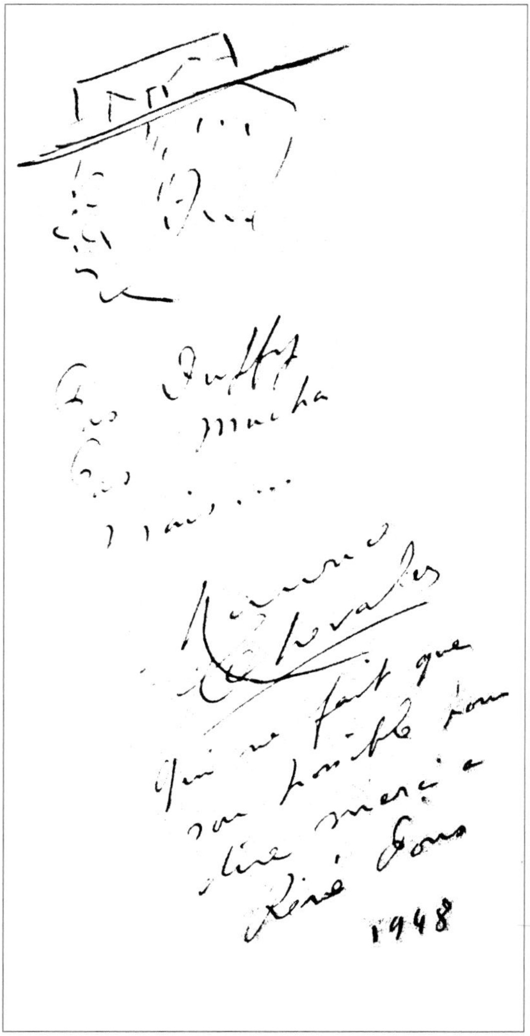

Maurice Chevalier
page, the Livre d'Or

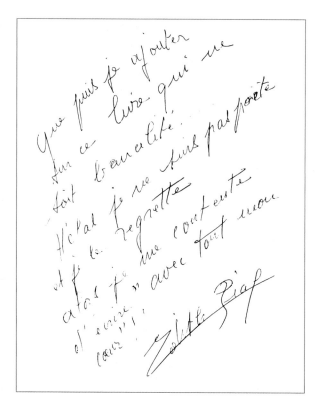

Edith Piaf page,
the Livre d'Or

Edith Piaf asks:

"What can I add to this book that would not be banal. Alas, I cannot paint and that I regret. So I am happy to write "with all my heart"

Edith Piaf

"She came to Collioure several times. She always stayed with us..."

Every page tells a new story, each story begging to be told.

Pignon, Pierre Brune, Poncelet, Perrot, Picasso, Matisse... Jojo pauses, "A delicious man, a wonderful man. He was a close family friend. My father would go and stay with him every year on the Côte d'Azur." In fact René Pous took the Livre d'Or to Nice one summer so that Matisse could add his page to those of the growing number of artists who had followed in his footsteps. His picture is of the Hotel de la Gare in memory of his first summer in Collioure with Derain in 1905.

A pencilled bull's head, Picasso 14th August 1953. "It took him about three seconds" said Jojo.

Antonio Machado plaque,
Collioure

1964 and Dalí has a Matador twirling in concentric circles down a page. "He didn't come here much, he was more Cadaqués, the other side... I never say Spain..." There are quite a few pages of artists and writers from "the other side". Many came to pay homage to Machado, the Spanish poet, buried in the little cemetery of Collioure. At the outbreak of the Spanish Civil War, a staunch republican, Antonio Machado left Madrid for Valencia and then Barcelona. In his elegy to the death of his close friend Lorca, "The crime was in Granada" it is easy to feel the despair that was beginning to affect Machado. He took the road to exile. At Portbou, a friend explained to the French police commander "Antonio Machado was to Spain what

Paul Valéry was to France..." and that "he and his mother were ill and could not continue on foot." The good police chief lent them his car in which they were driven to Cerbère. There they had to shelter in sub zero conditions in a railway wagon before driving to Collioure the next day. Dispirited and depressed, Machado, his frail, aged mother and his brother found lodgings in Collioure. He died on the 22nd of February 1939, his mother died three days later. It is easy to recognize his tomb. It is always covered with flowers.

Charles Rennie Mackintosh the Glaswegian architect/designer/ artist, did not sign the Livre d'Or. He had a closer connection with Port-Vendres where he lived and worked for the last four years of his life. However he and his wife Margaret were also part of the art scene in Collioure in the mid twenties and probably stayed a few months there. Margaret was remembered by René Pous, as "the woman with the red hair". She cut a striking figure with her blaze of auburn hair, dressed in the clothes she designed herself. Mackintosh described her as his "spirit key. My other half... more than half, she is three quarters of all I have done... I had the talent but she had the genius. We made a pair."

Musicians are also well represented. Saint Saens in 1973, Rostropovich signed in 1983, Josephine Baker never sang in Collioure but she stayed at the Templiers and she too signed the book.

Jojo laughs at a double page signed by the artist, H. Dirosa. In vivid colours the bell tower of the church has a nose, two eyes and large ears... "He said that's my nose!" All around the page in capital letters "For the first time in Collioure: The adventures of Jojo la Tour! He is a brilliant artist, abstract, impressionist, surreal, real, funny too."

Desnoyer, Savary, Jean Pau, Julien Py... the pages turn, the list goes on. Bernadi, "he was Hanicotte's best pupil and yes, I was one of the Gosses de Collioure and no, I have never been a painter. No time. Hanicotte was a wonderful man..." Again Jojo smiles as he remembers.

Pierre Brune. He too was an habitué of the Templiers bar, he too has a page.

Robert Savary page, the Livre d'Or

A René [...] et Collir.
De SETE [...]
DESNOYER

Francis Desnoyer page, the Livre d'Or

Jean Jacques Prolongeau, another page where Jojo hesitates. "He knew all the family well, he did the balcony here at the Templiers, a great artist, great ceramicist too. He used to work with Dufy...with Desnoyer as well... He was Director of the Beaux-Arts in Perpignan. He died too young, his widow moved away. I bought his house, we live there now..."

He stops again at a page covered with bold red cubes. The work of Claude Viallat. At Jojo's invitation he painted the walls of the restaurant... In Paris Viallat's work is exhibited behind safety barriers, in the Templiers restaurant it lives and breathes, admired and enjoyed by all who dine there.

On another page, after the dedication in French to René and Jojo Pous with much praise for the *soupe de poissons* of Pauline Pous, is a description of Collioure in English "...Down the middle runs a dried-up river-bed, a street on its left hand, the aorta of the town. On summer evenings the vital flow goes by peacefully, both to and fro for this is where the village heart is found, a restaurant, a café and a place where you can eat like a lord or where you and fishermen and masons may play most passionately at cards or sit mutely happy in the warmth

Pour René et Jojo Pous, en souvenir de je ne sais combien
de bons dîners (ah le soupe de poissons de Pauline, oh le
pigeon de mer sur son lit) toujours succulents mais surtout
... dans une ambiance aimable, détendue, amicale

    A tight-packed village like a swarm of bees
    the sea in three great curves and they
    divided by a holy lighthouse and
    a vast great castle quite as old a lime
    A village loved by Matisse Derain Picasso and the sun

    Down the middle runs a dried-up river-bed,
    a street on its left hand, the aorta of the town
    on summer evenings the vital flow
    goes by perpetually, both to and fro
    for this is where the village heart is found
    a restaurant a café and a place
    where you can eat like a lord or where
    you are fishermen and mascus may
    play music passionately at carts
    or sit simply happy in the warmth surrounded by the general sound of talk
    while geckos walk upon the wall
    and the small owl calls gloc gloc

                Patrick O'Brian

Patrick O'Brian
page, Livre d'Or

surrounded by the general sound of talk while geckos walk upon the wall and the small owl calls gloc gloc." The signature is that of Patrick O'Brian, historical novelist and biographer of Picasso. He too lived for many years in Collioure.

Jojo took over in the '70s. The huge collection of paintings had no order. Some have been stolen, some destroyed in a flood. Many remain, and Jojo adds to them from time to time. His second wife, Joséphine Matamoros, was the Director of both the Museum of Modern Art in Céret and in Collioure. How different the ordered art on their walls from the "pagaille" (higgledy-piggledy clutter) as Jojo calls it of the art in the living museum of his hotel. Recently, they have been re-hung, the nicotine stained walls repainted, but the impression of abundance, of artistic exuberance, remains.

Jojo Pous with H. Dirota page, the Livre d'Or

Jojo Pous is a charming man. His father's son, he is the perfect host, generous with his time, faithful to his friends. He says he had a charmed childhood, "*une enfance radieuse*". He is right. Under his family's roof the stars of the art world, plus the actors, musicians, singers, journalists and writers met. The bull-fighters changed in the room in which he was born. He may, as he claims, have no artistic talent, he has, nevertheless, a talent for cultivating artists.

Les Templiers letter heading

Part 1

Gustave Fayet – Maison d'Utrillo

Chapter 1

The history of art
in the first half of the twentieth century

In which the story of the part the Roussillon played in the history of art in the first half of the twentieth century begins to unfold.

In the second half of the nineteenth century, the far south western corner of France known as the Roussillon, was a bit of an artistic backwater. Remote, windswept, rugged, and predominantly (albeit sparsely) populated by Catalan people, many of whom spoke not a word of French, it was not exactly centre stage in terms of art. But, from 1856 onwards, from this backwater sprang five artists all of whom would play a part in changing this perception of their birthplace. And, in the same period, two more artists were born, one in the north of France and the other in the south of Spain, who were to place the Roussillon firmly on the art map of the world forever.

The locals...

George Daniel de Monfreid was born in 1856. His mother, Caroline, was a talented and successful singer from Toulouse when, in Paris, in 1854, she caught the eye of Gideon James T. Reed, a visiting jeweller and dealer in precious stones from Boston. His enterprise was called the Reed and Tiffany Company, later known simply as Tiffany & Co. Both were married: Gideon James T. Reed to Rebecca, a fervent spiritualist; the young singer to a solid citizen of Toulouse, called Jacoby. Reed, aware that the puritan atmosphere of nineteenth century Boston would not allow for extra-marital affairs, even with glamorous French singer actresses, installed his mistress in Paris. Despite the distance involved, so great was his passion and so boundless his energy (and wealth) that he managed to lead a double life on both sides of the Atlantic. No planes, no internet, this was no mean feat in the mid 1800's.

He also managed to have Monsieur Jacoby removed to South America.

Le Château St Clément,
Corneilla-de-Conflent

When George Daniel was born, he took his mother's invented name of de Monfreid, a name she felt suited the life of the wealthy aristocrat she aspired to be. "Uncle Reed" was a frequent visitor in their Paris home.

The family enjoyed taking the waters at Vernet-les-Bains, a spa town in the foothills of the French Pyrenees. They fell in love with the area and built a gracious country mansion on the site of farmhouse in the valley. Caroline de Monfreid indulged her taste for the grandiose by adding towers and called it le Château St Clément. George Daniel spent much of his childhood holidays surrounded by mountains and orchards in the grounds of his mother's country retreat.

He was educated in Switzerland and, at an early age, decided to become an artist. Thanks to "Uncle Reed" this posed no problem, and, by 1874 he was studying at the Académies Julian and Colarossi in Paris.

A year later, a precociously talented seventeen-year-old Etienne Terrus (1857-1922) also arrived in the capital. A couple of years younger than George Daniel, he had been born in Elne, the ancient Roman capital of Roussillon on the plain between Perpignan and the Spanish frontier. His father was a house painter and glazier whose family had, for generations, lived in the shadow of the vast cathedral, high up on the huge river stone ramparts of the old town.

Old postcard of Elne Cathedral and town ramparts

Young Etienne Terrus excelled at art at an early age and was apprenticed to Alexandre Cabanel in Paris where, in common with his fellow students, he was set to copying the old masters.

Paris life did not suit Etienne Terrus. He longed for the rural peace of his beloved Roussillon countryside. He got through his Beaux-Arts years under Cabanel as swiftly as possible.

Banyuls-sur-Mer was just a small fishing village when Aristide Bonaventure Jean Maillol was born there in 1861. In Banyuls, men who did not fish, worked the vines. Indeed the word *maillol* means a young grapevine in Catalan. The Maillol family, then, as now, produced the naturally sweet wine for which the town is famous. They farmed olives, kept goats. When the railway arrived in the mid eighteen fifties, a few rather grand villas were built along the sea front promenade. Bathing in the sea was becoming fashionable

Old postcard of beach of Banyuls-sur-Mer

despite over a hundred fishing boats being pulled onto the beach daily. The river was still used by the local washerwomen, and, on the whole, life in Banyuls was pretty simple and basic.

Aristide, the fourth of six children, was brought up by his forty four year old maiden aunt, Lucie, who had returned from Algeria to look after her father, a retired fisherman and part time smuggler. Being so close to the Spanish frontier, smuggling was a common enough sideline for fishermen at the time. Salt, tobacco, silver, sugar, rice, textiles, and leather were smuggled through Banyuls, almost always with impunity. The young boy adored his grandfather, listening spellbound to his tales of seafaring and contraband. Each day he would lead his grandfather to a sunny bench on the seashore so that, as he later told his close friend, Henri Frère "...he could meet other sailors like him. They sat there, having a kind of reunion, passing the time. I myself was so small that I sat leaning on my grandfather's legs. I used to listen to the talks. I still remember my grandfather's knees, which were so big..."

At thirteen, Maillol's first painting was of a sailor. He had already decided on a career as an artist.

This decision was not popular in a family of drapers, winemakers and fishermen. However, Tante Lucie ran a small shop whose proceeds allowed her to pay for Maillol to have art lessons after school in Perpignan. The only portrait he painted of her shows her sitting bolt upright, simple and neat, her large, work worn hands resting in her lap. It is clear he respected her immensely. It remained the only picture in the dining room of Maillol's Banyuls house to the end of his days. It is now in the Maillol Museum in Paris.

His art lessons consisted mostly of copying art in the museum. Aristide formed a low opinion of his art teacher and, considering him to be a waste of Tante Lucie's money, refused his lessons, preferring instead to go to the museum to study alone. The furious and offended teacher had him banned from the museum. Tante Lucie pleaded with the Mayor of Perpignan to get the order revoked without success. He was not allowed back. However he had had time to admire the work of Gabriel Farail, an up and coming local sculptor. Farail's sculpture of a girl with a snail, still in Perpignan's Musée Rigaud, enchanted Maillol.

He also realised that to succeed in art, it was essential to go to the capital.

It took him until 1882 to get there.

Farail's Young Girl with Snail

At the northern extreme of the Roussillon, actually in the Languedoc, on the 20th of May 1865, Gustave Fayet was born in Béziers into a family of wealthy land owners and wine producers. He was to become both a firm friend of Maillol and, thanks to George Daniel de Monfreid, one of the most extensive collectors of Gauguin ever known. It was the beginning of Béziers's golden age, a period of economic and cultural development in which members of Gustave Fayet's family were among the leading lights. He had a charmed childhood. His father, Gabriel Fayet and his uncle, Léon Fayet, were art collectors, artists themselves and lovers of music. Young Gustave followed naturally in their footsteps.

Old postcard of Béziers

Fayet was educated at the Dominican Brothers college in Sorèze, as were Maurice Fabre and Déodat de Sévérac, both of whom were to play a part in his later life.

His own description of his home upbringing "by symphonies of colour, by love of pure lines and a knowledge of precious materials and objects ... in an artistic atmosphere leading to art..." allowed and encouraged him to grow up loving and appreciating all forms of art.

It was felt he had no need of a Beaux-Arts education. His natural artistic and musical talents, fostered by his father and uncle, saved him from the rigours of a Paris *Académie* just as his family's wealth ensured he never suffered the poverty-stricken-Paris-from-the-garret experience of so many of the young artists pouring into the capital at the time. His family knew Paris well. Gustave Fayet was no stranger to the salons, galleries and dealers concentrated around the Ecole des Beaux-Arts.

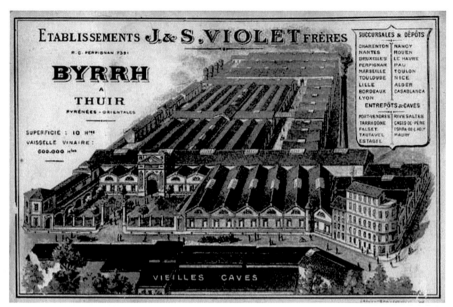

Etablissements Byrrh

Marshalling yard at Byrrh designed by Eiffel

Just as de Monfreid was beginning his student life at the Beaux-Arts in Paris, Gustave Violet, the fifth of our local heroes, was born in Prades in 1873. His father Pallade and his uncle Simon, had, in the early 1800's, been market traders, selling haberdashery all over the Pyrénées Orientales. In the middle of the century they opened a shop in the market town of Thuir. Soon afterwards the brothers invested their haberdashery takings in a small wine cellar in which they created an aperitif they called Byrrh made of local wine laced with quinine. It was first sold in pharmacies as a tonic and became so popular that, by the time young Gustave Violet was born in 1873, the family had become immensely wealthy.

When his father, Pallade, died leaving his mother with five children, the ten-year old Gustave was sent to live in Prades with his maternal Aunt Lavail.

Today, when driving round Prades towards Villefranche-de-Conflent, Corneilla-de-Conflent and the de Monfreid's Château St Clément, it is possible to catch a glimpse of a small chapel and, through the trees, the crenellations and towers of a large white mansion. Nowadays a tall wall of massive quarry stones protects it from the road and the outbuildings look in a sorry state, windows broken, the garden overgrown. A hundred years ago it was a lively and creative place, one of the preferred venues of the Roussillon artists. It is the home Gustave Violet built when he married, and where his children Pallade and Jeanne were born and grew up...

But that is getting ahead of the story...

From 1883 he spent the rest of his childhood and adolescence with his aunt, arriving in Paris to study architecture at the Beaux-Arts in 1894 when he was twenty-one.

Chapelle St Marti, Prades

And it is to PARIS, or, at least mostly, Paris that we need to go next...

George Daniel de Monfreid's student life in Paris was interrupted when, in 1876, he became ill. His doctor recommended that he spend time by the seaside. Swimming in the sea was a popular cure at the time. Leucate, a windswept seaside town between Narbonne and Perpignan and not too far from Corneilla-de-Conflent, was chosen. Dominated by lagoons, with vast expanses of sandy beaches, pine trees bent double by the wind, Leucate-La Franqui was becoming a fashionable and successful *Station Balnéaire*. The Domaine de La Franqui was owned and run by Antoine Bertrand and his wife Anna. They had a beautiful, brown haired, blue-eyed daughter called Amélie. She was older than George Daniel by seven years, had been married and had a daughter. However, her alcoholic husband had died of excessive drinking and the child had also died before reaching the age of three.

Amélie and George Daniel fell in love and were married the following year, in Paris. A strangely assorted group consisting of "Uncle Reed" with limited French and a strong American accent, a nervous Caroline de Monfreid and the bronzed Antoine and Anna Bertrand, away from their native Languedoc for the first time, celebrated the marriage in the Grand Hotel, a venue much favoured by visiting transatlantic businessmen.

Amélie and George Daniel de Monfreids' first son was born at La Franqui but only survived five days. Two years later, in 1879, in the coldest November weather of the century, their son, Henri Léon Romain de Monfreid was born, also at La Franqui. He was their only child, and grew up to be an adventurer, drug runner and writer. George Daniel wished him to have a free and wonderful childhood, running wild by the sea. This he did while his parents divided their time between 31 rue Saint-Placide, Paris and La Franqui. In La Franqui, George Daniel bought *le Follet*, a ten-metre yacht with a typically Mediterranean triangular lateen sail. He became known as the *capitaine à la casque blanche*. He began writing up his voyages for the prestigious magazine *le Yacht*. He was passionate about sailing often spending whole summers on his yacht with friends.

When autumn came he would return to Paris and resume his studies. A fellow student at the Académie Colarossi was Emile Schuffenecker, a stockbroker turned artist known familiarly as Schuff. Schuff, a small, dark-bearded Alsatian, had a mild and hesitant manner. He was timid and prudent and he could be extremely boring. Unlikely as it seems, his best friend at the time was another ex-stockbroker turned artist, Paul Gauguin. Their friendship followed the course of most of Gauguin's relationships: patronising affection on Gauguin's side, an admiration not far short of worship, on the side of Schuffenecker.

Seascape from the cliffs above La Franqui

In Paris, from 1880 onwards, the de Monfreids entertained a wide range of artists, writers and musicians every Saturday. Degas, Vuillard, Renoir, Valtat, Maurice Denis, Déodat de Sévérac as well as Terrus, Louis Bausil, and, later, Gustave Violet were all frequent visitors. It was an illustrious group and friendships were formed that would last their lifetimes.

George Daniel took particular care of the newly arrived Aristide Maillol.

The Paris that greeted Maillol on his arrival in 1882 was a Paris that had already been re-designed by Haussmann. It was beautiful, impressive and scarily imposing for a young man from a small seaside town in one of the most distant corners of France. Furthermore Maillol had very little money. His family's wine fortunes were foundering thanks to the phylloxera plague that was sweeping French vineyards. He had to survive on his allowance from Tante Lucie and the scholarship from the Préfecture in Perpignan amounting to a total of two francs a day.

He repeatedly failed the entrance examination for the Ecole des Beaux-Arts and so enrolled in the sculpture course of the Decorative Art School. He rented a room in a dark slum district.

Maillol suffered from chronic malnutrition, and was often in hospital. Sometimes he thought of "bringing things to an end by throwing myself into the Seine." His daily journey was a forty-five minute walk from his room to the school passing the Louvre Palace, crossing the Seine and entering the gate of the art school. There he started drawing classical sculptures in Professor Gérôme's class. Finally, on 17 March 1885, at the age of twenty-three, Maillol was accepted by the Ecole des Beaux-Arts. He was sixty-fourth of the eighty successful candidates out of the two hundred and twenty three seeking entry and attended the class of Cabanel for four years.

George Daniel de Monfreid visited Maillol in his first "studio". De Monfreid's description sums up Maillol's situation pretty succinctly: "He rented a cheap attic which was well lit by its two dormer windows and called it "his atelier". The room was without a ceiling and was directly beneath the zinc roof. It was freezing in winter and the heat in summer was intolerable. To get there, one had to climb up the stairs in the dark, hitting lead sewers on the wall that were open to let the tenants dispose of dirty water and worse. The place was filled with bad smells of ammonia but due to the darkness one could not see much. One followed a sticky handrail as if it had been the string of

Ariadne, and I have to admit that certain courage was needed to go higher up on this staircase. Fortunately there were only three storeys, and in the end it got a little bit better lit by a skylight obscured by spider's webs.

There were many doors. Onto one of them, a small paper was tacked by a pin: **Aristide Maillol, Artist-Painter, knock hard."**

De Monfreid's own life was very different. In 1883 a generous gift from Uncle Reed had enabled him to purchase his second yacht, a twenty-two a metre schooner, from a ruined Marquis. He called her *l'Amélie* and took his wife and six-year-old son to Algiers on a memorable voyage made difficult by quarantine restrictions in both Spain and Algeria. He continued to write illustrated articles for *Le Yacht. Le capitaine à la casque blanche* was a familiar sight along the French and Spanish Mediterranean.

For three years Maillol shared his room with Achille Laugé, a fellow student. They also shared their scant resources and ate sparingly of bread, sausages, or potatoes. Tante Lucie sent him as much money as she could and also a hamper of good Roussillon fruit and vegetables each month. His pride, his determination and above all the solidarity of his fellow student artists kept him going.

Laugé prepared the fire and peeled the vegetables that Maillol then cooked, following recipes he'd learned from Tante Lucie. With no money to hire models, they painted apples.

"I had not met Cézanne but painted more apples than Cézanne. It was the period of apples," said Maillol, referring to it also as "the period we wasted our time."

It was a period of amusing memories as well...

"It was at the Café des Ambassadeurs that I made my first decoration after my arrival in Paris. Yes, I decorated the Ambassadeurs!" Maillol and some friends had been employed to do some interior decorating in order to earn a little money but in the end, Maillol was the only one among them to be paid. The director found him completely incompetent and fired him. He settled Maillol's outstanding pay, but the others, who continued to work, did not get paid as the employer went bankrupt. It was a story that amused Maillol, as was his tale of decorating the Moulin Rouge: he painted two clowns to replace a painting that had been burnt in a fire a few years before. The completion of the decoration was celebrated with much revelry. Maillol was disguised as a charcoal crayon in a costume of green tights and black sleeves and gloves. The festivities were concluded by the dancers of the Moulin Rouge carrying him in a triumphant march ending with them ripping off all his clothes. Including the green tights.

In common with all artists at the time, Maillol learned to work in every medium possible. Painting, drawing, tapestry, engraving, sculpture, ceramics. Tapestry had always been one of his passions, and, inspired by the beautiful late fifteenth century examples he saw in the Musée de Cluny, he experimented with making his own dyes from plants and herbs he collected in the countryside surrounding Banyuls.

George Daniel de Monfreid – Hommage à Gauguin (détail)

Chapter 2
Under the Influence

Under the Influence – in which de Monfreid falls under the influence of Gauguin.

As the nineteenth century drew to a close, France could boast 22,967 artists, painters, musicians, writers and sculptors and most of them were registered in Paris. The de Monfreid Saturdays were a part of the social round that made up *l'Art Moderne* and George Daniel was a perfect host. Modest as far as his own paintings were concerned, he gave away more of them than he sold. He loved good wine and pretty women. He was a faithful and wonderful friend, an unfaithful and less than perfect husband. He had abandoned the Académie Julian but still frequented the Académie Colarossi where he and Emile Schuffenecker had been students some years earlier. And it was in Schuffenecker's studio in 1887 that de Monfreid first met Paul Gauguin.

Gauguin was a giant of a man, godlike, immensely proud though often penniless, with a huge beak of a nose, hooded green eyes and a lazy voice. He was fond of describing his exotic genealogy, claiming descent from a Borgia of Aragon and the viceroy of Peru. He was proud of his Inca and possibly even Polynesian heritage. His grandmother, Flora Tristan y Moscoso had the blood of France, Peru and royal Spain in her veins. Therefore he, Paul Gauguin, had it too... He would announce, proudly "I'm a savage," explaining later, "I come from the Borgias of Aragon, but – I am also a savage." He was also fast becoming the artist whose paintings and life-style would shock, inspire and enrich artists and collectors for generations to come.

Their first meeting was not a great success. De Monfreid, eight years younger than Gauguin, was a tall, distinguished looking man with a long, aristocratic face; he was bronzed and golden bearded and had rather prominent blue eyes. Although de Monfreid appeared both daring and courageous, neither quality was apparent in his painting. Gauguin knew only too well that Schuff's friends were often suspect in terms of their artistic skills and his first impression of de Monfreid was of a man playing at being an artist.

De Monfreid noted that, "at first he was unsympathetic towards me..."

Old postcard of **Paris** *Exposition universelle*

However, de Monfried had money, a fact Gauguin could not ignore. And, as soon as de Monfreid had seen Gauguin's painting, he became a gentle but unshakeable follower. "It was a revelation to me", he said, "I understood what Gauguin was seeking and at the same moment I realised the falsity of all that I had learned about art." From then on, as Maurice Denis said, "he consecrated his life to his friendship for Gauguin and sacrificed his personal pride as an artist to the glory of Gauguin"...

Paris, in 1889, was celebrating the centenary of the French Revolution. The Eiffel Tower had just been completed and, on the esplanade of the Champ de Mars, the great *Exposition Universelle* was about to open. The academic painters would be represented in the Palais des Beaux-Arts Pavilion whilst the more revolutionary, unacademic painters, amongst whom featured Gauguin, Louis Roy, Anquetin, Bernard, Schuffenecker and de Monfreid, not at all. The much vaunted world fair would attract large crowds and would provide precisely the publicity needed by Gauguin and his group.

It was the trusty Schuffenecker who had the innovative idea of persuading Monsieur Volpini, proprietor of Le Grand Café des Beaux-Arts, to cover his walls with the paintings of Gauguin and his friends. The mirrors that were to decorate the Café walls in time for the opening of the *Exposition Universelle* had not arrived, their paintings could hang in their place.

Poster of **Volpini** *Exhibition 1889*

The "Volpini Exhibition" in the summer of 1889 at the very gate of the *Exposition Universelle* was a brilliant move. Gauguin, de Monfreid, Schuffenecker and their companions had a poster and an illustrated catalogue printed, on the cover of which was Gauguin's *Woman and Wave*. The faithful Schuff had proved himself not only a good friend but a skilful negotiator. Gauguin, Louis Roy, Anquetin, Bernard, Schuffenecker and de Monfreid filled the café with their pictures...The Volpini Exhibition was both a success and a scandal. The public contemplated the host of "*strange*" canvases through a haze of tobacco smoke, lulled by an orchestra thoughtfully provided by the astute Volpini. Leaning back in their seats they joined in the choruses of the popular songs and wondered what had become of the Impressionists whose paintings they were just beginning to appreciate.

Nothing sold.

This was hardly a problem for George Daniel who had few financial worries.

One person particularly affected by the Volpini Exhibition was young Aristide Maillol. De Monfreid introduced him to Gauguin. As it happened Gauguin had already seen Maillol's work in Brussels where, in the 1880's, a series of exhibitions were held of an avant-garde group of artists known as the le *Cercle des XX*. Maillol had been showing a tapestry, Gauguin several paintings.

"Gauguin's painting was a revelation to me," declared Maillol. "L'Ecole des Beaux-Arts, instead of leading me to the light, had led me away from it. When I looked at Gauguin's pictures, I felt inspired by the same spirit which had prompted his work."

Gauguin encouraged Maillol to concentrate on his tapestry. Later, in his long correspondence with de Monfreid, Gauguin would often ask for news of Maillol. "You haven't written of Maillol recently. Is he still making masterpieces of tapestries?" (May 1899) or "It is deplorable that poor Maillol is suffering from his extreme poverty. He is an artist, a man with a heart of gold." (August 1899) There is no record of Gauguin ever writing to Maillol himself.

Fittingly, in 1898, in the salon of Monfreid's Château St Clément in Corneilla-de-Conflent, next to one of his many Gauguins, George Daniel de Monfreid hung one of Maillol's tapestries.

Maillol always claimed that "It was Gauguin and Maurice Denis who, after I left the school, opened my eyes. Thanks to them, I succeeded in clearing the first hurdle."

Much later Maillol's advice to beginners was to "Start by copying masters. One time, when I was at a loss," he would say, "I said to myself, 'I shall do a Gauguin.' And I work in Gauguin's way. This gives me an idea, makes me get out of mumbling. It is necessary to have an aim. Then, one can forget it and start doing something else on one's own. But the idea of what is the art remains."

Gauguin once said he felt he was "trying to try everything and liberate a new generation." Maillol certainly felt "liberated" by seeing his work.

At about this time Gabriel Farail, whose *Girl with a Snail* had so impressed him in Perpignan, introduced Maillol to a wealthy industrialist cousin. Following Farail's advice, the cousin commissioned Maillol to paint his three daughters. They were romantic paintings, one of which, *Young Girl in a Hat*, hangs in the Musée Rigaud in Perpignan.

The Conseil Général required a painting a year from him in exchange for their grant. Maillol always sent the smallest canvas possible. They asked for something larger. "If you send me more money I would be able to afford larger canvases!" he replied. They sent more money and received a large and most beautiful painting of the Farail girls in a meadow by a river, making crowns of flowers.

His paintings were filled with the light and the breeze of the first day of summer. In them time stands still; the girls and young women are dreamlike, eternal.

Commissions followed.

Gauguin's influence over Maillol was considerable. His paintings of this period resemble those of Gauguin in their luminous colours, their flat and decorative composition. However, behind Gauguin's one can almost sense a man of middle age with a difficult and troublesome ego whereas Maillol's have the lyrical feel of a child playing by the seaside.

Indeed his seaside life in Banyuls-sur-Mer continued to have a certain childlike charm about it. Maillol and his group of friends and fellow artists would meet from time to time at Château l'Esparrou, home of the Sauvy family on the coast near Canet. On one occasion they decided to stage Shakespeare's The Tempest. Maillol painted the scenery.

Gustave Violet's mansion in Prades was another popular venue. He had a kiln in the grounds and Etienne Terrus had a room in one of the towers. Together Violet and Terrus would paint the neighbouring landscape, talk and drink long into the night. There they felt in tune with their surroundings, and, firmly rooted in the south, strove to get away from the academic painting imposed by Paris, in order to maintain the simplicity and strength of their southern roots.

Back in Paris, before leaving for Tahiti, Gauguin had become a frequent visitor at the de Monfreid's home at 31 rue Saint-Placide. The young Henry de Monfreid watched the hold Gauguin had over his father and drank in the artist's tales of travelling and adventures. George Daniel had lent Gauguin his studio. The two men had fallen into the habit of walking together during the previous winter. They made a striking couple, the dark, broad almost corpulent Gauguin and the tall, thin, gaunt-faced de Monfreid with his hollow eyes, receding fair hair and long yellowish beard. De Monfreid knew Gauguin to be a difficult man but had no doubt about his greatness; Gauguin responded to the aristocrat in de Monfreid.

Although both were suffering from difficulties with their marriages, they had very different agendas for solutions. De Monfreid was separated from his wife and hoping for a divorce. Gauguin, estranged from his Danish wife and five children, was ready to sympathize with the trials of any husband and would listen coolly to stories of divorce, but the thought of permanent separation from his own wife and family never crossed his mind.

When he left for Tahiti, George Daniel promised to look after Gauguin's last model, Annette Bofils, with whom he fell in love. In 1892 the de Monfreids separated. George Daniel took up residence in Château St Clément in Corneilla-de-Conflent. He gave La Franqui to Amélie. He made a few voyages on his yacht and began making studies of *Le Calvaire* his monumental and only sculpture which can now be seen in the new church in Vernet-les-Bains. With his fellow Roussillon artists Violet and Fayet, he began experimenting with stained glass.

Gauguin wrote from Tahiti:

> "... I see by your letter that you have been in the South and that you are busy with the divorce. But you don't tell me how it is turning out. Inevitably one makes so many troubles for oneself by marriage – that stupid institution!

...see what I did with my household... I want to finish my life here, in this house, in perfect quiet. Ah, yes, I am a great criminal. What does it matter? So was Michelangelo; and I am not Michelangelo.

Many greetings to our friends and to Annette. Yours as always, Paul Gauguin."

Gustave Fayet, at much the same time, was happily marrying Madeleine d'Andoque. They honeymooned in Venice, installed themselves in a comfortable house in rue du Capus in Béziers and had five children. He visited all the grand European capitals, drawing inspiration from each visit. His grandson, Gilles d'Andoque, remembers his much loved grandfather as a man who, "radiated joy and kindness and consideration, a man who spread happiness among all around him." He was, according to Gilles, "an exquisite being, delicate, generous and spiritual, adoring his children, adoring nature, adoring his friends..." He loved the modern art he collected while painting himself; admired famous composers while playing the piano with a skill learned from playing four hands with his father as a child. He had a sharp wit and no time for pretensions.

He was no stranger to Paris and it was there that, through his old school friend Maurice Fabre, fellow proprietor of many vineyards and a serious art collector, that he met many of the artists whom Fabre considered to be the masters of the future. Van Gogh, Cézanne and Odilon Redon for example, were proof of the accuracy of Fabre's judgement.

One day, in a salon on the Champs-Elysées, Fayet noticed a couple he later described as, "as strange as they were magnificent". The man was large, his look hard, strikingly splendid and energetic. He wore a Bolivar hat and a long blue overcoat with golden buttons and carried a cane. His companion, a tall negress, was dressed in canary yellow with an orange scarf around her head and, on her hands, white gloves : "Gauguin," Fayet was told, "a man who likes to be noticed but who has no talent..." The young woman, Annah la Javanaise, originally from Malaysia, was thirteen.

Maurice Fabre introduced Fayet to writers, musicians, artists and dealers and to George Daniel de Monfreid. In de Monfreid's studio in rue Liancourt, on the 24th of October, 1900, Fayet bought his first two paintings by "the untalented man who liked to be noticed...". They were the beginning of a collection of over a hundred Gauguins, more than any museum in the world has ever possessed.

Fayet's own early paintings, glowing with rich colours, were shown in regional salons as well as the Paris Salon des Artistes Français in 1896, 1897 and 1898. He favoured dramatic violets and oranges and always wrote his letters in purple ink.

In the mid 1890's when Gustave Violet arrived in Paris to study architecture at the Beaux-Arts under Gaston Redon, most of our local heroes were in the capital.

All, that is, except Maillol who, with the trusty Tante Lucie, had started a tapestry studio in Banyuls. They took on three young workers, Angélique, Narcisse and Clotilde, daughters of Narcisse the baker. Maillol and Clotilde fell in love. Maillol was thirty-two and Clotilde sixteen. She loved accompanying him on his mountain walks in search of herbs for dyeing, a time he remembered as among his "most beautiful hours; the whole mountain saw my wife nude. She was beautiful... It was the happiest time in my life."

He continued his studies, exhibited paintings and portraits, designed tapestries. In the tapestry studio he began carving oddments of cherry and olive wood. He enjoyed what he made and continued to experiment, firstly with bas-relief then with small statuettes. The workshop was supported by Princess Bibesco who bought several tapestries including *Music for a Bored Princess* that can now be seen in the Statend Museum fur Kunst in Copenhagen.

Maillol took Clotilde back to Paris with him where they lived in considerable penury. He tried to make a living by teaching drawing. "She posed for me in the cold. In the period of great poverty, she endured hunger with me without complaining. This is unforgettable."

Who knows how they would have survived without the friendship and hospitality of the de Monfreids, as extracts from George Daniel's diary relate:

> "5 May 1897. I came home to find Maillol trying to fire several pieces of pottery in my stove but they had already been cracked. His wife arrived around half past eleven to have lunch with us, as they are without money. The Maillols arrived again at half past seven for dinner. Remaining in their cash box: zero francs and zero centimes."

> "8 May. I visited Maillol. I invited him and his wife for lunch, as they are without a penny."

"11 May. In the morning Maillol came to fire ceramics. I went for Mme. Maillol at their house on the Saint-Jacques Street."

"12 May. Maillol came at half past eight to cast a small statuette and to fire clay. Mme. Maillol came around half past six to join her husband, who came back to finish his casting, and they had dinner."

"15 May. The Maillols came to lunch. As they have nothing to eat, we feed them."

"17 May. The Maillols had lunch."

"18 May. The Maillols came to have lunch and told us that they would be able to leave for the country thanks to a statuette they had sold."

A friend remembers the firings of the ceramics as somewhat dramatic: "Maillol heated his oven. The glaze he wanted to have on his ceramic fountain needed even more heat, but then his neighbours started to shout, 'Fire in the attic!' Maillol heated the oven even more, climbed up to the attic with buckets to stop the fire, descended to heat the oven again, and then returned to the fire."

Maillol and Clotilde were married in Paris in July 1896. Pictures of the Maillol family taken by de Monfreid in this period show a young, handsome and sturdy Clotilde.

Their witness was Gustave Violet. His son, Pallade, remembers vividly his father's description of the event, a frequently recounted story that would make his father shed tears of laughter every time he told it: "…the bride and groom, flanked by their witnesses and friends, were waiting patiently to be wed in the church of Saint-Sulplice…time passed and the impatient Aristide became more and more nervous, grumbling in Catalan and finally crying out "One is really only well served in the Grandes Maisons. Let's go to Notre Dame!" And so they did. And so it was that Aristide Maillol was married in the grandest of our cathedrals. Like a King of France!"

Clotilde was to be a wonderful wife to him, modelling for his first sculptures, *La Méditerannée*, *Action Enchaînée* and *La Nuit*. One day, to demonstrate a point he was making to Gerald Kelly, a young painter (later Sir Gerald Kelly, President of the Royal Academy), Maillol scooped up her skirts and, raising them above her head, pointed out what Kelly described as "her admirable legs, of a massive construction, covered with hand knitted stockings, which stopped a little above the knee with great garters, and then, above that, there rose her red, mottled, splendid thighs. "And then," said Kelly, "he said this beautiful thing. "I rediscover marble"…"

Their only son was born in October. Maillol named him Lucien after his Tante Lucie, the woman who had played the role of a mother and had been one of the most important figures in his life.

By now, in Paris, Gustave Violet was enjoying a lively social life. He was a man who, within five minutes of knowing someone could make them his friend. He was tall, slim and a brilliant storyteller and actor. His deep-set eyes looked out at the world from under bushy eyebrows, always interested, never judgemental.

His studio in Auteuil was a popular meeting place for his fellow Catalan artists. Terrus spent as little time in the capital as he could, much preferring to meet up with Violet in Prades when he was at home. The others enjoyed the challenge of Paris life and profited from contact with the all important collectors and dealers, and in the case of de Monfreid and Fayet, doing a certain amount of collecting and dealing themselves. Aristide Maillol, despite the age gap of a dozen years, became Fayet's life long friend, as did Fernand Dumas, the banker and art collector from the village of Finestret in the Roussillon. Frequent visitors included Maurice Denis, André Maginot (he of the Maginot line) and the American dancer Loïe Fuller, as famous for her floating draperies as for their absence.

19th century cyclists mural, Els IV Gats, Barcelona

When Violet was in the Roussillon he would often get together with de Monfreid. They had both taken up the comparatively new sport of cycling. De Monfreid treated himself to a bicycle equipped with John Boyd Dunlop's new-fangled inflatable tyres. His son Henry had been given a bike by his mother for passing his *baccalauréat*; it was a splendid machine, albeit with solid tyres. Henry and his father agreed to meet for some mountain bicycle riding together.

In 1896 cycling was far from integrated into the French psyche. There was even criticism of the auto-erotic nature of the new sport. On the roads cyclists were considered eccentric looking insects, dangerous to both pedestrians and horse drawn vehicles. To scare off pursuing dogs, George Daniel took to carrying a pistol charged with *gros sel* (literally large salt, it was used in firearms to frighten without harming. The salt could enter the skin and shock and sting but inflict no lasting damage).

On one memorable occasion, Henry de Monfreid met his father at Perpignan station. George Daniel was dressed for the occasion in a white beret, white cycling trousers and, despite being only forty years old, his now almost white beard. They mounted their bicycles and set off for St Clément, fifty kilometres away. En route an incident occurred that quite justified de Monfreid senior's firearm. A horse and cart was blocking their way and refusing to budge. George Daniel with an adventurous manœuvre terrified the horse, causing it to swerve to one side. The furious driver set his dog on the two cyclists. George Daniel fired off his pistol, a noise that had the animal tumbling to the side of the road. The driver, thinking his dog dead, lost all control and whipped his horse into hot pursuit of the departing de Monfreids. Henry, the slower of the two, was about to be crushed by the horse and jumped into the ditch. But it was George Daniel whom the driver wanted. The road narrowed and came to a sharp bend. The driver was beating his horse forward with increasing vigour aiming to cut off the cyclist. With a superhuman effort George Daniel increased his speed. The poor animal lost control and crashed into the irrigation canal.

George Daniel and Henry arrived safely at St Clément to tell the tale. A tale that was to be retold many times over a glass of Banyuls...

George Daniel's post-divorce life was not lacking in pleasure and amusements. He enjoyed playing polkas on the piano in the Château St Clément living room, the music drifting out of the long French windows onto the terrace where his friends would gather. Here he would receive Maillol, Terrus, Violet and later Matisse. Gauguin's paintings would arrive from the South Seas via Paris and he would show them to Gustave Fayet, the Finestret banker Dumas and Calmel, the dentist from Béziers. It was to St Clément direct that Gauguin was to send his carvings which, on his first visit, would so amaze Matisse.

He cycled many kilometres, often with Louis Bausil the Roussillon painter best known for his pictures of blossoming peach trees. They would tour the Cerdagne or descend to Collioure to meet up with Terrus or Maillol. He was a frequent visitor at Violet's house in Prades.

In the summer of 1897 de Monfreid made an excursion to Spain by bicycle with Henry. De Monfreid took Henry to visit Annette whom he had installed in the pleasant Spanish seaside town of Llançá, just across the border. The visit was a success. There was only nine years difference in age between Annette and Henry, and Henry could not help admiring the "magnificent body one could make out beneath the light dress" that Annette was wearing. The dreamy pictures of Annette that George Daniel painted at this period confirm young Henry's assessment of his father's mistress.

Gauguin, in his letters, always sent good wishes to his former model as well as "... waiting impatiently for news of the pictures I sent you... If you have a bit of luck with the sales, I wish you would send me a few bulbs and flower-seeds. Simple dahlias, nasturtiums and sunflowers of various sorts, flowers that stand the hot climate, whatever you can think of..."

In 1899 George Daniel and Annette's daughter Agnès was born. At the christening on the 11th of June, Clotilde Maillol was godmother.

Gauguin wrote to them in July 1899:

> "...and you have a daughter; what a bother in Europe! Now I have a boy who is almost pure white and who costs no more than any animal that is nourished by its mother. And anyhow, children do not bother me, because 'I abandon them,' and 'I am a scoundrel of the worst sort who has deserted his wife and children.' What do I care! With best wishes to Annette, Cordially yours, Paul Gauguin."

De Monfreid spent the summer in the south and painted local landscapes, warm and gentle pictures, full of light and beauty. Villages such as Prats-Ballaguer, Fetges and Fuilla, vases of flowers and still lifes that in winter he exhibited in Paris with the Indépendants...

So it was that by the turn of the century our five Roussillon artists were well set on their artistic careers. A bond had been formed that would lead to joint exhibitions at home in Roussillon and in Barcelona as well as to meetings at the all-important Paris Salons each year.

Meanwhile, in the capital, the two men who were to become both friends and rivals and who would come to dominate the history of Modern Art in the twentieth century were beginning to make their presence felt.

Once again, in order of age, we will start with Henri Matisse...

*George Daniel de Monfreid – **Gorges de Fuilla***

Studio at Académie Julian, Paris

Chapter 3
Matisse in Paris

Matisse was born in a tiny, tumbledown weaver's cottage in 1869 in the northern French town of Le Cateau-Cambrésis near the textile centre of Bohain. He never forgot the rain that fell through a hole in the roof onto the beaten earth floor of his room. His family of weavers, grain merchants and tanners had lived in the area for centuries. Life in industrial Bohain was predominantly cold and muddy and seemed to have changed little since the Middle Ages. Even after the coming of the railway virtually everyone travelled on horseback or on foot.

His mother, an accomplished painter on porcelain, ran the section of his father's shop that sold house paints. Matisse later claimed he got his love of colour from watching her advise the customers on their colour schemes. At ten his father sent him to the Lycée in St Quentin. He was an awkward youth, by his own admission dreamy, frail and not outstandingly bright.

His father had decided his future lay in a career in law and it was only after a long and major struggle against the wishes of his family that he arrived in Paris in the autumn of 1891 to study art.

Paris was a large, bustling and dirty city, full of noise and colour. The iron wheels of horse drawn buses, carts and wagons rattled and screeched on the crowded, cobbled streets. Everywhere were brilliant posters whilst handbills distributed by sandwich-board men littered the roads amongst the horse dung. There were exhibitions of established and up-and-coming artists to be seen, the wonders of the Louvre to discover and the huge annual Salons to aspire to (or not, as Matisse was about to find out).

He enrolled at the Académie Julian under William Bouguereau. The Académie Julian (where de Monfreid had studied) had a good reputation. Its students would be put forward for the coveted *Prix de Rome* that Bouguereau had won at the age of 25. Bouguereau also had a seat on the academic governing body of the Ecole des Beaux-Arts and was President of the *Société des Artistes Français*. On seeing Matisse's first still lifes he commented "Aha, so we don't understand perspective! Never mind, you'll learn..." and enrolled him for a year, the tuition fees of 306 francs paid in advance.

The conditions at Julian's were grim. Too many students in too small a space, no supervision, rowdy singing of popular songs, overturned easels, much flicking of paper pellets, no fresh air. All overwhelming for young Matisse who felt inadequate, very unsure of himself and quite unable to reproduce the technically brilliant but emotionally empty canvases that hung on the studio walls. He found the rigid academic teaching difficult and uninspiring. He became depressed, feeling he would never make up for lack of early training. He did learn though, and, later, he was glad of the knowledge he had acquired in those early months. Even the plumb line Bouguereau advised him to use became a habit that amused his friends and fellow artists for the next decade. Particularly in the revolutionary summer of 1905 in Collioure where the running joke was whether or not the plumb line would or would not melt in the heat of the midday sun.

He failed his first round of the Beaux-Arts entrance exam and had a depressing meeting with his father in Lille. Back in Paris, he switched from Julian's to Moreau's Académie. Gustave Moreau was one of the few professors prepared to accept students despite their examination results. He was open-minded enough to see the need for change from the rigid academic tyranny at the Beaux-Arts that was beginning to foster strong feelings of revolt and an overwhelming need for freedom of expression. His fellow academicians regarded Moreau as dangerously permissive, but for Matisse he offered real hope and a belief that he could, at last, make progress. Matisse spent six years at Moreau's. In common with most of his fellow students he was permanently penniless, living in garrets, surviving on below minimum rations in Montparnassse, Montmartre and the Latin Quarter.

He met Camille, a vivid, fragile looking model of nineteen. Matisse, in love for the first time, noted, "She loved life, she made you want to live." Their bohemian life might have been hard but it was also full of fun. Whenever they could they would visit the music halls. Matisse and Camille were popular and behaved outrageously at art student parties that often got out of hand, even ending with police baton charges.

He enrolled at the under-equipped and overcrowded Ecole des Arts Decoratifs where he began studying in the evenings for a teaching diploma. He met and became friends with Albert Marquet and Henri Manguin. All three were determined to succeed as painters and, at Marquet's urging, took their sketchbooks into the streets to capture the Paris life in rapid drawings. Marquet was a timid man, quite shy and unassuming until he had a paintbrush or a crayon in hand, at which point he became the self assured leader of the group. Marquet's Paris scenes were to be some of his most successful paintings for the rest of his life.

The two followed Matisse to Moreau's where they were encouraged to "think in colour! Have imagination! If you have no imagination you will never make beautiful colour. That is what makes an artist!". In the Louvre Moreau would move amongst his students as they copied the old masters and, as Matisse said, "roused our imagination in front of the life he found in those paintings".

Matisse set up house with Camille in 1894. They moved to a tiny garret on the fifth floor of 19 quai St Michel. Their daughter, Marguerite, arrived the same year. This child, born amongst the paintbrushes and canvases of his student studio, was to become one of the dearest and deepest attachments of his life.

Matisse filled the studio with his collection of scraps of fabrics, embroidered cloth and chipped French faience. Their life revolved around his easel. When Moreau came to visit a couple of years later he remarked, "It's magnificent, it's extraordinary, he has really organised his life for painting." By now Matisse was one of the rising stars of Moreau's studio. He passed the Beaux-Arts entrance exam and, in 1896, had five paintings accepted by the Beaux-Arts *Salon de la Nationale*.

Matisse had arrived. His father was thrilled and wanted his son to compete for the *Prix de Rome*, a scholarship for promising art students providing an annual bursary. The competition was extremely difficult. Moreau was against it, causing the art critic Roger Marx to write in his review of the 1896 Salon du Champ-de-Mars, "In the heart of the Ecole des Beaux-Arts a flame of revolt has been kindled." Of Matisse, Marx wrote: "In his twenty seventh year, in 1896, Henri Matisse exhibited at the Champs-de-Mars with exceptional brilliance." His promotion to Associate Member of the *Société Nationale* went unchallenged, his pictures swept into private and public collections with no interference.

But he was not to build on his success. His relationship with Camille foundered as he struggled with insomnia and a growing need to follow his own course artistically as opposed to the traditional one laid down by the Académie. Colour and light began to infuse his painting, self doubt and fear of failure dogged his sleepless nights. The paintings he brought back to Paris from a summer on the island of Belle-Île, off Brittany, overturned all the teachings of Moreau's studio. John Peter Russell, an Australian artist, had settled there and established an artist's colony. He introduced Matisse to impressionism and the work of the comparatively unknown Van Gogh. Matisse would later say "Russell was my teacher, he explained colour theory to me."

Moreau, dying of cancer, emaciated and thin, made demands on his students to which many could not respond. But Matisse understood. He would have starved rather than compromise his artistic principles. He turned his back on the overtures of the official art world and with it the successful career he could have had. "A splendid career as a state functionary," was how he described the opportunity thirty years later.

Camille, who had supported him through thick and thin, modelled for him, borne his child, worked long hours for their survival, could not understand him. Her ambition to see him rise through the ranks of the artistic establishment was no different from that of Madame Cézanne or Madame Pissaro for their husbands. Matisse dismissed her argument, describing the two wives in question as "uneducated peasant women who knew no better".

On the 16th of October 1897 he was best man at a wedding in Neuilly. At the meal that followed he sat next to a certain Mlle Amélie Parayre. Years later she said she had intended never to marry a redhead, or a man with a beard, or a painter. She also said she knew from the moment they met that she would marry Henri Matisse.

He warned her from the start "Mademoiselle, I love you dearly, but, I shall always love painting more."

In 1898 they honeymooned on Corsica. Matisse painted the Mediterranean spring as Van Gogh had done ten years before him predicting that "The painter of the future will be such a colourist as has never been seen before."

The Matisse's first son, Jean, was born in Toulouse twelve months after their marriage. Matisse could delay no longer, he needed to earn a living. He returned to Paris. There he sold nothing and found no work. Instead he fell in love with Cézanne's *Three Bathers*, a painting he saw in Vollard's gallery. Amélie pawned an emerald ring and they bought it. She opened a hat shop so that they would have some income. The family lived above it in three tiny rooms.

At Carrière's studio where Matisse was studying, he met the eighteen year old André Derain, observing: "... He didn't work like the others. He interested me, little by little we began to talk..." Son of a pastry chef cum town councillor, Derain had hated school and had left with a reputation of being a "bad, lazy and noisy scholar" but with

Le Grand Palais, Paris

a prize for drawing. He and Matisse became friends. One evening, as a small protest against artistic penury, he, Amélie and Derain staged a dramatic scene for passers-by culminating with a body being hurled into the Seine. The victim was a dummy, dressed as a Beaux-Arts professor.

Strapped for cash as ever, Marquet and Matisse joined the team of decorators working at the Grand Palais preparing the Universal Exhibition. Amélie continued to work as a milliner. Despite their near impossible financial situation she decided to take on little Marguerite who was desperately missing her father. It was a decision she never regretted. The child grew up to be a daughter to her, the lynchpin of their family and adored by her half brothers. A second son, Pierre, had been born in 1900. Camille had no choice but to accept the situation, knowing it to be the best for both her and her child. Life as a penniless unmarried mother in turn of the century Paris was well nigh impossible.

By this time Matisse, tormented by rejection, isolation, and financial desperation was, nevertheless, beginning to disturb the Paris art world. And, unknown to him, Pablo Picasso, the man who was to become his friend and rival for the rest of his life, had arrived in the capital.

In 1901 Matisse showed at the Salon des Indépendants for the first time. Nothing sold.

In that same summer Marguerite fell ill but was almost miraculously saved. Matisse painted her portrait, huge dark eyes looking straight at the spectator, a striped pinafore dress and a black ribbon round her neck, hiding the ugly scar where her windpipe had had to be cut to allow her to breathe.

And, later in the same year, he met the dealer, Berthe Weill. When she came to his studio to look at his work, there was not room, even with the door open, for the three of them to squeeze in. She took some paintings to hang in her new gallery in Montmartre. It seemed his career was about to take off. But, at the same moment the Parayre/Humbert scandal broke. Amélie's parents, the Parayres, had been working for and with the Humbert family for many years. Blinded by faithfulness to their employers, they failed to notice that a considerable part of the Humberts' wealth came from unscrupulous dealings concerning pension funds. The dealings were supposedly secured by immense wealth in bonds in a strong box in the Humberts' Paris mansion. Public hysteria was growing, fuelled by two lawsuits against the Humberts. Finally, on May 11th 1902, when police forced an entry, the Humberts were nowhere to be found. A locksmith broke open the safe and found an old newspaper, an Italian coin and a trouser button.

The Parayres were ruined and suffered from the reflected disgrace of the Humberts. Amélie's hat shop was ransacked, her health collapsed. In addition to himself, his wife and three children, Matisse now had to support his parents-in-law. He almost gave up. It was a dreadful and black period for all of them, but, with the help of his family and the encouragement of his fellow artists Matisse struggled on.

Gustave Fayet, as well as investing in works by Cézanne, Monfreid, Fantin-Latour, Sisley, Van Gogh, Gauguin and, above all, Odilon Redon, began to buy from Matisse.

Meanwhile in the Roussillon...

After his father's death in 1899, Fayet had begun his own collection by buying that of Armand Cabro: an impressive assortment that included works by Degas, Monet, Manet and Pissaro. Fayet was now the curator of the Museum of Béziers. He also managed the extensive five hundred hectare family wine business he had inherited. Each domaine had its manager but the business was run from the Fayet family house in rue du Capus in Béziers. His daughter Yseult often accompanied him on his tours of the vineyards remarking afterwards how his eagle eye missed nothing and how his smiling instructions to his personnel were regarded as the word of god.

Through all this activity Fayet's passion for art flourished. In the Salle Berlioz in Béziers he arranged an exhibition that marked the arrival of Modern Art in the Roussillon. Fabre described it as "rivalling the capital". Redon, Degas, Renoir, Cézanne, Pissaro, Gauguin, Rodin and a certain nineteen year-old "M. Picasso, Espagne" were all represented, as, with the organizational skills of Terrus and Bausil, were the Roussillon artists. So great was its success that Fayet planned an hommage to Monticelli for the following year and, maybe for Gauguin the year after...

In summer Fayet would visit de Monfreid at Château St Clément in Corneilla-de-Conflent, sometimes making painting excursions further up into the mountains, sometimes meeting up with other local artists: Maillol, Terrus, Louis Bausil. Fayet's friendship with Maillol was made easy by their shared admiration of Paul Gauguin.

Both through de Monfreid and on his own account, Fayet was in contact with the artist himself in his self imposed South Seas exile and Gauguin was more than pleased by his correspondence with the new patron de Monfreid had found him. He wrote to Fayet, praising the catalogue de Monfreid had sent him of the exhibitions Fayet arranged in Béziers, and saying how delighted he was to feature among such illustrious masters. George Daniel de Monfreid himself Gauguin described as having "the most loyal, frank and beautiful nature of anyone I have ever known. Impossible to meet him without noticing it..."

Without doubt de Monfreid did all he could to promote Gauguin. In a letter in February 1901 the exile remarked that "...your last letter breathed a number of good hopes as to Béziers (possibly the collector and dentist, Calmel, or maybe Gustave Fayet) ...I have been busy hunting some wood to carve, and it is not easy in Tahiti..." only to complain in April "...and what a gamble it is! Think of that picture thrown aside as worthless you gave away to your friend the dentist, who leaving Marseilles went to live in Béziers ..." but... "The only way is to do good work, and then, sooner or later things will go well. Criticism passes, good work remains."

Gauguin often asked about de Monfreid's own work, in the same letter writing "... you are talented. I am thinking of your exhibition with the Indépendants when I was in Paris; and I think that you also have found great support in Béziers... I should be so glad if you would tell me something about it in your letters for I should like to know that at last you have taken the place in the world you deserve... When you have time, in exchange for the wood carvings which I insist on your having, I wish you would send me some little canvas of your own – a portrait, for instance. I should love to have it to put up in my little room in the Marquesas. I will make a pretty little carved frame for it.
Best wishes to all your crowd.
As always, with all my heart,
Paul Gauguin."

Gustave Fayet invited de Monfreid to paint a portrait of his wife. He began on the 8th of May, leaving home at 4.30 in the morning. Fayet would meet him at Béziers at midday and he would paint the afternoon away. On the 22nd of May, at Fayet's suggestion, he took his friend Calmel, whose portrait he had painted in 1893, to see the finished work. It was much praised.

De Monfreid's self-portrait of the same year shows an austere man, receding hair close cropped, beard grey, cheeks sunken. Long fingered hands are clasped over a soft white shirt, a blue spotted cravat tied loosely at the neck. Good looking, slightly supercilious, George Daniel's view of himself stares back at the viewer. On the wall behind his head is a painting of Château St Clément.

Gauguin had great hopes for Fayet's planned 1903 exhibition in Béziers. He wrote to de Monfreid sugesting that he might come back himself for the event. De Monfreid immediately wrote to discourage him: "It is to be feared that your return would only derange the growing and slowly conceived ideas with which public opinion has surrounded you. Now you are that legendary artist, who, from out of the depths of Polynesia, sends forth disconcerting and inimitable work – the definitive work of a man who has disappeared from the world. Your enemies (and you have many, as have all who trouble the mediocre) are now silent, they do not dare to combat you, do not even think of it : for you are so far away! You must not return. Now you are as are the great dead. You have passed into the history of art."

Fayet was completely in agreement with de Monfreid that Gauguin should not risk destroying the myth that was growing up around him by returning to France to be at the proposed 1903 exhibition in person.

Though Fayet and de Monfreid were both wealthy, well educated, patrons of the arts and artists themselves, from some of the many letters de Monfreid wrote to his good friend Louis Bausil, one gets the impression that he felt more at ease with his painting and cycling companion, the painter of peach trees in bloom. In a long letter from St Clément in August 1902 he writes to Bausil: "Your letter arrived as we were waiting for the Fayets who were to visit for a couple of days. Despite their simplicity, we have been a little overtired preparing to receive them. They make four extra people in the house. (M. Fayet, Mme Fayet, their son and the chauffeur.) And, given their millionaire status, we are obliged to offer them accommodation other than the improvised camping arrangements that suffice for our good chums like you or Gustave (Violet) or Mössieur Dumasss." (de Monfreid often wrote the name of Dumas, his friend the banker from Finestret, in a way to mock his Catalan accent).

Bausil was also a close friend of Terrus having taken, upon his father's death, to using his family's house in Elne for his holidays. He and Terrus were founder members of the Group of Roussillon Artists who, with Maillol, Monfreid, Violet and Gaudissard first exhibited their work in Perpignan in 1901.

"So," de Montfreid continued, "your letter has remained unanswered..." He goes on to tell Bausil of painting projects, of cycling excursions, of Dumas's car, the first in Finestret and not without mechanical problems. He talks of Gauguins he has brought back from Paris that he hopes Fayet will buy, of visiting Fayet in Béziers to admire three "superb" Van Goghs, a "delicious" Renoir, some Forains, Toulouse-Lautrecs and a Monet that Fayet had bought... "You must go one of these days! It's worth the effort!" he advises his friend. He finishes with sending "milles amitiés" to Terrus and to Violet, to wishing Bausil would conquer the Cerdagne on his bicycle so long as it did not deter him from his art, "shakes his hand with all his heart" and adds that "his wife sends best wishes..."

His friendship with Fayet was often coloured by their art dealing, especially in de Monfreid's self appointed role as Gauguin's agent. In Gauguin's last letter to de Monfreid in April 1903 telling him he had sent him three paintings for Fayet, he asked de Monfreid to beg Fayet to "save" him, adding "If the pictures don't suit him he can take others from you, or, could he at least lend me 1,500 francs with any guarantees he wishes..." De Monfreid told Fayet who sent the money immediately. The post to the South Seas was slow. The much needed funds eventually arrived several weeks after Gauguin's death on May 8th.

At the beginning of August, still unaware of the event, Fayet and de Monfreid met at Château St Clément to discuss Fayet's purchase of enough of Gauguin's paintings to allow the artist they both so admired to work free from financial worry for the rest of his life. On August 14th de Monfreid wrote to Gauguin telling him the good news. A letter he never received.

A week later, on the 23rd of August, at St Clément, de Monfreid learned of Gauguin's death.

Gustave Fayet was the first person he telephoned.

When, later, Fayet came to de Monfreid's Paris studio to be painted, de Monfreid posed him seated in a red arm chair behind which can be seen Gauguin's painting La Barque and his sculpted Masque de Tehura.

Frederick O'Brien's foreword to his book of Gauguin's letters to de Monfreid captures the essence of all Gauguin stood for: "... to his last breath he had been a rebel against convention in life and art, ... his whole life as a painter was an outcry, almost a curse, against materialism, against accepted success; against laws, morals, money, critics and clerics... his courage was unfaltering. He was a tremendous individualist; an example of strength against the powers of disintegration, of organised society, hardly to be found in modern years. He abandoned one by one every hold on ordinary things in order to be the savage he made his goal, and despite the certainty that he would not survive the attainment..."

In the year that Gauguin died, Gustave Violet, despite being a great success both socially and artistically in Paris, returned to Prades. The house he built, next to the little chapel of St Marti, overlooking a lake in the meadows, reflected his multi-faceted character and many artistic skills. The white façade, the terraces, the fountains and balconies were typical of his style, the ceramic tiles and chandeliers he made himself. In the grounds he built his studio, with his kilns for ceramics and sculpture. Aristide Maillol came to fire his first bas-reliefs in the kiln.

Meanwhile Maillol's life had been moving on apace. Ambroise Vollard, the dealer who gained both fame and fortune by investing his entire inheritance in the then complete works of the unknown Cézanne, was the first to become interested in Maillol's sculpture. He widened Maillol's audience from his circle of fellow artists to collectors and international museums. While enjoying this increased exposure, Maillol felt he was not benefiting enough materially. Vollard, having bought ten of his statuettes in terracotta, had a thousand cast in bronze, which he then sold. Maillol, exaggerating his accent, amused his artist friends by referring to Vollard as "*Voleurrr*" (thief)...

In June 1902, Maillol had his first one-man-show at Vollard's gallery. Thirty-three pieces of work, including sculpture, ceramics, tapestries and furniture, were exhibited. The well-known writer, Octave Mirbeau purchased *Leda* and showed it to his friend Auguste Rodin. Rodin studied it for a long while before saying "Maillol is a sculptor as great as the greatest. There is, in this little bronze, a lesson for everyone, for the great masters as well as for young beginners..."

Mirbeau, writing to Maillol about Rodin's reaction, told him: "He picked up your Leda, just as I had done, and looked at it intently, examining it from every angle, turning it round in every direction. "It is most beautiful"; he said, "what an artist!" He looked at it again, and went on: "Do you know why it is so beautiful and why one can spend hours looking at it? It is because it makes no attempt to arouse curiosity." And there was a look of melancholy in his eyes. "I do not know, I swear I do not know of any modern piece of sculpture that is of such an absolute beauty, and absolute purity, so evidently a masterpiece." Maillol could not have had praise from a more encouraging quarter. Rodin seems to have recognized an innocence that had remained intact in Maillol from childhood days spent alone on the seashore of Banyuls forty years before.

Maillol was determined to remain faithful to his own ideals, his own style. As he often said "I am not looking to be fashionable. One fashion follows another fashion. If you are beaten today, it's not serious. You will be understood tomorrow, and that tomorrow is for eternity."

Legend has it that, having seen an exhibition of Monet's recent work, Maillol renounced painting as an art form he could never accomplish. The reason could also have been the eye infection that forced him to stop his beloved petit point tapestries. In any case, from then on, he only drew and painted for his own pleasure. Sculpture became his speciality.

He worked in many sizes and many mediums, always from sketches and drawings. Figures he had sculpted draped and clothed he often reworked in the nude. His small terracotta statuettes were very popular, often featuring in the paintings of his friends Bonnard and Vuillard. He experimented with sitting, crouching, standing and reclining the same figure until he arrived at the perfect balance and harmony he sought. He broke with tradition, opening the way for a new generation of sculptors. By 1905, the simplicity of his forms was beginning to define a style all of its own. Just as Matisse was to reduce drawing to a single line, Maillol was to continue to simplify his statues till they became the forerunners of much modern sculpture.

Back in Paris, on 31st of October 1903, Matisse showed at the first Exhibition of the Salon d'Automne. When it opened on a bitterly cold night in the basement of the Petit Palais, most of the visitors found it electrifying and the works on display the art of the future. The actual electricity was very erratic, many of the paintings were difficult to see and the viewers needed torches to see the work. Nevertheless, Matisse, although he hardly recognised it, was on his way.

*Catalogue cover of 1903
Salon d'Automne*

Chapter 4
Collioure 1905

The Matisse who arrived in Collioure in his gold-rimmed spectacles and well-trimmed beard on the 16th of May 1905 was thirty six years old, depressed, full of self-doubts and very short of money. The pointillist picture *Luxe, Calme et Volupté* that he had presented at the Spring Salon des Indépendants in Paris had brought him neither luxury nor calm nor voluptuousness.

Old postcard of rue de la Gare, Collioure

As he got off the train he glanced around. He was struck by the vitality of the little Catalan fishing port. His depression lifted. Everywhere he saw colour and light, almost violent in its intensity. Signac, with whom he had stayed the previous summer in St-Tropez, had advised him to come. In 1887, in his painting *Collioure, the Beach and the Town*, Signac had captured the very colour, magic and light that Matisse now saw all around him. Matisse was about to paint his feelings, the sensations flowing from his surroundings, colours reflecting those sensations. He did not yet know it but he was about to start a new movement in the history of art. It was to be the summer that, thanks to Henri Matisse, "fauvism" would explode into existence in Collioure.

He and his wife had left their two sons with his wife's parents and their daughter with her sister in Perpignan. They set up house in the Hôtel de la Gare, the first artists the redoubtable Dame Rousette had ever taken. She was deeply suspicious of anyone not speaking Catalan. Fortunately Mathieu Muxart, who met her customers at the railway station and carried their bags to the hotel, spoke some French. His persuasion and Matisse's well-shined shoes and clean appearance won her over and they moved in. Mathieu not only worked for the hotel but, in his spare time, grew the Mediterranean vegetables that were to delight and impress Matisse. The aubergines from Mathieu's garden would feature in many of Matisse's interiors and still lifes.

Old postcard of fishermen pulling in the boats, Collioure

Tourists had yet to discover Collioure in 1905. The lower slopes of the surrounding mountains, vine covered, came down to the edge of the town; the fleet of brightly painted Catalan barques filled the bay, traditional fishing boats whose triangular sails could catch every breath of wind, their sloping masts casting geometric patterns against the vivid blue of sky and sea. The Château Royal, ancient Summer Palace of the Kings of Mallorca, dominated the harbour on one side. On the other, seawater lapping its walls, was the church of Notre Dame des Anges with its famous phallic clock tower. Narrow alleys of tall houses led down to the bay, washing strung across them, open drains running down the cobbles. On the beach, sardines and anchovies were landed, nets were mended, the catch sold. Omnipresent was a strong smell of fish, an odour augmented by the women of the town emptying chamber pots into the sea each night.

Picturesque, smelly, vibrant, sun-soaked, windswept, Collioure paid little attention to its new residents. For Matisse it was the opportunity to break free of the restrictions both of the Paris Académies and the strict rigours of pointillism as practiced by Signac. Here, at last, he was free. Free of criticism, the locals had little interest in art and, in any case, he did not understand the Catalan they spoke. Added to which, seriously liberating, he was as free as he had ever been of money worries. Living was cheap and his wife's family in Perpignan were helping with the children. As he rid himself of pointillism, the tiny dots gave way to daubs, sensual brushstrokes of colour, expressing the emotions each scene aroused in him. Holding nothing back, he allowed his painting to flow onto the canvas in a way no painting had before.

He drew as well: the fishermen at work, the nets drying in the sun, the fleet leaving harbour in the evening for a night's fishing, the women gossiping on street corners, mending the nets on the beach, carrying pots on their heads, carts and donkeys trundling past. Sketch after sketch dashed off with an accuracy that leaves a vibrant record of daily life at the turn of the century. None foresaw that the artist, painting the everyday scenes that delighted him, would cause the

Old postcard of rue du Château, Collioure

Fishermen with Nets on Collioure Beach, sketch by Phil Monk

small Catalan fishing port to become internationally famous, the scenes he captured now hanging in the houses of the very rich as well as in the best art galleries in the world. Some of these sketches can be seen in the Museum of Modern Art in Céret.

A week after his arrival, Matisse wrote to Manguin that he had met Etienne Terrus, a friend of Maximillien Luce, the pointillist painter Matisse had left in charge of his Paris studio.

It was at the Hôtel de la Gare that Etienne Terrus, already known as the painter of landscape from Elne, sought him out. Described by many as "*petit, trapu, poilu, bourrou, têtu*" (small, stocky, hairy, moody and obstinate) Terrus was to become a loyal and close friend of Matisse. He had the look of a rustic faun, a faun with strong cyclist's legs and metal-toed boots. He often cycled the twelve kilometres to Collioure to have a glass with his friend the winemaker, Paul Soulier, who lived next door to the hotel. Sometimes he would shorten the journey by riding through the railway tunnel.

Terrus showed his work at the Paris Salon des Indepéndants where Signac was the president and Matisse in charge of hanging. Matisse had always admired Terrus's painting and was more than glad to benefit from his local knowledge. Terrus wasted no time in taking him to visit his friend Aristide Maillol in Banyuls-sur-Mer.

Maillol's house was in the old quarter of Banyuls. Set in steep, narrow streets, an ancient pine tree dominating the garden, the house was homely and comfortable. His studio was in the old wine cellar. When Matisse and Terrus arrived he was working on *La Mediterranée*, the deceptively simple and sensual statue that now adorns his tomb in the garden of the Musée Maillol. Bits of plaster had stuck to his flowing beard. He was dressed in soft and simple clothes, a black beret on his head, canvas *espadrilles* on his feet. His face was fine and long, his nose also, but it was his eyes that struck Matisse, eyes of a deep clear blue.

Maillol's La Maison Rose, Banyuls-sur-Mer

Aristide Maillol embraced his good friend Terrus and shook Matisse by the hand. They set to work together on a small part of the rounded form, Matisse much flattered to be of assistance. The pure lines of Maillol's sculpture were to encourage Matisse to seek simplicity and purity in his own work.

Clotilde, Maillol's wife, had prepared a lunch of baked monkfish, a favourite of Terrus's. They often ate together. That day, with Matisse welcomed into their midst, the sun was going down by the time they had finished their meal. Suddenly, they heard the noise of a motor in the street. The hoot of its klaxon brought all the neighbours to their windows. An Hispano-Suiza drew up outside the house. In it were Fernand Dumas, the portly banker from Finestret, Louis Bausil, the local artist well known for his paintings of peach trees in flower and George Daniel de Monfreid. De Monfreid, wearing his large white beret, led the others inside.

"Allow me to present the artist, Matisse!" said Maillol. Terrus, watched, and, sucking on his pipe, smiled. Later, in flowing violet ink, de Monfreid noted in his diary, " 22nd May 1905, met the artist, Matisse."

An invitation followed...

On June 12th 1905, Henri Matisse rose early and made his way to Collioure station. Etienne Terrus, joined the train at Elne. At Perpignan

Villefranche-du-Conflent (Pyr.-Or.) — La Gare

Edit. Fau, lib., Perpignan N. B. (Pyr.-Or.)

Old postcard of Villefranche-de-Conflent train station

they changed trains and boarded one bound for Villefranche-de-Conflent, the station serving the popular spa resort of Vernet-les-Bains. At Villefranche, international passengers taking the cure were met by coaches from Vernet-les-Bains's luxury hotels. Matisse and Terrus were greeted by George Daniel de Monfreid on his bicycle. They walked towards Vernet, Mount Canigou, still capped with snow, gleaming white ahead. At Corneilla-de-Conflent the three men, deep in conversation, turned right onto a dirt track. The track meandered through fruit orchards until, before long, surrounded by trees, they saw the Château St Clément. Two pointed towers, warm ochre rendering, long French windows giving onto a wide terrace, the perfect gentleman's residence.

Dumas, the banker, Bausil the artist and Calmel, the dentist and collector from Béziers, were already there with their wives. They all knew each other well, conversation was easy and Gauguin was the subject of most of it. It was in this house that de Monfreid had learned of his friend's death two years earlier. He had been executor of Gauguin's will. He had received many canvases via his studio in Paris with urgent requests to sell them. As we know, Gauguin's livelihood had depended on the sales. In his many letters from the South Seas the constant refrain had been of money worries. Matisse looked around. He had bought a Gauguin from Vollard in Paris, back in 1899. On the walls of Château St Clément hung many of Gauguin's paintings, among them a self-portrait with the inscription "for my dear Daniel". There were none of de Monfreid's own pictures.

After lunch, in honour of his new friend, de Monfreid had decided to show his guests the wood sculptures that, on 22nd March 1901, had been sent directly to Château St Clément, avoiding Paris where Gauguin had feared they would be un-saleable. De Monfreid had already shown them to Maillol who had been unimpressed, saying that, in his opinion, "it had been a mistake to imitate Negro sculpture... he should sculpt as he paints, from nature, not these women with small legs and large heads..."

The primitive carvings could not have been further removed from Maillol's sculpture. So-called "Primitive Art" was only just beginning to excite and inspire European artists.

De Monfreid led them up to his studio in the left hand tower. Slowly, he unwrapped the dark figures. Matisse was silent, his heart beating fast. Sceptical and enthusiastic by turns, he found himself admiring the blend of primitive and western art, and pondering over Gauguin's rejection of familiar values in order to immerse himself in a simpler, purer society, pursuing his artistic goals far from friends and family despite financial insecurity, ill health and ultimately the knowledge that he was unlikely to survive.

Matisse had previously visited de Monfreid's friend Gustave Fayet in Paris and seen there the carvings Gauguin had done for him. He was fascinated by all de Monfreid's stories of his friend whom he described as the "chief of the symbolists", especially his anecdote of Gauguin dismissing the Paris salons for their claiming a distinction between "a painting" and a "decorative panel". According to Gauguin, "... all

View of Canigou from le Château St Clément, Corneilla-de-Conflent

painting consists primarily of decorating a surface by means of colour and design..." Matisse never lost sight of that simple idea, claiming to the end of his life that "Expression and decoration are but one and the same thing".

They returned to the terrace where Gauguin's work, his life as a painter and his influence on the world of art were discussed at length.

Night fell and the moon rose, bathing Canigou in silver light. As de Monfreid was later to record, a certain amount of drink had been taken. Calmel, Terrus and Matisse decided to stay the night. George Daniel de Monfreid heard them leaving at four the next morning to catch the first train.

Matisse moved to a house overlooking the main beach of Collioure owned by Terrus's friend, Soulier the vigneron. He visited Maillol, occasionally helping him with his mould for *La Méditerannée*.

One day Maillol took him to visit la Métairie (now La Musée Maillol), his dream retreat some four kilometres out of Banyuls. They walked through the vines that covered the mountainside, following the dry bed of the Roume river. Cicadas sang, the sun was hot and prickly pear cactus sprouted from the rocky sides of their path. As they approached the cool clearing where the old stone Mas stood, Maillol murmured, "This is where I will work and where, later, I will be buried". Matisse understood him completely. The spot was almost religious in its intense peace and tranquillity.

The Maillols and the Matisses met often that summer. Clotilde Maillol taught Amélie Matisse the needlework skills her husband had used for his early tapestries. Maillol was full of support for Matisse the artist. Nevertheless Matisse was often besieged with self-doubt. He felt the need of one of his Paris companions with whom to work and discuss his ideas. He had suggested to Marquet, Manguin and Camoin that they come and join him. None of them could. He sent a simple postcard to André Derain. "Venez!" it said, "Come!"

And Derain came, just in time to celebrate his 25th birthday. When he appeared at the Hôtel de la Gare, over two metres tall, with a fine moustache and the eyes of a cat, dressed all in white but for a red cap on his head, Dame Rousette had no intention of allowing him in. She took some persuading. Mathieu Muxart was, once again the key and, eventually, with Matisse, accompanied Derain to the station to pick up his trunks, suitcases and large umbrella.

Derain, with his friend and collaborator Maurice de Vlaminck, had been painting the Paris suburbs, Chatou in particular. Postcards were becoming popular, photography also. Painting and drawing were no longer the only method of recording scenes and events that a photograph could reproduce so accurately. The task of the artist was changing. In fact the camera liberated the artists: they were almost forced to use colour and free brushstrokes to distance themselves from the camera and its perfect reproductions. As Derain said "...it was the era of photography, this may have influenced us and played a part in our reaction against anything resembling a snapshot of life." Since the 1860's, self-consciously modern art had defined itself as "post-photographic", aiming to offer something other than the surface impression of the world.

Despite the fact that it is unlikely anyone accused Derain of painting "snapshots", he was restless and Matisse's invitation could not have come at a better time. It had been thanks to Matisse that he had exhibited at that year's Indépendants and consequently sold the contents of his studio to Vollard. Also it was thanks to Matisse and Amélie's visit to Derain's parents that they allowed their son to pursue his dream to be a painter.

Collioure was to seduce André Derain just as it had Henri Matisse. He seized the opportunity to learn from the "Master", describing what he learnt to Vlaminck in his frequent letters, particularly the conception of light as the negation of shadows. "In Collioure," he wrote, "every shadow was a whole world of clarity and luminosity contrasting with sunlight."

Matisse, always generous with his ideas, loved to share them with his fellow artists. Older than his friends, he was often portrayed as "the Prof". He certainly did like teaching and was prone to pontificating, his early sense of fun constrained by financial worries and personal self doubt. In his 1908 *Notes to an Artist*, he explained that he was striving to create works of art "harmonious in their entirety..." That he dreamt of "..an art of balance, of purity and serenity, devoid of troubling and depressing subject matter; an art which could be for every intellectual worker, for the businessman as well as the man of letters, a soothing, calming influence on the mind, something like a good armchair which provides relaxation from physical fatigue."

The artists and their wives were all dedicated letter-writers, their correspondence giving a vivid insight into their day to day painting problems and progress, as well as their family ups and downs. Money worries dogged most of them. Matisse wrote constant letters to Berthe Weill asking for his share of the modest proceeds from the sale of one of his paintings in order to repay Manguin a hundred and sixty francs he had borrowed at the start of the summer. Manguin, though better off than Matisse, was also short of money. "When shall we ever feel easy?" he asked Matisse in an August letter.

The art critic, Louis Vauxcelles, living out the summer under grey skies in Paris referred to Signac, Cross, Camoin, Manguin and Marquet in St-Tropez and Matisse and Derain in Collioure as "a flock of migratory birds", working in an idyllic trouble-free Mediterranean as opposed to the northern mists of Paris and its environs.

The lure of the Midi was strong for many artists at the start of the twentieth century. Matisse, of course, Derain and, by association, Vlaminck, Marquet, Camoin, Manguin, all friends since Gustave Moreau days in Paris, as well as the Normans, Othon Friesz, Dufy and Braque all painted the summers away in the south, all met at least twice annually at the Salon des Indépendants in the spring and the Salon d'Automne in the autumn.

This new generation of up and coming painters were all influenced to a greater or lesser degree by three artists: by the massing of bright colours and abrupt colour changes in Gauguin's paintings, by Cézanne's strongly geometric volumetric elements and by Van Gogh's freedom and expressionist qualities. They had moved through the "Pointillism" of Georges Seurat to the "Divisionism" of Henri-Edmond Cross and Paul Signac. The mix of influences varied from artist to artist so that no two artists produced the same style. They benefited from working together, often with easels side by side, discussing the theory while putting it into practice.

Derain was aware of the crisis Matisse was going through when he arrived, describing it to Vlaminck and adding that "...on the other hand, he is a more extraordinary type than I had believed, from the point of view of logic and psychological speculation..."

They were both passionate about Collioure. Derain, once again in a letter to Vlaminck, praising: "above all the light. A blond light, a golden hue that suppresses the shadows..." Later, Derain was to remark, that the colours of Collioure that summer of 1905 had been as "sticks of dynamite". The two artists certainly went into battle together, painting Collioure from every angle: the bay, the church and clock tower, the Château, the boats on the beach and the nets drying amongst the glistening fish scales. Derain would come bounding up the staircase of the Matisses' seaside house. On the terrace Amélie Matisse would place a jug of water on a small table and stretch out an awning. Derain in his red cap and, next to him, Matisse in a

Plage de l'Ouille, Collioure

large straw hat, pipe in his mouth would be working away. They both delighted in the freedom from criticism that Collioure afforded them. Painting at speed, capturing the heat of the day on their canvases, ignoring all traditional convention, they worked the colour direct from the tube. Sometimes Amélie dressed in her Japanese kimono and posed barefoot on the rocks of the little bay of l'Ouille. Derain painted her there, modelling for her husband. It was a setting Matisse was to develop in his large *Bonheur de Vivre*. The bay became a favourite spot where the whole family could bathe away from the hustle and pollution of the town beaches. They bought rope soled espadrilles, threw off their town shoes and got into a routine of work that always allowed time for a daily swim.

For the paintings Matisse did of Amélie, nude in a forest clearing, they would set off very early in the morning, worried lest she be spotted by a wandering Colliourenc. Fortunately in 1905 the woods came right down to the shores of the Mediterranean, making it comparatively easy to find a private glade.

Derain painted a double portrait of Matisse and Terrus against a backdrop of Collioure's clock tower. "Two solid fellows sunburned and bearded." He got on well with Terrus. "...and I have found here a true anarchist!" he wrote to Vlaminck. "...wherever I go I find anarchists. By night they destroy the world...every morning, they rebuild it." Two of his fauve portraits are of Terrus; in one he used Terrus's favourite colours, painting him with a red face and blue beard.

Beards were very much in vogue at the time, worn to a greater or lesser extent by most of the men in this book. Only one or two, Dumas the banker, for example, and the musician Déodat de Sévérac settled for generous moustaches.

Matisse loved using open windows to frame scenes alive with colour. Red and pink, blue and green. Colours that had never been used to such effect before: red sand, pink sea, he painted what he felt. Derain's sand was often yellow but his use of colour was every bit as powerful as that of Matisse. A keen photographer, Derain introduced a perspective in his landscapes often missing from those of Matisse. It is easier to recognise Collioure scenes and the daily life of the village in Derain's paintings whereas Matisse's seem to flow straight from his emotions. They worked well together, were often each other's model. The colour danced off the walls, sparkled on the sea, hung on the white sails of the Catalan barques, glistened on the fish scales clinging to the black clothing of the women mending the nets. The two artists captured it all on their canvases. Blue/green, rose/pink, reds, deep blues, violets, they painted from their very souls.

Derain discovered Spain where he bought brightly coloured pottery and met Spanish painters in Cadaques. He visited Maillol, the lynch pin of the local artistic community, the link between Paris and the Roussillon. 1905, such a great year for art in general, was particularly important for Maillol. Through Vollard and Rodin he had met Count Harry Kessler. As soon as Kessler saw the work of Maillol he offered him freedom from any monetary problems so that he could consecrate himself to art. Maillol accepted. He would illustrate a number of books published by the Cranach Press, Kessler's publishing house which had been inspired by Willian Morris's Kelmscott Press. It was through Kessler that Maillol was to meet Eric Gill and other artists of the English Arts and Crafts Movement. Through sales in England as well as in Germany and Switzerland, Aristide, Clotilde and Lucien Maillol were able to move out of Tante Lucie's house and install themselves in a house and studio in Puig del Mas, just outside Banyuls town.

Maillol had been commissioned by Clemenceau to make a monument in homage to Auguste Blanqui. "Who was he?" asked Maillol. Clemenceau went into a passionate description of the man that lasted an hour. He described in detail Blanqui's life dedicated to revolution, how he had spent thirty six years in prison, and how, upon his death in 1881, an immense crowd all waving red flags had accompanied him to his grave in Père Lachaise cemetery. "How do you see the statue?" asked Clemenceau.

"I shall make you a beautiful woman's bottom, it will be called *Liberty unchained*", said Maillol. This reply so pleased Clemenceau he immediately put down seven thousand francs. Actually it was not enough to cover the cost, but Maillol was happpy to accept. However, when it was about to be erected in front of the church in Puget-Thénier, Blanqui's birthplace in the Alpes Maritimes, it caused such a scandal that the priest refused to say mass unless it was removed. It was moved from place to place, narrowly escaped being melted down during the Second World War, miraculously missed bombardments while in a warehouse in Nice and, finally, in 1944, was renamed "*Marianne*" by the citizens of Puget-Théniers and became a symbol of unity and pride for the town. A second version is now to be found in the Tuileries in Paris.

His *Hommage à Cézanne* met with a similar reaction. The reclining nymph was refused by Aix-en-Provence, Cézanne's birthplace. She was to resurface, lightly clad, as the War Memorial in Port-Vendres. The original, in bronze, can also be seen in les Jardins des Tuileries. Maillol, all his life, dreamed of his statues being in the Tuileries. And he was right so to dream, the eighteen that are there now look perfect.

Derain visited de Monfreid in Corneilla-de-Conflent where, inspired by his collection, he did a painting in the style of Gauguin.

In Collioure, he painted a new signboard for the hotel as a gift for Dame Rousette. She rejected it, claiming it was nothing but a mess of colours. Muxart hid the sign on top of a rabbit hutch in the yard "so that Monsieur André should not have the pain of seeing it in the ditch." One evening, during a storm, taking pity on Derain, Dame Rousette allowed him to paint the saloon door. He

Clocher and beach at Collioure, sketch by Phil Monk

chose to paint Don Quixote and Sancho Panza. Muxart watching, and commenting afterwards, said "A yellow moon in a green sky! No one had seen anything like it! Wherever did he get hold of these things, Monsieur André? How he made us laugh, la patronne, me and everyone else who saw that door!"

When, forty-five years later, Matisse remembered that summer in his sketch in the Livre d'Or of the Templiers Hotel, he called it "le Bonheur des Peintres". In it, clearly depicted, were Dame Rousette's hotel, the studio he shared with Derain and the boats in the bay of Collioure.

It had been a happy summer. Derain was always Amélie's favourite of her husband's artist friends. Young Pierre Matisse had ridden everywhere on his shoulders...

Derain and Matisse would never work together again, but, for that summer in Collioure, they had given each other the courage they needed to break the rules in order to pursue their artistic goal.

The end of August was stormy. Matisse was having difficulty getting his paintings finished.

Derain headed back to Paris via Marseilles and l'Estaque at the beginning of September, writing to Vlaminck: "Thirty canvases, twenty drawings, and fifty or so sketches!"

He would never return to Collioure. Dame Rousette threw out all the sketches he left pinned up in her hotel. Years later Muxart remarked reproachfully that no one had told him they were worth more than the calendars they had replaced.

Matisse wrote to Signac: " What a harvest!...To autumn!"

At the beginning of September most of the "migratory birds" were back in Paris. Marquet saw both Matisse and Derain's Collioure canvases and immediately wrote enthusiastically to Manguin that "they have done some stunning things!"

Matisse saw Manguin and Marquets' Côte d'Azur paintings, admired them and noted the differences to tell Signac.

On September 18th Signac bought *Luxe, Calme et Volupté* for 1,200 francs. Matisse promptly repaid sixty of the hundred and sixtyfrancs he owed Manguin.

At the end of September Derain signed a receipt with Vollard for 3,300 francs for the results of his summer's work...

Matisse wrote to Signac telling him that works by Camoin, Marquet and Manguin had already been accepted by the Salon d'Automne, adding, with reference to his own work, that "If I had not been on the committee and strongly supported by friends, mine would not have been accepted."

On October 18th 1905 the Third Salon d'Automne opened in the Grand Palais.

1,625 works by 397 artists. In Room 7 Maillol's magnificent sculpture *La Mediterranée* went almost unnoticed thanks to the uproar caused by the surrounding paintings:

10 by Matisse,
9 by Derain,
5 by Vlaminck,
5 by Marquet,
5 by Manguin.

Catalogue cover of 1905 *Salon d'Automne*

In his Gil Blas review, Louis Vauxcelles described the room as "*La Cage aux Fauves*" and "Wild beasts!" was the scandalised cry taken up by the art loving public who flocked to see them. It was not a compliment. But the name stuck, Fauvism was born and Matisse was chief Fauve.

While one critic described their painting as "a pot of paint thrown in the face of the public", the critic for Le Radical, perhaps with more vision than his fellows, wrote "There is much better than just hopes and promises (in this salon) and these youth's names now unknown by the snobs who rush to society openings will be celebrated tomorrow..."

Recently returned from his military service, the unknown Georges Braque was among those most impressed by the paintings of the "wild beasts", saying later that, in 1905, Matisse and Derain had opened the way for him.

Matisse said "Fauve painting is not everything, but it is the foundation of everything."

Barques catalanes

Chapter 5
Meet Picasso

In which we go back a bit in time, return to Paris and meet Picasso, the Steins, some dealers, and a few other collectors and artists.

The artist who was to be Matisse's life long rival in the field of twentieth century art had been working in Paris for a few months every year since 1900.

He was short of stature but had a commanding presence and an enormous personal magnetism. He was to become one of the most prolific innovators in the history of modern art.

Son of a painter and teacher of art at Málaga's City Art School, when *Pablo Diego José Francisco de Paula Juan Nepomuceno María de los Remedios Cipriano de la Santísima Trinidad Mártir Patricio Ruiz y Picasso*, better known simply as Picasso, was born in 1881 in Málaga, he failed to draw breath until a resourceful uncle blew cigar smoke into his nostrils.

He drew and painted prodigiously from a very early age and went on to study art in Madrid before moving to Barcelona where his father had become Professor of Art. By the late '90's he already enjoyed a certain following. The painter Casagemas, his best friend and constant companion, paid all the bills including the bulk of the rent for Picasso's loft studio. It was both vast and light. On its walls Picasso painted the essentials he could not afford to buy as well as the inessentials, covering them with images of a richness beyond belief. Console tables groaned with fruit, there was a safe for valuables, a page to run errands and an extremely buxom maid to care for the master of the house (later, when Fernande Olivier, his Parisian mistress, visited it, she remarked that this strange decoration gave the impression of a stage set). Casagemas collaborated on some of the "masterpieces" and the accompanying facetious inscriptions.

Barcelona, at the turn of the century, was bristling with all that was new in art, literature, the theatre and architecture and Els IV Gats Café was the bohemian meeting place of all young talent. Picasso and Casagemas, together with the sculptor Manolo, Manuel Pallarès

Bar at Els IV Gats, Barcelona

and Sabartès the poet, were habitués. In February 1900, the nineteen year old Picasso had an exhibition there of a hundred or so portraits. His portrait of the Patron's wife hangs in the Museum of Modern Art in Céret.

It was an exciting period. Close friendships were formed, Picasso and Casagemas went to bullfights together, and partook of the infinite variety of entertainment Barcelona had on offer. They dreamed of going to Paris. And it was in the autumn of 1900 that they first went there. Casagemas found in Paris "...nothing as good as Els IV Gats nor anything like it. Here everything is fanfare...tinsel..." He sent a " a little inventory..." of their accommodation to a friend back in Barcelona: "One table, one sink, two green chairs, one green armchair, two chairs that aren't green, one bed with extensions, one corner cupboard that isn't corner shaped, two wooden trestles that support a trunk, one oil lamp, one mat, a Persian rug, twelve blankets, one eiderdown, two pillows and a lot of pillowcases, four more pillows without cases, some cooking utensils, glasses, wineglasses, bottles, brushes, a screen, flowerpots, W.C., books and a pile of other things. We even have a mysterious utensil for private use by ladies only.

Goodbye and next time I'll be more lengthy..."

They met Odette, who spoke no Spanish and became Picasso's mistress, and Germaine, a well known artists' model, who was partly Spanish and for whom Casagemas developed an instant passion.

He, unfortunately, was unable keep up with her considerable sexual requirements.

Picasso fared better. Odette was more than satisfied by her Spanish lover. Furthermore, when Berthe Weill sold three of his paintings, Mañach, a Spanish art dealer whom Picasso had met through her, offered him a contract for a hundred and fifty francs a month.

Picasso and Casagemas visited the International Exhibition, spent time in the Louvre and did the rounds of the rue Lafitte galleries. After two months they returned to Barcelona.

Picasso was in Madrid when he heard of Casagemas's dramatic suicide.

Jilted, inevitably, by Germaine, Casagemas had gone to Paris to remonstrate with her. She said she would always be his friend but insisted their affair was over. Despite days and even weeks passing she could not be persuaded to change her mind. Finally Casagemas said he would return to Barcelona and a farewell dinner was arranged at the Hippodrome Restaurant. Manolo, Pallarès, Ramon Pichot and several other friends, mainly Catalans, were present. At nine o'clock Casagemas, the pocket of his velvet suit bulging with suicide letters and a revolver, stood up. As Casagemas fired shouting "Voilà pour toi!", Germaine dived under the table and hid behind Manuel Pallarès. Assuming he had killed the woman he loved, Casagemas turned the revolver on himself and, crying "et voilà pour moi!" shot himself and fell, dead, into Manolo's arms.

Picasso did not go to the memorial service held at Els IV Gats but the suicide of his friend affected him greatly, literally colouring his work. Paintings of beggars, poverty, old age and death ensued which then became known as his "Blue Period". Several of them were later exhibited in a group exhibition at Berthe Weill's Gallery.

On his second trip to Paris, Picasso headed to Casagemas's old apartment which he shared with his dealer, Pedro Mañach, who organised a show of his paintings with Vollard. It was at this show that he first met Max Jacob. Max Jacob was a poet, an extremely amusing man, homosexual and poverty stricken. He and Picasso had no language in common. Max Jacob records that towards the end of that evening "all the Spaniards went away… while Picasso and I spoke in sign language until morning…"

Picasso also met Maillol who, with Clotilde, had moved to Villeneuve-Saint-Georges where rents were considerably cheaper than in the Latin Quarter. Maillol described Picasso as "slender, delicate and beautiful like a girl" remembering fondly that the young Spaniard visited from time to time and sang Catalan songs for him.

Germaine became Picasso's mistress. This did not please Odette. It did not please Manolo either who had been sleeping with Germaine since Casagemas's suicide. Nevertheless Manolo and Picasso's friendship continued. They were both small, dark, intense and energetic, both had a great sense of humour and mischief. Unusual amongst their friends, neither liked getting drunk, though this fact never deterred them from having wild nights on the town.

By 1904, Picasso, aged 23, had taken over the painter and collector, Paco Durio's studio at 13 rue Ravignan in Paris. The building was ramshackle, constructed mostly of wood, zinc and dirty glass with stove pipes stuck out of it at random. So steep at that point is the Butte de Montmartre, that from rue Ravignan it seemed like a one floored shack, while from the rue Garaud side, five stories of rickety studios soared up with virtually no visible means of support. Vast and comfortless, it was boiling in summer when the sun streamed in through the dusty skylights; in winter Picasso's tea, left overnight, was frozen by morning.

Old postcard of Le Bateau Lavoir, Paris

Picasso was no stranger to poverty. In 1902 he had shared a studio with Max Jacob, so small that the one narrow bed was used by Picasso by day while Jacob worked in a shop and by Jacob at night, while Picasso painted by candlelight. Near destitution struck when Max Jacob lost his job in the shop. They were down to their last sausage, bought from a local street vendor which, when warmed, swelled and swelled and finally exploded, showering Picasso and Max Jacob with its skin and putrid flesh. Both they and their friendship survived and their lives lurched on. Max Jacob had one of the studios in rue Ravignan. He likened the building to the vessels moored along the Seine in which laundresses washed clothes. From that time on it was known as the Bateau Lavoir. Given that originally there was only one tap for the entire building, this was something of an irony. In fact some laundresses did indeed live there, along with numerous painters, actors, sculptors, writers and itinerant greengrocers.

In Picasso's time Kees van Dongen, Juan Gris, Constantin Brancusi, Modigliani and, of course, Max Jacob were fellow residents. Frequent visitors included Henri Matisse, Georges Braque, André Derain, Raoul Dufy, Frank Burty Haviland, the Steins and Ambroise Vollard.

The Bateau Lavoir burnt down in 1970 and was rebuilt in cement.

La Bande à Picasso

It was there that Picasso met the tall and strikingly beautiful Fernande Olivier who became his mistress. His painting changed from "Blue" to "Rose". He was a jealous and possessive lover and, forcing her to give up her career as a model for other artists, kept her a virtual prisoner in his freezing Bateau Lavoir studio. However, her pre-Picasso life featuring abuse as a child, followed by a disastrous marriage during which she had suffered rape and a miscarriage, had been so devoid of affection, that Picasso's love and devotion more than made up for her lack of freedom. Later, she remembered those days with great fondness as a time when Picasso and his friends were "sustained by hope and their illusions... How little money one needed then, when fifty francs could last a month and there would sometimes even be enough to settle up with the paint shop..."

Manolo was a frequent visitor and core member of the *Bande à Picasso*. As well as stealing Durio's Gauguins and selling them to Vollard, he also stole Max Jacob's sole pair of trousers while he slept, only returning them when he could find no buyer. Yet everyone loved Manolo, including his victims. He was witty, amusing and the only man from whom Picasso would take teasing, criticism and contradiction. Manolo's friends regarded him with a mixture of pleasure and suspicion. He was always involved in the most complicated, unlikely, usually fruitless and utterly fantastic deals. He would also enjoy playing the most outrageous tricks on people. He organised lotteries for his own profit. The draw was often hotly disputed as the same number came up repeatedly. Fernande remembers one that ran for three years.

Picasso's circle of friends expanded rapidly to include André Salmon and Apollinaire.

Vollard took some of his "Rose" paintings. He would arrive at the studio and buy everything Picasso had painted. In one swoop he took thirty canvases for which he paid 2,000 francs. Picasso worked at night, going to bed in the early hours of the morning and getting up in the middle of the afternoon. Clovis Sagot, a picture dealer Fernande described as "a bit too wily to be likeable but having something attractive about his audacity and his taste for advanced art, which he managed to combine with a rather more ordinary taste for profit and money," was Picasso's dealer of last resort. When he was completely out of money, food, canvases and paint he would go to the shop of Clovis Sagot, ex clown of the Medrano Circus and invite him to visit his studio. He sold pastels of bull fighting scenes to Berthe Weil and exhibited at the Gallery Serrurier... But it was really through the Steins that his rise to fame and fortune was assured and it was through the Steins that he met Matisse.

Enter the Steins

Doorway of 27 rue de Fleurus, Paris

Leo Stein and his sister, Gertrude were wealthy Americans of German Jewish extraction. They were not immensely wealthy in the manner of the Potter Palmers of Chicago or the H. O. Havemeyers of New York and their ilk who, at the turn of the century, swooped into Paris buying up whatever caught their fancy to fill their mansions back in the United States. The Steins were of more modest means, and, rather than spiriting their collections back to California, they chose to live in Paris, keeping their collections with them.

Soon after their arrival in Paris, Leo became an art student. A collector by nature he was always on the lookout for paintings that intrigued or interested him. From 1903 onwards the pair began to buy and collect contemporary art, displaying it on the walls of their apartment at 27 rue de Fleurus for anyone who was interested to see and enjoy. It has been said of Gertrude Stein that she "collected geniuses rather than masterpieces. She recognized them a long way off..." Soon the fruits of their intuition began to fill their living space.

They were a striking pair. Leo was tall and thin; his sister, Gertrude, the opposite. Both dressed in flat sandals and matching brown corduroy suits. Their brother Michael, his wife Sarah and their son Allan had also moved from San Francisco to Paris. They too were enthusiastic collectors.

GERTRUDE STEIN

1874 – 1946

ÉCRIVAIN AMÉRICAIN

Vécut ici avec son frère LÉO STEIN
puis avec ALICE B.TOKLAS
elle y reçut de nombreux
artistes et écrivains
de 1903 à 1938

*Gertrude Stein plaque at
27 rue de Fleurus, Paris*

Rue de Fleurus, near the Opéra, was situated conveniently just around the corner from the auction house Hôtel Drouot and the short stretch of rue Laffitte where most of the city's best known galleries were to be found. Vollard at no 6, Berheim-Jeune at no 8, Hessèle at no 13 and Durand-Ruel at no 16...

When the Steins first visited Vollard he was comparatively unknown, just beginning his career as a dealer. He was born on the Île de la Réunion in 1866, had arrived in Paris in 1887 and had neglected his law studies in favour of trawling the Seine-side book stalls for prints. He opened his first gallery in 1893 on the rue Lafitte at the age of twenty seven.

Clovis Sagot, where the Steins had bought their first Picasso, was higher up the street and Berthe Weill sold her mix of books, paintings and bric a brac, higher still on rue Victor-Masse in Montmarte.

A year later Vollard moved a few doors down to a better space. He took a chance on buying up the paintings of an unknown artist named Paul Cézanne, who, taking advantage of the new fangled paint in little metal tubes, was painting landscape in situ. The first five Vollard bought set him back 902 francs and made him Cézanne's sole agent. Despite having to compete with well established dealers such as Petit and Durand Ruel, he never looked back. Gertrude Stein described him as a huge dark man who lisped a little. The gallery, unlike any other she had visited, had a couple of paintings turned to the wall and, in a corner, an untidy heap of large and small canvases. Vollard himself stood in the middle of the room "*glooming*". This, she said, was Vollard cheerful. When cheerless he would put his huge frame against the glass door that led onto the street and gloom darkly out of it. Gertrude and Leo bought their first Cézannes from him.

Later, when selling an early Cézanne portrait of a woman to the Steins, he appeared to study it intently for a while before telling them that, of course, ordinarily a portrait of a woman is always more expensive than a portrait of a man; "but", said he, looking at the picture very carefully, "I suppose with Cézanne it does not make any difference"...

Vollard had an eye for hitherto unrecognised talent. He had supported Gauguin, sending him a small allowance in his South Seas exile (in Gauguin's opinion an insultingly small amount).

Vollard had given Picasso his first exhibition in 1901 and did the same for Matisse in 1904. His gallery became one of the most important centres of innovative art and his clientele included some of the leading collectors of the day.

He had been one of the first dealers to become interested in Maillol's sculpture, managing to widen Maillol's audience from his circle of fellow artists to collectors and international museums.

By 1903, thanks to his improved financial position, Maillol built a studio and summer house near the station in Marly-le-Roi just west of Paris. Other artists had also settled in Marly and Maillol's house, studio and garden became a meeting place for many of his artist friends as well as poets and writers. Vuillard painted him there, working in his studio. From then on Maillol divided his time between Paris and Banyuls, working on tapestry, painting, drawing, sculpting and engraving. He and his group of friends were inspired by Gauguin to experiment with all forms of contemporary art. Although Maillol gave Gauguin no credit for any influence on his sculpture, he admitted that, in painting, his liberty from the restrictions of the academic conventions of the time was much inspired by Gauguin

In 1905, following the death of his mother the previous year, Gustave Fayet bought a mansion in Paris and, with his family, began spending more time in the capital. He dedicated the salon to Gauguin's works. Above the chimney was the wooden bas relief *La Guerre et la Paix* that Gauguin had sculpted especially for him and Gauguin's paintings covered the walls. Matisse, the Steins, the Russians Shchukin and Morozov, Maurice Denis, Gide and Cocteau came to admire them. The homage Fayet wanted for the *Maître des Marquises* had begun. The same year, with Fabre and de Monfreid, Fayet lent his Gauguins to Maillol's patron, Count Henry Kessler, for a retrospective exhibition in Germany, and again, in 1906, for the Salon d'Automne in Paris. In 1905 Fayet bought, from Vollard, a Maillol bronze of a crouching woman, adding a bas relief in stone and a wooden statue of a naked woman standing, for which Vollard charged him 2,000 francs. "*Quel Volleurrr*" cried Maillol on being told.

Fayet would often go to Marly, Maillol's studio, to chat to the sculptor and study his drawings. Through Druet he bought twenty four of them. When Maillol admitted his only laziness was the dispatching of his work, Fayet went to Marly and collected the precious bundle himself.

Fayet, possibly under the influence of Fabre, had become interested in the paintings of Matisse. Certainly de Monfreid considered it to be thanks to Fabre that Fayet started investing in what de Monfreid described as "Matisseries."

Visiting the 1905 Salon d'Automne, de Monfreid talked only of the success of Maillol's *La Mediterranée*, not mentioning the Collioure paintings of Matisse and Derain.

All the Steins attended the Salon d'Automne in 1905 and were fascinated by the uproar caused by the Fauves in Salle VII. They were pleased to see paintings there by Manguin, whose work they had recently begun buying, and were interested in those by Camoin, Derain, Vlaminck and, above all, by Matisse. They had certainly heard of him. He was constantly mentioned in the Paris art press and Vollard and Weill must also have spoken of him to them.

After five weeks of staring at the strange and vivid portrait of Amélie, her face all turbulent colours, a blue/green line down the nose, an explosion of more colours in the dramatic hat and dress, the Steins finally decided it was worth the 500 francs asking price. It was Sarah who persuaded Leo to buy it. Advice she later regretted, wishing she had bought it herself as she found the portrait bore a striking resemblance to her mother. Be that as it may, the purchase of *Woman in a Hat* was a bold move when the rest of Paris was too busy ridiculing the work of the Fauves to recognize the unfolding of a new movement in the history of art. They were encouraged, however, by the salon secretary to offer 400 francs for it as opposed to the 500 Matisse was asking. To Matisse's consternation, Amélie refused the offer saying the extra hundred francs would clothe little Marguerite for a year. She was right. They got their money and Matisse's first Fauve painting to be sold went to the Steins.

Picasso, who had not at that point met Matisse, felt considerably out-flanked. Although twelve years older than Picasso, Matisse had been a slow developer. Nevertheless, by 1904, he had taken on the colour theories of his friends Signac and Cross and, by 1905, had exploded them into fauvism and was on the way to becoming one of the most revolutionary colourists in the history of art. Picasso, quintessentially Spanish, relied on more sombre shades. "The only real colour is black, Spaniards understand this. Look at Vélazquez's blacks. If you don't know what colour to take, take black." Both Matisse and Picasso drew on the paintings of Van Gogh, Cézanne and Gauguin for inspiration, coming up with very different interpretations. Both were beginning to recognize in each other their rivalry for pole position in the art of the twentieth century. It was a rivalry much fostered by the Steins.

Leo Stein introduced the German collector, Hans Purrmann to Matisse. Other foreign collectors began to follow suit and the Paris dealers started to show an interest. From October 21st to November 20th six paintings by Camoin, six by Derain, five by Dufy, fifteen by Manguin, seven by Marquet, six by Matisse and five by Vlaminck were on show at the Berthe Weil Gallery. Dufy's inclusion in the exhibition so infuriated Matisse that she had to place his work in a separate room at the back.

Leo Stein, writing to his friend Mabel Foote in November 1905 said, "The Autumn Salon is over... Recent acquisitions are unfortunately by people you have never heard of..." He describes Matisse's *Woman in a Hat*... "made everybody laugh except a few who got mad about it... " he also described two pictures by "a young Spaniard named Picasso whom I consider a genius of very considerable magnitude and one of the most notable draughtsmen living..."

It wasn't long before Leo and Gertrude Stein bought their first Picasso. They took to Picasso immediately and invited him and Fernande to dinner. Fernande described Leo as "a typical American Jew" and Gertrude as "fat, short and massive, with a broad, beautiful head, noble, over accentuated, regular features and intelligent eyes which reflected her clear sightedness and wit. Her mind was lucid and organized, and her voice and her appearance were masculine." Fascinated by Gertrude's appearance, Picasso asked if he might paint her portrait. Ever astute, he also painted swiftly executed portraits of Leo and Allan.

Both Gertrude and Leo dressed, as Fernande said, "à la Raymond, brother of Isadora, Duncan who was a friend of theirs..." they were, in her opinion "Too intelligent to bother about whether people found them ridiculous, to sure of themselves to care what people thought of them..."

The large portrait of Gertrude took many sittings during which they became friends. They remained close for many years, long after Picasso had any need of buyers.

From the autumn onwards Matisse was working on his huge canvas *le Bonheur de Vivre*, a painting that not only shows Gauguin's influence but was a clear forerunner of Picasso's *Les Demoiselles d'Avignon*. Its setting was the beach of l'Ouille, near Collioure. The ring of dancers could well be dancing the Sardane (the traditional Catalan dance of unity, forbidden under Franco as subversive. Anyone can join the circle of dancers but no one may leave until the dance is finished) and were a preview of his own "*Danse*" of 1909. It was his only submission to the Salon des Indépendants in March 1906 and caused just as great an uproar as his "*Woman in a Hat*" had done in October of 1905.

Ceramic panel of sardane dancing, St Laurent de Cerdans

It, too, would be bought by the Steins.

In his copy of the Indépendants catalogue, next to Matisse's name, Apollinaire noted, "At the moment Stein speaks only of two painters, Matisse and Picasso."

It was through the Steins that Matisse and Picasso first met. That winter of 1905/6, Leo and Gertrude took Matisse, with little Marguerite, to visit Picasso in his Bateau Lavoir studio. Fifty years later, Marguerite still had vivid memories of the occasion; of Frika, the impressive and vast dog, and of Fernande's extraordinary beauty and the way she served sugar by taking a handful out of the cupboard and depositing it on any clear space on the filthy table. Marguerite also never forgot the dinner they ate afterwards at the Lapin Agile, of steak, topped with ham and crowned by a fried egg.

Le Lapin Agile, Paris

Matisse and Picasso, apart from their devotion to painting, could not have been more dissimilar. Nevertheless they would remain friendly rivals, reacting to each other's achievements all their lives. Leo Stein noted that, in his opinion, from then on twentieth century art was to be a two-man race.

Fernande made her own comparisons of her lover and Matisse. "There was something very sympathetic about Matisse. With his regular features and his thick, golden beard, he really looked like a grand old man of art. He seemed to be hiding behind his thick spectacles, and his expression was opaque, gave nothing away, though he always talked for ages as soon as the conversation moved on to painting. He would argue, assert and endeavour to persuade. I think he was a good deal less simple than he liked to appear. He was nearly forty-five (in fact Matisse was thirty-seven to Picasso's twenty-five) and very much master of himself. Unlike Picasso who was usually rather sullen and inhibited at occasions like the Steins' Saturdays, Matisse shone and impressed people. They were the two painters of whom much was expected."

Much later Françoise Gilot, Picasso's mistress during the 40's and the mother of Claude and Paloma, summed up their relationship rather charmingly: "Like a ballet dancer, Pablo would try to charm Matisse but it was always Matisse who ended up seducing Picasso. 'We need to talk to each other as much as possible' Picasso would say. 'When one of us is dead, there will be so much left unsaid that can never again be discussed'."

There was an unspoken competition between them for the friendship of the Steins. The maid, Hélène, had no doubt who her favourite was. In Gertrude Stein's autobiography, (the misleadingly titled *Autobiography of Alice B. Toklas*) Hélène tells Alice B. Toklas that she did not appreciate Monsieur Matisse. In her opinion "a Frenchman should not stay unexpectedly for a meal, particularly after asking the servant what was for dinner."

One time on being told Matisse would be staying to eat she told Gertrude Stein: "In that case I will not make an omelette but fry the eggs. It takes the same number of eggs and the same amount of butter but it shows less respect, and he will understand."

Nevertheless the Matisses were often at the Steins and the Steins often ate with the Matisse family, especially if one of the Matisse relations had sent them a hare. Gertrude Stein remembers with enthusiasm the jugged hare Amélie Matisse prepared from a Perpignan recipe and served with the naturally sweet wine from Banyuls-sur-Mer they had already sampled with Aristide Maillol.

Picasso, although his fame was beginning to spread, spoke little

French and had not sold much. Matisse, who always passed on any good luck that came his way to younger artists and always shared any good fortune with Picasso, introduced him to Shchukin, the Russian collector, who Fernande described as "a little tallowy swine-faced man with a large head and a terrible stutter." Picasso and Matisse understood the importance of wealthy amateur collectors. They both sought the recognition and praise that was, to them, as important as the money.

Both benefited from the friendship of the Steins even if it could be, from time to time a little intrusive as on one Sunday afternoon, when Gertrude Stein, wishing to show off her participation in Parisian bohemian life, took a young woman friend from California to visit Picasso in his Bateau Lavoir studio. Annette Rosenshine described the event: "(Gertrude) suddenly decided it would be interesting to drop in at Picasso's studio… She turned the doorknob and pushed - there on the bare floor of a completely unfurnished room lay an attractive woman between two men – Picasso on one side… they were fully clothed… lying there to rest from a Bohemian revelry the night before… (Since) Picasso and his companions were disinclined to get up or incapable of it and did nothing to detain us, we left. As we stepped into the dimly lighted hall, closing the door behind us, Gertrude gave me a quick quizzical look that told of her interest in my response to our Bohemian foray. She obviously expected me to be shocked. I resolved to display nothing but aplomb."

Gertrude herself described Picasso as "a little bullfighter followed by his squadron of four" or, later, as "Napoleon followed by his four enormous grenadiers. Derain and Braque were great big men, so was Guillaume (Apollinaire) a heavy set man and (André) Salmon was not small. Picasso was every inch a chief."

The bohemian life of the Bande à Picasso attracted earnest young Germans. Visiting Montmartre for the first time, many sought Picasso out. Most bored him but one, Wilhelm Uhde, became both a friend and a collector. He had bought his first Picasso in a shop for ten francs, a picture by an unknown artist of a woman taking a bath in a blue room. A few days later, as Uhde was eating in the Lapin Agile, buying wine for the gathering of painters and writers who surrounded him, he learned that the artist was the young man sitting next to him. The famous Blue Room now hangs in the Phillip's Collection in Washington D.C.

Many of the more successful of the Montmartre painters of the time owed quite a debt to the Germans for making them so well known. The Russians and later the Italians were other major contributors.

Derain, meanwhile, had been spending six weeks in London where he was much impressed by Turner. He haunted the British Museum and visited all the art galleries. He also visited a tailor in Savile Row where he ordered a suit.

"I couldn't have been more English... except that I added an element of fauvism to the tailoring..." he said. He spoke the truth. Returning to Paris, he wore it for the opening of the Salon des Indépendants. The trousers and jacket were a startling shade of green, the waistcoat red; to set it off, on his feet, he wore a pair of the yellowest of yellow shoes.

Fernande had always maintained that his "elegance was English and slightly over done."

The trip had been the result of a commission to paint some London scenes for Vollard following the success of the 1905 Salon d'Automne. Derain spent the summer painting in l'Estaque and the next year signed a contract with Kahnweiler.

As a result of his improved financial situation Derain felt he could marry Alice Princet. Alice Princet had long been a friend of Fernande Olivier. Gertrude Stein describes her as "a madonna like creature, with large lovely eyes and charming hair." Fernande told Gertrude Stein that Alice Princet was "the daughter of a working man and had the brutal thumbs so characteristic of working men". She had been, explained Fernande, for seven years with her husband, Princet and had been faithful to him in the "manner of Montmartre", which, according to Fernande, was to stick with him through sickness and health while amusing herself along the way. Now Princet had become head of his small government service department and would need to invite other heads of departments to his house, their relationship needed regularising. They were to be married. Max Jacob remarked that "it is wonderful to long for a woman for seven years and to possess her at last." Picasso wondered, prophetically, "why they should marry only in order to divorce?"

And, sure enough, as soon as they were married Alice Princet had met Derain. It was love at first sight. They were, as Fernande put it, "mad for each other." Princet tried to bear it but couldn't. In his anger he tore up Gertrude Stein's fur coat, the first one she had ever had and which she had purchased especially for his wedding. Within six months Alice and Derain had run off together. Gertrude Stein always liked Alice, particularly "her certain wild quality that, perhaps, had to do with her brutal thumbs, and that was curiously in accord with her Madonna face."

Fernande's description of her is remarkably similar... "Alice Derain at this period was so calm and beautiful that she was nicknamed "*La Vierge*". Derain she describes as "Slim, elegant (we know she considered his elegance somewhat overdone) with a lively colour and black enamelled hair, always a pipe in his mouth, phlegmatic, mocking, cold; an arguer..."

Just before the Salon des Indépendants in the Spring of 1906, Matisse's solo exhibition of fifty five paintings opened at the gallery of the photographer and dealer Eugène Druet. In the opinion of several critics the paintings would "only be of interest to those afraid to seem outdated"... The Steins, despite suffering from no such fears, bought several. At the Indépendants, Matisse showed only his large *Bonheur de Vivre*. It did not sell. Signac, on seeing it said "Matisse, whose attemps I have liked up until now, seems to have gone to the dogs."

Le Bonheur de Vivre was later bought by Leo Stein.

The Stein's highly visible collection was where Picasso's and Matisse's work was most on public show. It seems that Gertrude and Leo Stein rather relished the power their patronage bestowed and enjoyed pitting their two preferred artists against each other. Matisse was said to display "an astonishing lucidity of mind, was incise and intelligent and impressed people" Picasso, however, was perceived as "... easily irritated by people who tried to question him about his work, tried to make him explain what he was unable to explain."

The vibrant arcadia Matisse depicted in *Le Bonheur de Vivre*, with its revolutionary use of colour, form and line was a real challenge to Picasso, a challenge he was not about to ignore.

At first Matisse and Picasso would meet regularly, scrutinising each other's work minutely. As Picasso would say half a century later, "Nobody ever looked at Matisse's work as thoroughly as I did and he at mine."

Although they were both struggling with money, gradually, sales were coming in and each of them, come the summer, was able to leave the capital.

Picasso took Fernande to visit his family in Barcelona. It was the first time she had been to Spain so it was, as Gertrude Stein noted, necessary for her "to buy a dress, a hat, perfumes and a cooking stove. All women in those days, when travelling from country to country, took a French oil stove on which to cook"...

Fernande maintained Picasso became a different person as soon as he returned to Spain, especially in the Spanish countryside, gay, less wild, more brilliant. She found he radiated happiness as opposed to Picasso in Paris whom, she found, was oppressed and inhibited by an atmosphere alien to him. As an artist in Paris he flourished, as a man in Fernande's opinion, he would have been happier in Spain.

They met many friends in Barcelona, including Enric Casanovas, with whom Picasso planned to work. However, after all, Casanovas was not free to join them and they went on their own to the tiny village of Gósol, in the heart of the Spanish Pyrenees. There Picasso spent a prolific six weeks painting seven large canvases and a dozen medium ones. He produced some of his most stunning pictures of Fernande, filled two sketchbooks with drawings, made any number of gouaches, watercolours and carved some wooden sculptures. His output of work confirmed his joy at being in Spain. He practised speaking the Catalan he had learned eight summers before at Horta de Ebro.

"The locals were enchanted by us," said Fernande , "they sought out our company, brought us partridges and thrushes to vary our diet of bean and sausage stew, they made us play the peculiar games of the region."

Matisse had gone back to Collioure.

Chapter 6
Summer 1906
Winter 1907/8

As well as the Steins and Shchukin, Gustave Fayet had begun collecting Matisse's work. As early as February 1906 Fayet had called on him in Paris and bought a number of his Collioure watercolours. Gertrude and Leo Stein, encouraged by Matisse, had viewed Fayet's collection. Accompanied by Matisse and Fabre, Fayet went to 27 rue de Fleurus to visit the Steins. Competition was growing for Matisse's latest canvases. That summer, Vollard, primed by Leo Stein, had asked for a first viewing of the five paintings Matisse had sent to Paris for the salon jury. Druet got there first. The paintings were accepted and sold before the private view to Druet who sold them on to Fayet.

Fayet was glad of them when, in the autumn, he lent his Gauguin Collection to the Salon d'Automne and could hang the sixteen Matisses on the denuded walls of 19 rue de Bellechasse. Certainly one of the first to recognise the genius of Matisse, Gustave Fayet had an excellent eye. But much as he loved his pictures, he could never resist a profitable sale. He was as much a businessman as a collector, always selling enough as the prices rose to finance his own private collection.

Fayet visited Algeria a couple of times a year in connection with his wine business. Many artists and collectors at the time were interested in "Oriental" influences, both Far Eastern and North African. It may well have been at Fayet's suggestion that before settling for the summer in Collioure, Matisse made a side trip to Algeria travelling by ferry from

Shipping poster of Port-Vendres

Port-Vendres. Matisse was fascinated by the Algerian landscape and, to a lesser extent, by the people. He found Algiers a dispiriting version of Paris, "the casbah full of predatory whores, a filthy stinking Paris that has been inadequately cleaned for years" he wrote to Manguin. Despite this comment, the colours and decorations of Algeria were to crop up time and time again in his future paintings. The flute player, the goldfish, the princely Arab would all appear in later works. Rich coloured rugs and primitive carvings would also figure.

Fayet, later that summer, in the company of Fabre spent time with Matisse in Collioure. He allowed Matisse to take prints from Gauguin's Noa Noa wood blocks, asking him for lessons so that he could print from them himself. Matisse, of course, knew of Gauguin's carvings from his first visit to de Monfreid's Château St Clément the previous year. He had also admired those that Gauguin had carved specifically for Fayet that he had seen taking pride of place in his Paris mansion on rue de Bellechasse.

Matisse and Derain were corresponding about "primitve art", continuing their conversations of the summer before. Derain, in London, was sketching Maori carvings from New Zealand in the British Museum, promising to show them to Matisse when he returned. He wrote saying he was missing the violent light of the South that had so inspired them, missing the women of Collioure made, as he said, "for moving in full sun". At least the carvings he was copying were "forms born of the open air in full sun, forms called into being by strong sunlight." Matisse, Derain, Braque, Vlaminck and also Picasso were ardent collectors of "primitive art," often competing to see who could discover the most beautiful sculptures and masks. The inspiration it engendered had begun to play an important part in their development.

In the summer of 1906 Braque was painting fauvist canvases with Friesz and Dufy in l'Estaque near Marseilles. Dufy, Braque and Friesz: "The Three Normans." Fernande called them "Three ambitious, intelligent and shrewd Normans, whose success was due as much to their birth as anything else. Three friends who distrusted and certainly envied each other."

Collioure Beach, sketch by Phil Monk

Back in Collioure, Matisse put on his old rope soled *espadrilles* and got to work. Amélie and the three children joined him at Dame Rousette's Hôtel de la Gare. He sent a sketch of the reunited family to Sarah and Michael Stein. Amélie looking young but stern, himself peering through his thin rimmed glasses with bushy beard, Marguerite posing in pinafore dress, puffed sleeves and a ribbon in her hair. The little boys, shaven heads and sticky-out ears looking full of mischief, Pierre labelled "the naughtiest of them all". They were enrolled at the local primary school where René Pous, father of Jojo Pous and future owner of the Templiers Hotel in Collioure, was already a pupil.

Later Matisse told Picasso that it was around this time that he began to pay attention to the spontaneity of his children's artwork. He described to Picasso how, in a profile portrait, the child had placed both the eyes side by side as if full face. Picasso took a greater interest in children's art from that moment on. Young Pierre copied a painting Matisse had done of one of his Algerian jugs, telling his father he had "invented a new colour". For the rest of his life Pierre remembered the crushed feeling he experienced when his father told him there "was no such thing."

Matisse wrote to Manguin describing a typical Collioure day when he and Amélie left home at 6am to go to a forest or the mountains where she would pose peacefully. He wrote that he could only work till around ten or eleven because of the intense heat. He tells Manguin that "Collioure is just a village whose only regular visitors are some lower-middle-class people from Perpignan; to go swimming it is necessary to travel about one half hour to a small pebble beach." This was the beach of l'Ouille, over the headland from Collioure. He spent a lot of time painting the luxurious palms and shrubs in the garden of the Villa Palma. Ernest Py, the owner, allowed Matisse to paint in the garden to his heart's content but would not allow the artist in the house for fear of damaging the reputation of his two unmarried sisters.

For his models Matisse used Amélie, Marguerite and Rosa, an Italian girl who had posed for him in Paris. She became an honorary member of the Matisse family.

In St-Tropez, Manguin complained constantly that it was becoming impossible to find secluded enough spots for his wife to model for him nude in the surrounding landscape. On July 12 he arrived for a month in Collioure with his family. Jean and Pierre Matisse were aged seven and six, Claude and Pierre Manguin six and four. The boys played happily together. Amélie Matisse and Jeanne Manguin posed for their husbands and gossiped and tended their houses and families. The two Henris painted, examining and analysing each others' work with an easy frankness born of fifteen long years of friendship. Manguin, the gentlest of the Fauves, was described by his friend as having "a passionate tenderness of feeling..." Manguin admitted that "his goal is of obtaining harmony and luminous expression in his paintings. He admired Matisse immensely, describing him, with Cézanne and Gauguin, as "the golden triangle of modern painting."

The two men had much in common. Both relied on the support of their families, both their households revolved around the artist's studio. Manguin painted his wife Jeanne reading, sleeping, doing her hair, lying on her bed, on the grass, paddling, swimming. Matisse drew her as well. In his portrait she looks a bit matronly for her twenty six years, possibly because, in the summer of 1906, she was pregnant with the Manguin's third and last child.

In August, after the Manguins had left, Fayet visited Matisse in Collioure. He brought his friend and fellow collector, Maurice Fabre. Matisse remained in Collioure after Amélie took the children back to Paris in the autumn. He and Terrus saw each other almost daily, often working together in Terrus's studio in Elne.

In a letter to Manguin, he describes a performance they attended given by the local theatre group in Collioure, the sets designed and painted by Terrus. "The Grand Théâtre Moderne of Collioure... stalls 25 cents, gallery 15 cents... Count X goes without shoes in spite of being in formal court dress...In short, mon vieux, we make do with any amusement we can get..."

In November Matisse was back in Collioure for the best part of a year. In February Terrus instigated a round of excursions to visit the other artists of the Roussillon. They took the train up the Têt valley to see Gustave Violet in Prades where Terrus often stayed. Matisse then moved on to Narbonne to call on Fayet and Maurice Fabre. By the 12th of February he was back in the Pyrenees with Terrus and Amélie visiting Vernet-les-Bains near de Monfreid's Château St Clément, where the snow in places was over eight foot thick on the ground. The de Monfreids made plans to meet the Matisses in Collioure in the summer.

In the meantime, de Monfreid spent most of the winter and spring in Paris. Even after Gauguin's death, he was ever busy with his affairs. His notebook for that spring was full of meetings with Mme Gauguin, who was staying in Paris with the Fayets, and was wanting to sell more of her husband's canvases. With de Monfreid she visited Vollard, organised the sending of some paintings to an exhibition in Vienna, discussed restoring others. One evening, after dining with the Fayets, Mette Gauguin gave him a terracotta bust of her son Clovis. De Montfreid noted in his diary that, finding no horsedrawn cab, he had to return home on foot, in the rain, with the bust of Clovis under his arm...

On May 9th the Fayets and Mette Gauguin dined with de Monfreid. One of many occasions when Mette railed furiously against her late husband. Undeterred, de Monfreid, ever loyal to the artist he admired so greatly, continued to do all he could to support Gauguin's widow and her family.

In February 1907 Vollard went to Picasso's studio and purchased most of his Rose period work for 2,500 francs.

Ambrose Vollard was becoming a major character on the Paris art scene. For thirty years, every Thursday evening, he hosted dinners in the bare-walled cellar of his gallery, uproarious affairs at which Creole chicken curry was served and to which invitations were much sought after. Pablo Picasso, Odilon Redon, Maurice Denis, Aristide Maillol, Guillaume Apollinaire and André Derain were among those fortunate enough to enjoy his generous hospitality. In his *Recollections* of a *Picture Dealer* Vollard tells of a "foreign lady who heard of the "Cellar" through Count Kessler, the well known German collector of paintings who sometimes dined there with me. Coming on a visit to Paris from Germany, she jotted down her plans in a notebook, and alongside "visit to Maxim's" she wrote "Dine in the Cave Vollard". She imagined it to be a restaurant." Vollard goes on to say that, actually, it was more like a Montmartre cabaret than a restaurant.

As well as buying and selling paintings Vollard wrote and published books, encouraging and commissioning artists to illustrate them. *Les Fables de la Fontaine*, illustrated by Chagall during his time in Céret, is a shining example.

Many of the artists he encouraged painted his portrait... As Picasso was to remark "The most beautiful woman who ever lived has never had her portrait painted, drawn or engraved any oftener that Vollard."

St Martí de Prades
by Etienne Terrus

At the start of his career Vollard would exchange paintings when he could not afford to buy them, a practice that benefited him and the artists who were building their own collections. Picasso traded his own works for those of Degas and Matisse, Degas and Renoir drew lots for a Cézanne. A total of 678 works by Cézanne passed through Vollard's hands. It was chez Vollard that Matisse, having persuaded Amélie to pawn her emerald ring, purchased Cézanne's *Three Bathers*...

Manguin wrote to Matisse from Paris urging him to keep his prices up, adding that Fayet was selling many of the paintings that he had bought. He also mentioned a German dealer called Kahnweiler who was paying the prices asked by Braque, Friesz and Marquet.

Matisse followed his advice on pricing, returning to Paris to show one painting, his *Blue Nude: Memory of Biskara*, in the Salon des Indépendants in March. He was visited by Fénéon who offered him a one man show at the Berheim Jeune Gallery.

Cover of Gil Blas, illustrated weekly magazine

The influential art critic, Louis Vauxcelles, describing the Fauve Group within the Salon wrote in the weekly review, Gil Blas on March 20th 1907: "a movement I consider dangerous. (despite the great sympathy I have for its perpetrators) is taking shape among a small clan of youngsters. A chapel has been established, two haughty princes officiating, MM Derain and Matisse, a few innocent catechumens have received their baptism. Their dogma amounting to a wavering schematicism proscribes modelling and volume in the name of I-don't-know-what pictorial abstraction. This new religion hardly appeals to me. I don't believe in this renaissance. M. Matisse, fauve in chief, M. Derain, fauve deputy, MM Othon Friesz and Dufy, fauves in attendance, M Girieud irresolute, eminent, Italianate fauve, M Czobel uncultivated, Hungarian or Polish fauve, M Bérény, apprentice fauve, and M Delaunay (a fourteen year old pupil of M Metzinger) infantile fauvelet..."

Matisse's startling *Blue Nude: Memory of Biskra* stopped the Paris art world in its tracks once again. And, once again, it was bought by Leo and Gertrude Stein, ostensibly to replace a Bonnard they had sold a couple of months earlier.

On seeing it at the Salon des Indépendants, George Daniel de Mondfreid wrote in a letter to Louis Bausil that "it made a big impression on Picasso!"

In fact, at the time, Matisse's work was far more revolutionary than Picasso's whose "Blue" and "Rose" periods, although exciting in their own ways, were nothing like as dramatic as the Fauve paintings Matisse had been producing since 1905.

Picasso had shut himself away. He was working on his answer to Matisse's Salon d'Automne's, *Bonheur de Vivre*. As yet almost no one had seen *Les Demoiselles d'Avignon*. It was not shown to the general public until almost a decade later. Those who had seen it found it every bit as baffling as Matisse's work. Leo Stein actually burst out laughing.

After the added challenge of the *Blue Nude – Souvenir of Biskra* Picasso redoubled his efforts.

Picasso not only saw it on the walls of the Salon des Indépendants but also, later, on the walls of 27 rue de Fleurus. One of the Steins' guests, Walter Pach, was staring at it when Picasso, standing at his side asked him "Does that interest you?"

"In a way yes," Pach replied, "it interests me like a blow between the eyes. I don't understand what he is thinking."

"Neither do I," said Picasso, "If he wants to make a woman, let him make a woman. If he wants to make a design, let him make a design. This is between the two." Nevertheless he began drawing and painting a woman with a bent raised elbow and crooked knee, for all the world Matisse's *Blue Nude* rotated into a standing position, and incorporated her into his *Demoiselles d'Avignon*.

In Collioure, the start of that 1907 summer was overshadowed by the tragic death of a Matisse cousin who had been sent to stay with Matisse on health grounds.

The Roussillon countryside, too, was far from peaceful. There was unrest amongst the subsistence farming community, a growing rebellion resulting in an 180,000 strong demonstration in Perpignan by the peasant wine growers. There were strikes and riots all along the coast. The Wine Growers's Revolt was ruthlessly suppressed by Prime Minister, Clemenceau. Matisse painted on regardless.

Etienne Terrus – *Le Racou*

Old postcard of *le Racou*

On June the 13th Matisse wrote to Fénéon from Collioure telling him he was sending him four canvases on which several small areas of red were not yet dry.

The de Monfreids and their friend, Louis Bausil, were, as planned, spending the summer in the Roussillon. From time to time they visited the Matisses in Collioure. The men would often make the journey from Corneilla by bicycle, sometimes joining up with Terrus for boating excursions and picnics. De Monfreid noted one such occasion in his notebook. They arrived, with his daughter Agnès, at the beach of Le Racou in a dinghy around ten. "Prepared lunch in the hut (probably Terrus's) and had a swim. It was quarter past twelve before we ate, we were all starving. We feasted on fresh sardines. Exquisite! In the afternoon we took the dinghy and went with Bausil to Collioure dropping Agnès at Ouille. We saw various people, Mme Matisse, the Souliers, etc. We got back to the hut at le Racou around 7.30 and dined late. Then we slept in bunk beds..." The next day, de Monfreid spent the day with them all again, had a swim and returned by bicycle via Argelès, Elne, Thuir, Corbère, and Bouleternère, where he "drank water from a cool spring", and arrived home around 7pm, "Without excessive tiredness". A bicycle ride of some seventy-three kilometres.

Michael and Sarah Stein arrived as well and got together with the Matisse family. Matisse also spent a lot of time with Maillol and, of course, with Terrus. Idyllic memories: "... met up with Terrus, in some forgotten valley in the Albères, it was a great pleasure. We would sit under a laurel bush; Maillol dreaming of his monumental torsos, Terrus looking for a subject he wanted, an old farmhouse built by the Moors, its ancient walls baked in the sun. Beyond the valleys were glimpses of the sea. Terrus would be painting it..."

In July Matisse signed a receipt for Fénéon indicating that he had been paid 1,800 francs for four paintings. The next day he wrote to Fénéon that he was sending him several more...

The Matisses had been persuaded by Leo Stein to visit him in Florence. They set off at a leisurely pace, spending a week with Derain in Cassis and staying with the Manguins in St-Tropez, and Cross in St-Clair. Matisse had taken photographs of his paintings to show his friends. They were suitably and gratifyingly amazed. Derain reported to Vlaminck "It's brilliant! I believe he's crossed the threshold of the seventh garden, the garden of delight..." adding in a second letter "... He's getting younger... He's happy as a lark, and has the air of being ready for anything... I'm very fed up."

The Berheim Jeune Gallery had sent a payment of 18,000 francs just before they left. The Matisses could afford to travel in style.

Amélie enjoyed every moment of their Florence stay, telling Gertrude Stein that it was "a girlhood dream come true..." Henri was considerably less enthusiastic. He preferred solitary travel and became irritated by Leo Stein. "Leo was at my heels all the time except in front of great works of art. He would then move a few steps away and come back with the question "what do you think of it?" I could not reply... This manner of visiting museums paralysed me completely. So much so that I couldn't see anything any more. I looked at things with the one idea that I'd have to talk about them."

The summer was almost over, Matisse longed to get back to Collioure. He wanted to experiment with Terrus's recipe of mixing glue with his paints to give an Italian fresco-like glow to his work. Terrus was looking forward to his return.

Despite his grumpiness as Leo Stein's guest, on 21st August Matisse wrote to Fénéon telling him of the "many beautiful things I saw in Italy".

And, in Paris, the Steins, both Leo and Gertrude, and Sarah and Michael, were exchanging and updating their collections, often with Vollard and sometimes at auction. Their Californian friend Annette Rosenshine, who was becoming a small time collector of Matisse herself, remembers the excitement at one auction when Michael's last bid was accepted. Next day the press was full of wonder at "the crazy American who had paid one thousand francs for a Cézanne fragment..."

By the time of the 1907 Salon d'Automne, Matisse was already beginning to be recognised as being in a different class from his contemporaries. Apollinaire described him as the "Fauve of Fauves". The Salon was awash with fauves and false fauves. Upset by most of what he saw, Matisse went to the Bateau Lavoir to visit Picasso. There *Les Demoiselles d'Avignon* upset him as much as all the fake fauves had done. His opinion was much in keeping with the opinion of anyone else who had seen it. Braque, who was becoming a close friend of Picasso, said it made him feel as if he had eaten or swallowed petrol. Derain reckoned Picasso would end up stringing himself up behind his "*Demoiselles*".

Within six months Derain and Braque had reversed their opinions. Both transferred their allegiance from the Fauvism of Matisse to whatever nascent new movement *Les Demoiselles* was heralding. Inspired by both *Les Demoiselles* and the Cézanne exhibition at the Salon d'Automne, Braque and his new friend Picasso began to work out a system of painting based on the flattening of perspective and the simplification and geometrisation of forms. The subject was represented from several angles simultaneously, the colours became muted, predominantly greys and browns. Braque continued to paint landscapes strongly influenced by Cézanne until he abandoned them in favour of the still lifes for which he is so well known.

By now paintings hung five deep on the walls of the Stein's apartment, including Matisses and Picassos in numbers that grew till there were no walls left on which to hang them. The numbers of visitors who came to visit on Saturday evenings grew as well. Gertrude Stein attributed the start of the Saturday salons to the people who began visiting to see the Matisse paintings... and the Cézannes. "Matisse brought people," she said "everybody brought somebody, and they came at any time and it began to be a nuisance, and it was in this way that Saturday evenings began..."

All four Steins had become very friendly with the artists whose work they collected. They enjoyed Madame Matisse's rabbit stew as much as Fernande's gossip. They helped the Manguins in their search for a cheap villa to rent in Italy.

Letters from Picasso to Leo are full of requests both for money and to see paintings at rue de Fleurus.

Gertrude and Leo's apartment in rue de Fleurus and Michael and Sarah's in rue Madame overflowed with paintings created, to a large extent, by artists who had become their friends. Every Saturday evening the apartments filled with painters, sculptors, writers, collectors and dealers keeping up with all that was developing in the Paris art world.

On one occasion Gertrude Stein gave a lunch and invited all the painters and sat them opposite pictures they had painted. "You know how painters are, I wanted to make them happy so I placed each one opposite his own picture, and they were so happy, so happy that we had to send out twice for more bread, when you know France you will know that that means they were happy, because they cannot eat and drink without bread and we had to send out twice for bread so they were very happy. Nobody noticed my little arrangement except Matisse and he did not until just as he left, and now he says it is proof that I am very wicked, he laughed and said "I know Mademoiselle Gertrude life is a theatre for you but there are theatres and theatres, and when you listen so carefully to me and so attentively and do not hear a word I say then I do say you are very wicked."

Gradually, the Paris art world was dividing into two camps. Gertrude and Leo Stein gave most of their Matisses to Michael and Sarah. Gertrude had thrown her weight behind Picasso. Annette Rosenshine reckoned she might have been disappointed that Matisse had not volunteered to paint her portrait. She had also been joined by Alice B. Toklas who was to be her companion for the rest of her life and was concentrating more on her writing. In any case, the duel between Matisse and Picasso, fostered by the Steins, led to a rivalry that proved to be one of the richest and most productive in the history of Western Art.

Chapter 7
Paris of
"la Bande à Picasso"

The account of an evening held in Picasso's studio in November 1908 gives an extraordinary glimpse into bohemian life in Paris at that time: Picasso had purchased a Rousseau painting from Père Soulier's second hand shop in the rue des Martyrs. The dealer justified his price of five francs by pointing out that it was a large canvas and Picasso could always paint over it.

Picasso and Fernande, decided to celebrate the purchase by throwing a banquet in Rousseau's honour. The thirty friends and acquaintances they invited were all young and at the time comparatively unknown. Now the guest list reads like a who's who of the art world of the twentieth century.

Neither Fernande nor Picasso had given a banquet before. Fernande told Gertrude Stein's companion, Alice B. Toklas, that she planned to serve *Riz à la Valencienne* (paella) and had ordered it from the caterer, Félix Potin. Guillaume Apollinaire, already well known as a writer and poet, who admired and knew Rousseau, wrote a poem and persuaded others to write poems or songs. Aperitifs would be served at the café at the foot of rue Ravignan before dinner in Picasso's studio. It was all very exciting. Alice B. Toklas put on her new hat and, with Gertrude and Leo Stein, set off for Montmartre. When they arrived, in the midst of the crowd already assembled, they saw a tall thin girl Gertrude described as "swaying forward and back, with her long thin arms extended. I did not know what she was doing, it was evidently not gymnastics, it was bewildering but she looked very enticing." The girl was Marie Laurencin, Apollinaire's girlfriend, who, in Gertrude Stein's opinion appeared to have taken too many preliminary aperitifs.

Suddenly there was a violent noise at the door and a very angry Fernande burst in. Félix Potin had not sent the dinner. Alice B. Toklas suggested they telephone, later commenting that "in those days in Paris one did not telephone and never to a provision store."

When they eventually found a telephone that worked, Félix Potin was "either closed or dozing" and deaf to their appeals. Alice and Fernande ran from store to store until there were enough ingredients to add to an emergency paella they had previously prepared to cover the entire meal.

In Picasso's studio the Rousseau painting, draped in flags and flanked by large primitive statues, was in the place of honour at the head of the trestle table. The paella was cooking below in Max Jacob's studio that was also to be used for the men's overcoats. The ladies were to put their overcoats in the front studio. The party left the café and moved up the steep slope of rue Ravignan towards Picasso's studio, Marie Laurencin supported by Gertrude Stein on one side and Leo Stein on the other. Alice B. Toklas, already there with Fernande, had deposited her hat and overcoat and was admiring the arrangements. Chinese lanterns hung from the beams, coloured garlands circled the pillars and a great streamer read: HONNEUR A ROUSSEAU.

Just as the others began to arrive Fernande barred the entrance, crying loudly that she was not about to have her party spoiled by Marie Laurencin. Gertrude Stein remonstrated with her, saying she had not struggled up the hill with the girl for nothing and calling for Picasso who made his way forward from the rear. He persuaded Fernande to yield in the interest of getting everyone seated before Apollinaire arrived with Rousseau. Fernande was always a little afraid of Apollinaire. Marie Laurencin, very drunk, plunged into a plate of tarts and, covered in cream and jam began embracing everyone. Finally everybody was seated and Apollinaire and Rousseau made their entrance to loud acclaim.

"How well I remember their coming" wrote Gertrude Stein. "Rousseau, a little small colourless Frenchman with a little beard, like any number of Frenchmen one saw everywhere. Guillaume Apollinaire with finely cut florid features, dark hair and a beautiful complexion. Everybody was presented and everybody sat down again." Apollinaire slipped into a seat beside Marie Laurencin who, previously calmed down by Gertrude Stein, broke into wild movements and cries. Apollinaire got her out of the door, returning a little later with a slightly bruised but sober Marie.

Frédéric of the Lapin Agile, wandered in with his usual companion, a donkey, was given a drink and wandered out again. Some Italian street singers, hearing a party going on, came in. Fernande rose from the table and, forefinger straight in the air, said it was not that kind of a party. The singers were thrown out.

Everything was eaten and the poetry reading began. Apollinaire gave a solemn eulogy ending with the poem he had written which he half chanted, everybody joining in with the refrain. All of a sudden, the art critic and poet, André Salmon who had been having a serious discussion about literature with Alice's neighbour, leapt onto the table, declaimed a poem, drank a large glass, and, completely drunk, began a fight. The men all got hold of him. Georges Braque, a large, strong man, saved the statues, holding one under each arm while Leo Stein, an equally

Le Lapin Agile, Paris

large and strong man, protected little Rousseau and his violin. Picasso, small but also strong, dragged André Salmon into the front studio and locked him in.

In the peace that followed Marie Laurencin sang some charming old Norman ballads in a thin voice. Ramon Pichot, Picasso's Spanish artist friend from Els IV Gats days in Barcelona, danced a religious Spanish dance ending on the floor in the form of a crucified Christ. Apollinaire invited Alice B. Toklas to sing some native Red Indian songs, which, to his regret, she did not feel able to do. Rousseau blissful and gentle, played his violin and talked of plays he had written and memories he had of Mexico.

At around three am they went into the studio where André Salmon had been deposited to find him sleeping peacefully. Beside him were a half chewed box of matches and Alice B. Toklas's hat, also half chewed. He awoke, was very charming and polite and they all went out into the street. Suddenly, with a wild yell, Salmon rushed down the hill.

The Steins and Alice B. Toklas called a cab and escorted Rousseau home.

Matisse, much encouraged by Leo Stein, opened his own academy in the former Couvent des Oiseaux in January 1908, moving, with Rodin, to the Hotel Biron, which later became the Rodin Museum.

That summer he went to Germany with Purrmann while Amélie looked after her ailing mother. He wrote to Manguin in Naples that the "beer and cigars were good but he had doubts about the wine". In the Salon d'Automne, Matisse had his own section and received very good reviews from the critics... His life had definitely moved on.

At the end of the year he published his *Notes of a Painter* in which he discussed his compositions, tonalities and the modelling of his forms. He was becoming established. He bought a house and some land in Clamart, now a suburb of Paris. Gertrude Stein visited. "This home in Clamart was very comfortable... The bathroom, which the family appreciated from long contact with Americans, although it must be said the Matisses had always been and always were scrupulously neat and clean, was on the ground floor adjoining the dining room. But that was all right, ... in the new house Braque was building the bathroom was again below... they said because being nearer the furnace it would be warmer."

"The grounds at Clamart were large... There was also a glass forcing house for flowers... Madame Matisse with simple recklessness went out everyday to look at it and pick flowers, keeping a cab waiting for her. In these days only millionaires kept cabs waiting and then only occasionally... These were the beginning of very prosperous days for the Matisses."

Meanwhile, in the Roussillon

Gustave Fayet made a purchase that would change his life. In the arid rocky countryside behind Narbonne, where the Corbières meet

Abbaye de Fontfroide general view

Abbaye de Fontfroide cloisters

the Cévennes, the ancient Abbaye de Sainte Mairie de Fontfroide had been home to a community of Cistercian monks from 1093 until its abandonment in 1901. His father had known the last of the monks, particularly the Abbé Jean. On the 23rd of January 1908, with his wife Madeleine d'Andoque, he bought it for 49,925 francs. The other potential purchaser had been the American, Georges Grey Barnard, the collector of Romanesque sculpted cloisters, some of which came from the Abbey of St Michel de Cuxa near Prades. These can now be seen in the Cloisters Museum in New York. The state of the buildings and the beautiful Fontfroide cloisters was lamentable. Gustave and Madeleine Fayet set to work on their restoration, a task that was to take a good ten years but that would create an oasis of art and beauty where both local and Parisian artists, musicians and friends could meet. Aristide Maillol, George Daniel de Monfreid, Etienne Terrus and Louis Bausil, Odilon Redon, Déodat de Sévérac, Maurice Ravel and Richard Viñes were among the first to join in and appreciate the work in the church, the rose garden, the cloisters and the house, much helped by agricultural workers from Fayet's many wine domaines.

De Monfreid was horrified to learn Fayet had sold a number of his Gauguins at a large profit. Although Fayet never complained of the enormous cost of the restoration of the Abbey, his accounts show that the price he received for just two of his Gauguins almost covered the initial price of Fontfroide. "Impossible to say no," he explained to de Monfreid, "Just think of it, my collection will have cost me nothing."

In 1909, in total discomfort, Fayet and his family moved in. He was the project manager, the master of works. He oversaw the army of builders, electricians, plumbers, carpenters, blacksmiths, locksmiths, and craftsmen, visiting each phase of the work every morning, encouraging, advising, sometimes suggesting new techniques and generally adding the finishing touches that were to restore it to a glory it had never formerly had while simultaneously respecting the peaceful character of its ancient Cistercian origins.

In the spring of the same year, Count Kessler persuaded Maillol to accompany him on a visit to Greece. On arriving in Piraeus, Maillol was struck by the similarity of the Greek landscape with that of his own beloved Banyuls, claiming he found in Greece "the same soil, the same horizon," and that in Greece he could "breathe the same air". In Greek art he could see the basis of his own sculptures. He wandered, enchanted, through the countryside, feeling completely at home. Once, he clambered up to embrace one of the statues of the Erechtheion on the Acropolis of Athens and had to be ordered down by a guard. He filled his notebook with sketches, between each page of which he pressed wild flowers. For him it was an epic trip, confirming his choice of sculpture as his preferred art form. Maillol and Kessler stayed three months. Maillol was ecstatic. Kessler, having started out with such enthusiasm, towards the end was less so. "Conversation with him is impossible," he wrote, "he speaks his opinion and finds all deviations from it stupid. Though his opinion is often on the mark and mostly amusing and picturesque; the impossibility to add anything other that a flat "yes", over the long term, becomes unbearably fatiguing..."

Kessler succumbed to gout and articular rheumatism in Rome on the journey back. Maillol returned home with three blocks of marble.

Els IV Gats poster, Barcelona

The bohemian life of the group of painters, writers, poets, musicians and sculptors surrounding Picasso continued in Montmartre. Many were Spanish, of whom a few, such as Enric Casanovas, Ramon Pichot and Manolo, Picasso had known since his Els IV Gats days in Barcelona.

Ramon Pichot, according to Gertrude Stein, was "awe-inspiringly religious" and resembled one of "those primitive Christs one saw in Spanish churches." He was to become a major influence on Salvador Dalí's early work. Fernande Olivier described his wife, Germaine (one of Picasso's former mistresses and the cause of Casagemas's suicide) whom Pichot had married in 1906, as gentle and serious and having many sisters, all with different fathers, adding that she also had many lovers, most of whom she found at the Circus. She and Ramon ran the bar restaurant called the Maison Rose, across the street from the Lapin Agile.

André and Alice Derain were both very much part of Picasso's circle of friends, even more so when Derain illustrated *l'Enchanteur*, Apollinaire's first book of poetry.

Fernande had no love for Marie Laurencin whom she described as a "mysterious and horrible woman who made noises like an animal". An unkind description of the young and chic Marie who had studied art at the Académie Humbert at the same time as Georges Braque and had shown her work at the Salon des Indépendants. In 1907 Picasso, in Clovis Sagot's shop with Braque, had introduced her to Apollinaire. It was the start of a liaison that was to last until 1912, as tumultuous as it was passionate (when she died 1956 she was buried in a white robe in the Père-Lachaise cemetery. In one hand she held a rose, in the other a love letter from Apollinaire whose grave was just a few steps away).

He wrote poems to her, she painted portraits of him, one of the best of which is *Apollinaire et ses Amis*. Easily recognizable *Amis* are Picasso and Gertrude Stein. To Marie's delight Gertrude Stein bought it. She and Braque had also painted each other's portraits. She was the only woman painter of *la bande à Picasso*...

Manolo, a graduate of the Beaux-Arts of Barcelona, had had an adventurous life before arriving in Paris. The illegitimate son of a Spanish officer, he deserted as soon as he was drafted into the army, hiding out in Barcelona with gipsies, petty thieves and artists. As a sculptor he was briefly employed in a dairy to sculpt flowers and animals out of butter. He frequented Els IV Gats Café.

When Picasso left Barcelona for Paris, Manolo's only ambition was to follow him. The story goes that he had just been called up for his military service, and, finding himself in the cavalry and on the frontier, rode his horse into France, sold it and caught the train to Paris, disguised as a monk. On his arrival, the only French word he knew was "Montmartre" and that is where he went. Often dressing like a gipsy in wide brimmed hat and wielding a guitar he became known as "Sancho Panza of Montmartre". He fell in love with a barmaid called Jeanne de Rochette, better known as Totote, whom he later married. He relied greatly on the young Frank Burty Haviland.

Frank Burty Haviland was the third child of a wealthy American porcelain manufacturer of Limoges, and his second wife, Madeleine Burty whose father was the well-known art critic Philippe Burty. Both Philippe Burty and Frank's father were great collectors and knew many writers and painters. The Haviland's Paris house was filled with the canvases of the fashionable artists of the time. Paintings by Renoir, Degas and Manet adorned the walls. Frank grew up with a passion for both literature and painting.

His upbringing was strict and somewhat frugal despite his father's considerable fortune. Money was never discussed and meals were adequate but meagre. At the end of the first meal at which his mother was presented to the Haviland family, she was offered strawberries. "Please take plenty," she was told, "take two!"

When Frank was fourteen his mother shot herself following a dispute with her husband over his long affair with a Molineux mannequin. She had sought a divorce but, on being threatened with the disinheritance of her three sons, took her own life. Frank was devastated. (As an artist he was to forever sign himself "Frank Burty"...). He was sent to boarding school where he excelled at music. His piano teacher was Ricardo Viñes, a brilliant musician and friend of the composers Debussy, Satie, Ravel and de Sévérac to whom, in Paris, he introduced young Frank.

Déodat de Sévérac, Frank's elder by fourteen years, was also one of the central figures of la Bande à Picasso. They became and were to remain close friends for the rest of their lives.

When he left school, Frank spent some time in Germany attempting to learn the porcelain business and then a stretch in New York with his older brother, Paul, before returning to Paris and the company of his artist friends. By 1908 he was twenty years old and had grown into a charming and strikingly good-looking man. (His niece always remembers how, whenever he entered a cabaret, all eyes followed him, no one bothered to look at the stage).

He was large, both in stature and generosity and was nicknamed *"le riche"* by the mostly penniless artists with whom he spent his time. "Richness" is, of course, relative. In point of fact he had, by then, been disinherited by his father for refusing to go into the family business, deciding instead to become an artist. The support he received from his maternal grandmother did not actually make him "rich"... He did, however, have his own studio in 110 avenue d'Orléans and it became a regular meeting place for *la Bande à Picasso*. He admired Picasso immensely. Art was discussed, the piano and guitar played, much *Anis del Mono* was drunk and the poems of Apollinaire and Max Jacob were read. He was always happy to help his friends, particularly the diminutive and constantly broke Manolo.

Anis del Mono

Déodat de Sévérac left his native Toulouse and his aristocratic family to study in Paris at the Schola Cantorum. The many letters he wrote to his family are full of the music and gossip of Paris, interspersed with fond memories of his Lauragais roots. In one of March 1902 he describes a dinner he had with Fabre in the company of Odilon Redon, Ricardo Viñes and Fayet where an *outrade* (a bustard or field duck) from Castelnaudary was served.

He writes of the "glacial" reception received by the playing of *les Barbares* by Saint-Saens and mentions Fabre's wisdom on the fluctuations in the art collectors market in general and with the rue Lafitte dealers in particular.

He signed himself "Dodo".

Déodat took organ lessons, finding in the organ an instrument that allowed him full rein to develop his love of improvisation. He wrote melodies to accompany the poetry of Baudelaire and Verlaine and arranged choral texts in Catalan. His first opera, *Le Coeur du Moulin*, was performed in Paris on December 8th 1909 and established him as one of the rising stars on the Parisian scene. However "the Parisian Scene" was not necessarily one to which he wished to belong. His thesis that French music should diversify and filter out Germanic influences and that this could be achieved by incorporating folk and traditional elements of French culture was not always popular in the capital. It would take a return to the south of his birth to enable him to give full flight to his musical creativity.

He was, however, a popular member of Montmartre society.

* * * * *

Frank Burty Haviland had become a firm friend of the sculptor Enric Casanovas who divided his time between Paris and Barcelona and with whom he carried on a lively correspondence for many years. In June of 1909 he wrote to Casanovas telling him he was planning to leave Paris for Gósol, in the Spanish Pyrenees, spending a day in Toulouse en route and asking him about accommodation. He mentioned that Déodat de Sévérac was already in the south and that he had been posing almost every day for Manolo. Picasso, he adds, has sent a few words from Horta de Ebro where he is spending the summer...

"Dear Friend," writes Frank Burty Haviland on the 26th July 1909 to Enric Casanovas from Bourg Madame where Manolo was completing the bust of Frank he had begun sculpting in Paris, "We should have been in Gósol by now if we hadn't had to change our plans and stop at Bourg-Madame, on the French border near Puigcerdà. We couldn't cross the frontier because Manolo, seeing what was happening in Morocco, and knowing there would be a need of soldiers, feared that if he entered Spain he would be immediately sent to fight the Arabs.

So we can't go to Gósol; we will stay here till mid September..."

Manolo adds: "Novas, you can see how everything is in Spain, I am not only afraid but also I love France. Come and see us here, Your friend, Manolo..."

Old postcard of Bourg-Madame

Frank Burty Haviland and Manolo stayed on in Bourg-Madame...

Picasso, from Horta de Ebro, wrote suggesting he drove to visit them. He also wrote to Kahnweiler telling him he was hard at work. He added that Apollinaire had told him that Derain was illustrating his latest book saying that it was bound to be most beautiful. Fernande wrote to the Steins saying they were hoping to see Frank and Manolo in Bourg-Madame.

However neither Picasso and Fernande nor Déodat de Sévérac managed to get together with Frank and Manolo and, at the end of September, they returned to Paris full of stories of a wonderful summer in the Cerdagne. In fact, fifty years later, Frank Burty Haviland forgot they ever returned to Paris. In his mind (and in many accounts later written) he and Manolo moved straight from Bourg-Madame to Céret.

Back in his Bateau Lavoir studio Picasso showed his friends his summer's work. Totote could see from Manolo's face that the emerging cubist images were not to his taste and signalled to him to keep his thoughts to himself. Frank, however was very impressed and hesitated only over which one to buy. He chose l'Usine à Horta (Now in a private collection in New York).

When, in 1909, Picasso left his Bateau Lavoir studio and moved to 11 boulevard de Clichy it felt like the end of an era. The photograph Picasso took of Frank Burty Haviland in his studio there shows a clean shaven, handsome young man, seated in an arm chair, holding a hat and cane, his face half turned to the light. On the wall behind him hangs the portrait of Marguerite that Matisse gave Picasso in 1907.

Far more comfortable and in distance not far from the Butte de Montmartre, Fernande, now quite the lady of the house, felt more trapped than she ever had in rue Ravignan. In her memoirs she describes her feelings as "something like a premature aging," noting "an imperceptible flagging in their friendships, an occasional unwonted harshness (quickly repressed), an exhaustion at seeing the same old faces every day, at thrashing out the same ideas, at criticising the same talents and envying the same successes..."

A page had been turned.

Braque spent the summer in La Roche-Guyon, east of Paris on the Seine, Cézanne's old stamping ground. Derain joined him there.

In the Roussillon, in the Prades home of Gustave Violet, Terrus, de Monfreid, Déodat de Sévérac and Louis Bausil would meet, Violet's

211. PRADES (P.-O.) — Les Lavoirs du Chemin Neuf

*Old postcard of
Les Lavoirs, Prades*

young son Pallade remembered vividly times spent at St Martí. One afternoon that stuck in his memory was when he was walking with his father and Maillol from St Martí towards Prades. Near the old mill is a *lavoir* with running water which can still be seen. There, squatting down with her back to them, a washerwoman of ample proportions was beating her laundry. Maillol stopped dead in his tracks and, placing a restraining hand on Gustave Violet's arm while making an explanatory gesture, cried "... all the same! How beautiful that can be!"

Pallade's most distant memory of Maillol was of walking near Banyuls with his father and Maillol, when the sculptor, his habitual straw hat on his head, took him by the hand and lead them both through the vines to the Métairie, the small farmhouse that is his resting place today. The young Pallade imagined that the path, fringed by prickly pears, might be in Africa.

Another frequent visitor at St Martí, tall, bony, white haired and bearded with piercing blue eyes and usually riding a "Saint Etienne" bicycle, was George Daniel de Monfreid. Pallade writes of his charm and originality and the fondness de Monfreid had for his father. Violet made a magnificent bust of de Monfreid.

In 1909, Violet's translation of Daudet's *l'Arlésienne* was presented in the open air in Prades, the scenery painted by Terrus. Henry de Monfreid, son of George Daniel, with the help of one of Gauguin's sons, hung the scenery panels from the branches of two plane trees. It played again the following year in Perpignan.

Gustave Fayet's great grandson, Alexandre d'Andoque, remembers the end of that summer of 1909 at Fontfroide when, in contrast to the days of labour on the restoration, his family would gather on the terraces in the evenings to talk of literature and art, to read passages from Fayet's friend Saurès' writings or congregate round the piano where Viñes would play the latest compositions of Déodat de Sévérac, Debussy or Ravel. Fayet, in his *Souvenirs sur Odilon Redon*, recorded with particular affection his conversations with his friend... "Ah ! Those conversations with Redon, what substantial, confidential conversations! Bringing to life Montaigne, Shakespeare, Baudelaire, Flaubert, Rembrandt, Dürer, Delacroix, Berlioz, Schumann. And how he played the violin. He loved, above all, Bach, Monteverdi, Beethoven, not Wagner. Berlioz, lover of painters, Schumann, Debussy, de Sévérac..." He and Redon shared a fascination with the occult in the sense of a deeper spiritual reality. Redon was particularly interested in Hinduism; Fayet had a valuable collection of antique buddhas.

It was a magic pre-war period, marred only by the death of the Fayet's son, Gaby, the ambulance arriving at Fontfroide too late to save him from peritonitis. In the photograph of Gustave Fayet on the terrace with his family and Redon, Fayet's black armband is the one note of sadness in the otherwise idyllic scene.

Gustave Fayet and family with Odilon Redon

Chapter 8
Céret bound

Old postcard of Grand Café de la Loge, Perpignan

As 1909 turned into 1910, Manolo and Frank Burty Haviland were both keen to return to the shores of the Mediterranean. Déodat would follow when he had finished his *Coeur de Moulin*.

Manolo took the train to Perpignan. Forgetting the grand plan and feeling very at home in the alleys of the Catalan capital, he made the Café de la Loge his new bohemian meeting place, rather as Le Lapin Agile had been for *la Bande à Picasso* in Paris. However Perpignan

View of Canigou from Céret

was not Paris. The more conventional of the locals became alarmed by Manolo's "*Bande*". He was arrested on suspicion of "illicit acts" and threatened with expulsion. It was probably the intervention of Déodat de Sévérac that saved him. In any case it was Déodat who had been informed by both Totote and Frank Burty Haviland of his misadventures. Soon after, Frank Burty Haviland and Totote arrived in Perpignan and met a liberated Manolo at the station.

They made their way to Banyuls-sur-Mer to visit Maillol. They had recently seen him in Paris where he had assured them of a warm welcome.

Maillol's money problems had not completely disappeared but life had become much easier. For the most part thanks to Kessler, his large statues of naked women had started appearing in Russia and Japan. Meanwhile, the French public, remained far from ready to accept such revolutionary figures.

However, the day Frank Burty Haviland and Manolo arrived in Banyuls the tramontane wind was blowing particularly fiercely. They rejected Maillol's suggestion to settle in Banyuls in favour of seeking shelter in the Vallespir. They chose the thermal town of Amélie les Bains. There, they found the number of sick, old people walking the streets armed with spittoons, discouraging. Tossing a coin to decide whether to move on up or down the valley, they took the train to the next station down the line and arrived in Céret.

The little Catalan town of 4,000 inhabitants was surrounded by cherry orchards and vineyards, Mount Canigou dominating the Albères hills. Few if any tourists came to Céret a hundred years ago, Catalan was the main and often only language spoken and visiting Parisian artists were virtually unheard of.

Hôtel du Canigou building today, Céret

They booked into the Hôtel du Canigou (no longer a hotel, now two houses opposite Gustave Violet's monument to the Canal d'Arrosage) in rue St Ferréol. It was reasonably priced. Very reasonably priced, a coffee would cost ten centimes, fifteen if you threw in some rum. The home cooking was delicious and, most importantly, Manolo spoke Catalan. He was Catalan. The "Parisians" were made welcome.

Déodat arrived a few days later and set to work immediately, composing the music he had dreamed of in Paris. Inspired by the south, he mixed a blend of traditional *Cobla* music with gypsy tambourines in a haunting and passionate piece entitled *Héliogabale*. He became an important member of the Céret society, loved as much for his character as for having integrated popular chansons and the rhythms of the sardane into his compositions. He never seemed to care that, unlike Ravel and Debussy who remained in Paris, his choice of living and working in the comparative obscurity of Céret restricted his progress internationally.

In Céret, evenings of music and art related discussion took place in the Grand Café. Totote played nostalgic Spanish airs on her guitar to the delight of her husband, Manolo, Déodat and the assembled company. Manolo's anecdotes, based on his often somewhat dubious life in Paris, entertained the locals greatly. Full of charm and loved by all who knew him Manolo was, basically, lazy,

Old postcard of Le Grand Café, Céret

Céret bound **125**

Église St Pierre, Céret

idle and utterly unreliable. He was always broke but still refused commissions from the good folk of Perpignan saying he was "too busy". Frank Burty Haviland continued to support him.

The new "Parisians" were to make an indelible mark on the village they adopted so joyfully that summer. They joined in the local festivities and the Céretans enjoyed their company. Manolo was the first of them to form relationships with the local artists and writers, the Céret poet, Pierre Camo, Etienne Terrus in Elne and George Daniel de Monfreid in Corneilla-de-Conflent. Sometimes Maillol, in the company of friends with new fangled motorcars, would drive to the Vallespir. Terrus complained in a postcard to Matisse that there were now so many automobiles in Elne it was hardly safe to step outside. Occasionally the newly arrived Céret crowd made the journey from Céret to Banyuls on foot...

Much as Maillol loved to walk and talk with friends he continued to wander alone in the hills in search of plants with which he would colour the threads for his tapestries or for the herbs he used to flavour his cooking. He knew all the highways and byways surrounding Banyuls. The local Banyulenc were, for the most part, interested neither in him nor his art, unlike the Céretans who were intrigued by all the shenanigans of the "Parisians" who had chosen to live in their midst.

Sportive as ever, de Monfreid, well used to pedalling great distances on his bicycle, visited the new artistic arrivals in Céret as well as Maillol in Banyuls-sur-Mer and, of course, Gustave Violet in nearby Prades.

On February 4th, 1910 Totote wrote to Casanovas: "The skies are as they are described in Paris, the skies of the south... Apart from that there is no wind and very little rain. The roadsides are so beautiful; mimosa grows wild and is in flower right now... Make up your mind to come. Three francs a day for board and lodging and if you only knew how well one is fed! One would never arise from the table."

Déodat de Sévérac with his huge black moustache and love of the simple life, captured the hearts of the locals. He became the organist at the church of St. Pierre. One day the priest happened to be inside while Déodat was practising. He remembered long afterwards being "rooted to the spot... in his hands the organ produced a music never before heard. "What is that wonderful piece are you playing?" He asked... "Nothing really, I'm just improvising on an air of Debussy" replied de Sévérac... "He was such a modest man..." said the priest.

A few months after their arrival, Frank Burty Haviland took La Maison Alcouffe (sadly now demolished) overlooking the famous Devil's Bridge. Ever attentive to Manolo's needs, he rented for him, from Michel Aribaud, a local wine merchant and writer, a large house on the road to Maureillas where Manolo could get on with his sculpture.

Déodat's personal life was improved by the arrival of Henriette, an actress he had first known in Paris in 1907 and whom he would later marry. However nothing distracted him from working on the *Héliogabale*.

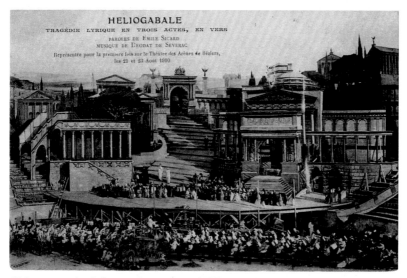

*Old postcard of the performance of **Héliogabale**, Béziers*

One of his most important works, it was first performed before 13,000 people in the *Arènes* in Béziers. Gustave Fayet was present. He had just moved all his Paris paintings and sculptures from the rue de Bellechasse to Château d'Igny, near Paris, close to Redon's house in Brièvres but, loyal as ever to his friends, he returned to Béziers for the opening night.

In the Fontfroide *Livre d'Or* Déodat wrote "Fontfroide where the water may be icy but the hearts are on fire and I am delighted by it all" signing himself "Dodo".

His *Héliogabale* was presented the following year in a concert version in Paris where it received high praise from both Debussy and Fauré.

Déodat often worked in close collaboration with Gustave Violet. They shared a love of theatre and music. Violet mixed easily with both his fellow Catalan artists and the visitors, most of whom he already knew from his Paris days. Déodat de Sévérac, as soon as he arrived in Céret, had used one of Violet's poems to create his hymn to the beauty of the region, *Lo Cant del Valespir*. Violet often visited Céret.

Mostly, however, Violet was involved in a prodigious output of, sculptures and ceramics from his St Martí studio and kiln. Exhibition followed exhibition, in Barcelona and Paris as well as locally and the commissions rolled in. Among them were the beautiful bas-relief allegoric figures representing Work and Science now flanking the entrance to the Collège Jean Moulin in Perpignan and the monument near Bourg-Madame to Jean Lax, the engineer responsible for the creation of the Little Yellow Train. His statue *L'Avia* was placed in the *Salle des Mariages* in Perpignan in 1910. In the entrance hall of Céret's town hall two bas-reliefs of agricultural scenes were installed. He opened a new kiln in Céret. He was also a frequent visitor at Fayet's Abbaye de Fontroide.

Studio and house at St Martí, Prades

Fayet, inspired by all the artistic activity at Fontfroide, had begun to paint again. "how strong are the spiritual fermentations during my long stays at Fontfroide!" he wrote to the ciritc, René-Louis Doyon. He commisioned Redon to decorate his library, giving him complete freedom of choice of subject matter. On the two huge panels, six and a half metres wide and two metres high, Redon decided on two paintings, one depicting "Day" the other "Night". In a letter he described the atmosphere at Fontfroide and the pleasure the project was affording him:

Abbaye de Fontfroide salon, painting by Richard Burgsthal

"I am writing to you from beneath the vaulted ceiling of the large room that I am decorating in the old cloisters. I have brought my work with me so that I can work in situ. I find this enormously stimulating. I have taken a risk with the representation (still not fully defined) of a quadriga driven by one or two winged creatures, sort of flowers, in a mountainous landscape rendered in a range of luminous greys. On the opposite wall is another panel that I have sketched in black, leaving myself the option to indulge shamelessly in every imaginable fantasy. Black on a large surface is wonderful. I realise that I must not take it too far, but you only really know, you only learn while you are actually creating a work. It's the first time that I have agonised over a surface like this. I am pursuing this project surrounded by extremely lively, happy guests, in the cheerful, bright Mediterranean sunshine. A beautiful region, not far from the landscapes Cézanne and Van Gogh painted. I see it through different eyes, of course".

Gustave Fayet had always possessed the gift of friendship. This quality was never more apparent than at Fontfroide where all his collaborators would become his friends and each friend would inevitably become a collaborator.

Richard Burgsthal, a musician, artist and friend of Ricardo Viñes, decorated two rooms of the house with scenes of myths and legend. In a medieval book in his extensive library, Fayet found recipes the 12th century monks of Chartres had used to create the richly coloured glass used in Chartres Cathedral. Later, in 1912, he opened his own glassworks. Burgsthal then designed the windows of the Abbey on a theme of St Francis of Assisi, and, using the jewel coloured glass he and Fayet had created, glazed the new Abbey windows.

Ricardo Viñes was a keen gambler, capable, as he had done one night in Mexico, of losing the entire takings from a concert on one turn of the roulette wheel. He remembered the afternoons playing at the table Fayet had installed in the grand parlour of Fontfroide, with Burgsthal as croupier, counters as currency rather than money and the evenings spent discussing astrology, 17th century literature and religion. Viñes recalled one evening ending with Fayet's imitation of a circus director performing a high wire balancing act. "What was he insinuating?" wondered Viñes. "That he lived balanced between life in Paris and life at Fontfroide? Between a life of business and that of an artist? Between the visible and the invisible?"

Picasso and Fernande had spent the summer in Spain, in Cadaqués. Derain was often with them. Fernande remembers a visit to Figueres where Derain found a tie of "astonishing vulgarity and garishness, which he bought and delighted in for quite some time."

Back in Paris in the autumn, Picasso befriended two cartoonists, both of whom had cubist aspirations. The first was Juan Gris of whom much more later, the second was a Pole, Louis Marcousis, whose pretty new mistress was Marcelle Humbert. Picasso enjoyed the Pole's jewish wit and Fernande got on well with and began confiding in Marcelle.

Max Jacob had been worrying both Fernande and Picasso. He overindulged in the drugs they all used to a greater or lesser extent, ether and opium being favourites, and had been found one evening in a seriously bad state in the gutter. They took him in to their boulevard Clichy apartment.

Picasso, needing "more room to work," took a studio in the Bateau Lavoir, just beneath his old one.

The following year, 1911, prompted by Manolo, Picasso took the train from Paris and arrived, in a horse drawn coach, outside the Hôtel du Canigou in Céret. He moved in, enjoyed the patron's cooking, bought *espadrilles* in the market in the place des Neuf Jets, promenaded beneath the town's tall plane trees and drank at the Grand Café.

Old postcard of place des Neuf Jets, Céret

Matisse may have been inspired by the dazzling light of Collioure, but it was in Céret that Picasso felt at home. Bull fighting, a passion of his since early childhood took place right in the centre of the town and the sardane, his favourite dance, was danced at every local festival. "It's a very serious thing, the sardane," he said, "and difficult! Each step must be counted, there is one person who does this for all the others. This dance is a communion of souls... It abolishes all distinction of class. Rich and poor, old and young dance it together: the postman with the bank manager, and the servants hand in hand with their masters."

And, as for bullfighting, he initiated both Braque and Max Jacob into the art of the *corrida*, claiming he would always choose to be the picador rather than the toreador.

He had travelled with the huge dog, Frika and a new pet monkey but without Fernande, content with the company of friends from both Paris and Barcelona who were already there. He lost no time in encouraging Braque, still working in Paris, to join him. Fernande, bored and lonely in Paris, began looking around for diversion.

Plane trees, Céret

Matisse, just a few kilometres away in Collioure must have been on Picasso's mind but, burying themselves in their art, they made no effort to see each other. Braque's imminent arrival goaded Picasso on. In Paris they had visited each other's studios daily to see what the other was doing. Neither felt a canvas could be declared finished until the other had agreed that it was.

On July 16th Picasso wrote to Braque from the Hôtel du Canigou saying how pleased he was to receive Braque's letter saying he would be coming to Céret. On the same day he wrote to Kahnweiler saying he had moved to a large room in Frank Burty Haviland's Maison Alcouffe and was working on his *Poète et Paysan*, a painting he finished but did not keep.

A month before arriving in person, Braque sent Picasso a present of hats.

"My dear friend Braque, I finally received the hats and what a surprise. You have no idea how much I laughed, particularly when naked... Last night Manolo and I put them on to go to the café. We had false moustaches and sideburns done in burnt cork..." One can only imagine they created quite a stir in le Grand Café.

Kahnweiler, from the moment he first saw Picasso's *Les Demoiselles d'Avignon* in 1907, had been the dealer both Picasso and Braque relied on. He had given Braque his first one man exhibition in 1908 and had shown both his and Picasso's work in his rue Vignon Gallery. He had then taken on Juan Gris, selling his first three paintings to the Steins. Kahnweiler saw his role as selling the paintings of his friends the artists to his friends the collectors so that the artists could get on with their work, living quietly and producing art. In his own words he set out to " offer for public admiration painters who the public did not know at all and for whom it would be necessary to clear the way." Picasso was sharp enough to wonder "What would have become of us if Kahnweiler had not had a business sense?" adding, "What I want is to be able to live like a poor man with plenty of money."

In the catalogue for Kahnweiler's exhibition of November 1908 Louis Vauxcelles, noted that "M. Braque is a very daring young man. The misleading example of Picasso and Derain has made him bolder still. And perhaps he is more obsessed than he ought to be by the style of Cézanne ...... He despises form and reduces everything, views, people, places and houses, to geometrical diagrams, to little cubes."

By 1909, Picasso and Braque, as well as Herbin, Léger, Picabia and Gris, thanks to Vauxcelles, were universally known as "Cubists".

It was the beginning of a ten-year period of intense collaboration for Picasso and Braque, the true start of Cubism and Kahnweiler, as dealer and friend, had a major hand in bringing it about.

In the course of this summer of 1911 Maillol's *La Méditerannée* was finally unveiled, perfectly placed in the arcaded courtyard of the Town Hall of Perpignan, the proportions of the twentieth century sculpture in total harmony with the architecture of their sixteenth century setting. Maillol's compatriots found the statue "massive and heavy". The nudity shocked, indeed the good ladies of the town declared it to be almost pornographic. However, the Russian collector Ivan Morozov recognized his genius and commissioned Maillol to make a series of large sculptures on a theme of the seasons. *Pomone*, *Flore*, *le Printemps*, and *l'Eté* were all completed in the years leading up to the outbreak of the First World War.

Maillol had yet to find the perfect model for his sculpture. In Paris there was no shortage of models but none of them had the Catalan shape he sought. In Banyuls, no one would pose in the nude. Clotilde, his model at the start of their marriage, stopped soon after the birth of Lucien. Nevertheless, he continued to paint her as she bathed nude in the creeks near Banyuls. Their marriage was a happy one; he often said that he had married one of the women he so admired, the woman whose grace, sweetness and gentleness had made him very happy.

Hôtel de Ville courtyard, Perpignan

Clotilde Maillol and Amélie Matisse, both strong women from the south, supported and believed in their artist husbands and it is no exaggeration to say that modern art owes much to their dedication.

Thérèse, Clotilde's maid, was the model for Maillol's *Venus*. Classical, simultaneously simple and majestic, sometimes nude, sometimes dressed with a necklace, he worked and reworked the sculpture in as many materials as possible.

It was ordered by collectors from all over Europe. The Russian collector, Morozov, was invited by Maillol to visit him and see the sculptures he bought in situ. A Swiss couple travelled to Banyuls to choose their sculptures from his studio. But, at home, in the village of vines and fishermen, his work was viewed very differently. Art was not considered a correct profession for a man. Indeed it was not considered to be a profession at all. It was only in 1950, several years after his death, that Mme Maillol and Lucien's' gift of a bronze version of Venus could be installed in the Place de la Loge in Perpignan. Only Mme Maillol knew that her maid, Thérèse, had been the model.

In 1914, some wondered if Maillol's art was inspired by his German connections. It had indeed been Kessler who had introduced him to Morozov. Few recognised its deep roots in their Catalan soil, how the work of this artist/artisan son of Banyuls grew out of the classic Mediterranean landscape in which he had been raised.

Picasso, for reasons that intrigued Maillol, avoided him. They had met in Paris. "...he has a mad talent" said Maillol of Picasso... "but he wants to do everything. He wants to do everything that others do... But he doesn't do it any better." Not particularly endearing if Picasso was aware of his opinion.

Maison Delcros viewed from the street, Céret

Braque, with Marcelle Lapré, joined Picasso in Céret on the 17th August. They both stayed with Frank Burty Haviland at the Maison Alcouffe before moving on to the Maison Delcros, a large house on the edge of the town where their names are on the doorbells to this day. During that summer of 1911 he and Picasso resumed the closeness and collaboration begun in Paris. Ever since the 1907 Salon d'Automne exhibition of Cézanne, Braque and Picasso had spent hours exchanging ideas, often joined in their conversations by André Derain.

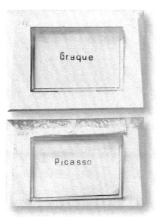

Maison Delcros door bells today, Céret

1911 was a summer of intense closeness and productivity... Braque described his relationship with Picasso at that time as "Very close... like a roped party of mountaineers, in those years Picasso and I said to each other things that no one will ever say to another, things that no-one would now be able to say to anyone, things that no one would now be able to understand... things that would be incomprehensible and which gave us so much joy... and this will end with us... Most of all we were in a state of great concentration."

They worked together with neither pretension nor vanity, signing their paintings on the back. Braque said the experimental input of their work was so intense that it had a laboratory quality about it. He also vowed that "when we made Cubism we had had no intention of making Cubism, we were merely expressing what was in us." Picasso said much the same. However, close as they were, their paths would diverge as each of them followed their own interpretation.

And it was not only a time of work. It was also a time of high spirits, fun and games. Picasso liked to bathe naked in the surrounding rivers. His monkey was considered an unusual companion. He, Braque and Manolo loved dressing up and Braque's hats were often worn.

Picasso was an indefatigable walker. He and Manolo would stride up to Fontfrède, above Céret, from where they could see Spain, the plain of Ampurdán and the Bay of Roses. On some days they even walked as far as the Spanish frontier town of Le Perthus. When Picasso returned to Céret in 1953, after an absence of almost forty years, it was at the Place du Belvédère, Fontfrède, that the town organised a celebration picnic in his honour. It was his first glimpse of a Spain to which he had sworn never to return under Franco's rule. But the Temple to Peace he dreamed of building there was never to happen.

Fernande remained in Paris. Picasso wrote to her there hoping she would come to Céret and telling her his work was going well and that the monkey was very amusing... He concludes by writing that he embraced her and loved her always...

When she did arrive her stay was short: just two weeks. They might not have been aware at the time but, as a couple, it was virtually their swan song. In her memoirs Fernande noted that in Céret "Picasso was living as he had in Spain, working all day, going to the café in the evenings and seeing either Manolo or Haviland..."

The Maison Delcros had plenty of space for studios for both artists. Fernande and Picasso lived in one of the vast high-ceilinged bedrooms but Braque and his wife, Marcelle stayed at the Hôtel du Canigou.

Picasso and Fernande and Braque and Marcelle were distinctive couples as they strolled beneath the hundred year old plane trees in Céret's evening *Passegiata*. Marcelle discreet, timid and tiny next to her tall good looking Braque, Fernande tall and beautiful; her abundant hair and fair skin protected from the last rays of the southern sun by a large multicoloured umbrella, escorted everywhere by the small, bronzed, dark-eyed Picasso.

Picasso and Braque worked on, continuing with their research. They dismantled and analysed, using superimposed planes and a high degree of simplification and scattering all the elements of the picture over the canvas. Braque was as sure of himself as Picasso was tormented by doubts. Braque, typically French, was as restrained and measured as Picasso, typically Spanish, was excessive.

Maison Delcros viewed from the garden, Céret

When Picasso proposed to "paint things as we know them, not as they are seen" Braque would respond "Things don't exist in you, they only exist through you... one mustn't only wish to reproduce things as we see them, one must penetrate into them, we must become them. In that way things will be not so much simply seen as seized or grasped..." and so the discussions continued. They were bringing their analytic cubism almost to the point of abstraction. For example, in Picasso's

Accordionist the work had become so abstract that, later, one of its owners mistook it for a landscape because of the word "Céret" on the back. He missed the musician entirely. In fact, it is not difficult to make out the general outlines of a seated accordionist.

Picasso and Fernande's sudden departure for Paris was precipitated by a report in the local daily paper, L'Indépendant, of the theft of the *Mona Lisa* from the Louvre. It had been stolen on the 21st of August, 1911.

In those days thefts from the Louvre were not uncommon. But Picasso had reason to be worried.

Only a few years before, he had acquired a couple of 3rd century BC Iberian statues from a bi-sexual Belgian, Honoré Joseph Géry Pieret, Apollinaire's secretary, who masqueraded as a French baron. Though Picasso would later deny it in court, he almost certainly knew at the time that both heads had been stolen from the Louvre. "Primitive" art was becoming more and more popular; in fact Picasso had used the heads as models in his 1907 *Les Demoiselles d'Avignon*. As he recounted years later. "You will recall the affair in which I was involved when Apollinaire stole some statuettes from the Louvre? They were Iberian statuettes… Well, if you look at the ears of *Les Demoiselles d'Avignon,* you will recognise the ears of those pieces of sculpture!"

Mona Lisa theft from le Louvre, 1911, Paris

Géry Pieret was suspected of stealing the *Mona Lisa*.

Picasso and Fernande rushed back to Paris. It was decided Picasso and Apollinaire had to get rid of the compromising 3rd century Iberian statues. Hastily, they put them in a suitcase and set off into the night with the intention of throwing them into the Seine. They found themselves unable to carry through the plan and returned home with the suitcase. The next day Apollinaire took them to *Paris-Journal* and asked for them to be returned anonymously… The promise to do so was not respected.

The police arrived at Apollinaire's apartment on the 8th of September and found proof of Géry's having worked for him. Apollinaire was arrested and incarcerated in La Santé prison, accused of harbouring a villain and suspected of being a member of a ring of international art thieves.

Two days later, at 7am, Fernande opened the door to a policeman ordering Picasso to follow him to be interviewed by a magistrate. Picasso was terrified; Fernande helped him dress.

When the handcuffed Apollinaire arrived, according to Fernande, "pale, defeated, unshaven, collar torn, shirt open, tieless, thin and in tatters, pathetic to see..." Picasso, terrorised by the judges' questions about his stolen statues, denied any knowledge of their theft. He also denied any close friendship with Apollinaire, saying he only knew of him as a famous poet. He was released.

Apollinaire was taken back to La Santé. Five days later, when Géry admitted full responsibility, Apollinaire was liberated. For years afterward he grumbled about being the only person in France arrested for the theft of the *Mona Lisa* (two years after it vanished from the Louvre, the stolen painting turned up in a Florence apartment only blocks away from where Lisa Gherardini, the subject of the painting, was conceived).

It is hard to believe that this episode did much to cement Apollinaire's friendship with Picasso.

It did nothing for Fernande's relationship with Picasso. Perhaps Picasso never forgave Fernande for seeing him in such a state of abject panic over the Louvre affair, perhaps she had flirted once too often the very good looking Ubaldo Oppi, an Italian artist on the fringes of the "Futurist Movement". As an intermediary in her affair Fernande chose none other than her new friend Marcelle Humbert soon to be better known as "Eva" not realising that Picasso was falling in love with the very Marcelle/Eva she had chosen as her confidante.

Gertrude Stein describes Guillaume Apollinaire as "very attractive and very interesting. He had a head like one of the late Roman emperors. He had a brother whom one heard about but never saw. He worked in a bank and therefore he was reasonably well dressed. When anybody in Montmartre had to go anywhere where they had to be conventionally clothed, either to see a relation or to attend a business matter, they always wore a piece of a suit that belonged Apollinaire's brother.

Apollinaire was extraordinarily brilliant and no matter what subject was started, if he knew anything about it or not, he quickly saw the whole meaning of the thing and elaborated it by his wit and fancy carrying it further than anybody knowing anything about it could have done, and oddly enough, generally correctly..."

Meanwhile, back in the Roussillon, Redon had finished his second great panel for Fayet's library at Fontfroide. Fayet was thrilled. He loved Redon's work, his meandering thoughts, sombre, dreamlike, symbolic. The two panels can be seen as a synthesis of Redon's art, the dazzling yellow of *Day* and the exuberance of the flowers contrasting with the darker, more sombre shades of *Night* where, woven into the shadows, half hidden but easily recognizable, are portraits of all the *Fontfroidiens*.

Abbaye de Fontfroide salon

A letter written by Fayet's youngest daughter, Yseult describes in detail the meals taken at her parents' table when the *Fontfroidiens* would gather on long summer evenings. Her parents both loved entertaining and kept an excellent table. Conversation was wide-ranging and lively, guided by her father while her mother was ever attentive to the quality of the service and the comfort of her guests. When conversation became philosophical, it was Odilon Redon who would lead in his soft voice, talking of the esoteric themes with which his paintings were imbued.

Musicians were almost always present. Fayet loved music and played the piano well. Ravel was sometimes present, Déodat de Sévérac often. Ricardo Viñes and the "Wagnerian" Richard Burgsthal were also there.

Sometimes George Daniel de Monfreid would come over, bringing with him Maillol and Manolo, Violet and Louis Bausil. The vaulted ceiling of the dining room would reverberate with passionate discussions. Yseult remembers the children, released from the table, hiding in the gardens, listening sometimes to the after dinner concerts under a star spangled night sky. At other times they would play at ghosts by dragging chains around the cloisters... Magic memories...

She also remembers how, as autumn came and the guests departed, the Fayet suppers around the grand table became, once more, simple and intimate family affairs.

In Céret, with Manolo and Totote, Braque and Marcelle spent sunny autumn days exploring the countryside, eating *cargolades* (great barbecue feasts featuring grilled snails), and going for long walks to Arles-sur-Tech, Les Cluses and even as far as Collioure. Braque continued painting. He started using collage, adding stencilled letters and fake wood to his pictures, his early skills learnt as a painter and decorator paying off.

He wrote to Kahnweiler telling of his progress and adding that one day, when he "went to Collioure...hardly had I arrived than I bumped into Matisse who showed me his latest canvases"

He was, as ever, short of money, asking Kahnweiler to send him some hundred francs so that he could settle the hotel bill and adding that he was happy in Céret and hoped to stay till January at least.

Braque's piano accordion often had the locals dancing under the plane trees. Their friendship helped him through lonely months after his Marcelle had returned to Paris. Manolo was his constant companion and Totote always made him welcome at their table.

Manolo and Totote had moved into a large house and had begun furnishing it as best they could. In a long letter to Frank Burty Haviland in Paris, Manolo described their furniture as "the minimum second hand or borrowed" adding that perhaps Frank would be able to send some of the sheets he had left in Paris. "However," he continued, he was "thrilled to have a large kitchen garden and was growing all their vegetables."

He also said that he was "happy to have several remarkable pieces, a negro mask that is very beautiful, two Greek earthenware lamps and a couple of beautiful amphorae... and some ivories;" telling Frank to "take note, maybe I could get you some, but you would have to come back first..."

In his next letter he mentioned that he was "a bit short at the moment" but was "surviving thanks to the ivories..."

It seems that, in Céret at the time, there was a somewhat dubious trade going on in African art objects and Greek and Roman amphorae from Ampuries in Spain. Contraband had always been a long established Catalan way of life. A way of life into which Manolo fitted very easily.

His own sculpture benefited from his increased self-confidence and, thanks to Frank's contacts with Parisian galleries, he started to sell.

It was in this October that he too signed a contract with Kahnweiler enabling his life to become more stable. Despite his success, Manolo never lost his fear of poverty, a fear he hid under the cloak of his habitual clowning and merriment that so entertained all with whom he came in contact.

Braque continued living and working happily and peacefully in Céret until mid January. He celebrated Christmas with Manolo and Totote and Maillol who always left his Marly studio for the end of year festivities in his native Roussillon.

Braque, who had become integrated far more closely into local life than Picasso ever did, was never to return to Céret. His collaboration with Picasso in the Cubist adventure would continue, but in Normandy, Paris and Sorgues.

Frank Burty Haviland summed the year up in the following words.: "The summer we spent in Céret has been delightful: we have had Braque and his wife, as well as Picasso and Fernande, Pichot and Germaine. All Paris and all Montmartre."

Panorama, Céret

Catalan fiesta

Chapter 9
1912, Céret

Braque may not have returned to Céret in 1912 and Matisse had deserted Collioure for Morocco, but Picasso was back. Over the winter, as Gertrude Stein had noticed, clouds had certainly been gathering over his relationship with Fernande. He had fallen deeply in love with "Eva", the companion of his friend Marcoussis. The words *Ma Jolie* cropped up on a painting, *La Table de l'Architecte*, a painting Gertrude had found him working on in January. Eva, in her opinion, was "a modest looking woman, far from "*Jolie*". Picasso was behaving like a lovesick teenager, needing to write the name of his beloved wherever he could, for all the world to see.

Eva had certainly used her position as Fernande's friend and confidante to her own advantage. When Picasso learned that Fernande had gone off for a few days with the young Italian painter, Ubaldo Oppi, he wrote to Braque saying that "Fernande has done a bunk with a futurist... so I am leaving Paris for a bit... and asking him to "Please look after Frika (the huge dog) for a few days..."

It was far too interesting an affair to go unnoticed in the Paris art world. Matisse, who sometimes went riding with Michael Stein, was provided by him with the details of the affair and Michael Stein lost no time in writing to Gertrude in Fiesole in June 1912. "I think I have the story of the Pablo business. Matisse told me he had a new model who lived with one of the Montmartre crowd and that she told him all about the affair. It seems that F. had been going with the Futurist for some time, and a note she gave her woman friend, who is always with her, to deliver to the Futurist, the friend gave to P. because she wanted P. herself. So P. confronted F. and they split up. P. went to K. got money, cleared all his things out of Ravignan (le Bateau Lavoir), discharged the maid, locked up the other place and decamped to Céret with the friend, where he is still working. The Futurist has no cash, so F. poses for Cinemas and says she is going on the stage and is living with the Pichots or however you spell it"

Many years later in her memoirs, Fernande rather mocked the "Futurists" remarking that their talents were "meagre" and noting that they had started a futurist fashion which consisted of wearing socks of different colours but matching their ties.

Picasso had departed from Paris on May 19th, in such a hurry that he left most of his possessions including his precious camera in the boulevard Clichy apartment.

He was happy to see Manolo's new house and to be amongst his Céret friends again. He also made certain no one in Paris knew his address.

From the Grand Café on May 20th he wrote to the ever-tolerant Kahnweiler asking him to sort out the animals ... "As for the dogs I have asked Braque to send me Frika, and the other animals, the monkey and the cats, to Madame Pichot who told me she would take them ..."

And again to Kahnweiler on May 24th, asking him to send on his paints, canvases etc. adding on May 25th that "I also need sheets, pillow, bolsters, blankets and my yellow kimono with flowers on it. I don't know how to set about to arrange this but I have more confidence in you than I have in myself."

Perhaps Kahnweiler was relieved to hear, on June 1st, that " Terrus has lent me an easel"

He worked in his studio in the Maison Delcros, the house he had shared with Braque the previous summer. "I miss you," he wrote, "I miss our walks, our exchange of feelings, I cannot write art discussions..." Braque was in Le Havre for a family celebration. Picasso worked solidly for almost a month.

He did a pencil portrait of Déodat at the piano and made some studies for a portrait of Frank Burty Haviland. He painted several still lifes.

For company he had Déodat, Manolo, Frank Burty Haviland, and others as well. They may not have had Braque's accordion but they had Casanova's guitar. They talked and walked and worked and cooked and ate together. Picasso's huge studio was strewn with scattered books and bags of beans.

And in June 1912, Eva arrived. She was a gentle woman, her sweetness and charm seducing all she met. She loved Céret, walking the surrounding countryside with Totote and Frika the dog. She took part in the cherry harvest.

But, all too soon, Picasso received a letter from Braque in Paris announcing the imminent arrival of Fernande.

Rapidly, he wrote to Kahnweiler: "I have had bad news from Paris. Braque wrote to me yesterday and said that he met Pichot who said that he, his wife and Fernande were thinking of coming to Céret for the summer and he was going to write to someone here to find out if I was here and I am quite upset about this because I do not want my great love, Marcelle (Eva), to suffer from the trouble they can cause and I don't want her to be upset either and I must be calm for my work.

With all these complications, I need to have here a reserve of one or two thousand francs... I don't want to be unable to leave for the lack of a few sous... and, if you should see Fernande, you could tell her to expect nothing more from me and that I would be happy never to see her again..."

Fernande had never liked Kahnweiler, describing him as "...clever, tenacious, cunning (though not so cunning as Vollard), a real Jewish businessman capable of taking a risk in order to make a profit." She did admit that he was also "Daring and busy. He wanted to have Picassos, Matisses, van Dongens, Vlamincks, and he got them...bargaining for hours on end until at last the exhausted painter agreed to a lower price..." (Actually Kahnweiler was highly cultured, had a deep understanding and appreciation of art and remained a good friend of Picasso for the following sixteen years).

Fernande arrived in Céret and there were terrible scenes between the two women. The events did not go unnoticed in the local artistic community. Terrus sent Marquet a postcard from Violet's house in Prades "there is fire in the cubist camp in Céret" he wrote, "the women are fighting and so are the men. Between Picasso's woman and Pichot's and between Picasso and a poet whose name I've forgotten..."

By June 25th Picasso and Eva had fled to Avignon and then on to the rather dull town of Sorgues sur l'Ouvèze where Braque and Marcelle, whom he had now married, joined them later that summer.

Picasso had been annoyed at having to leave the countryside that pleased him, the friends whose company he enjoyed and the work that was going well. Before he and Eva caught the train out

Abbaye de Fontfroide cloisters

he asked Manolo and Frank Burty Haviland to pack up his paintings and send them to Kahnweiler. On one of his frequent trips to the capital, Frank Burty Haviland duly delivered Picasso's canvases to Kahnweiler.

At the other end of the Roussillon, the creative intensity of Fontfroide and the encouragement of Redon inspired Fayet to take up his own paintbrush once again. He began working everyday, paintings rich in colour of the landscape around Fontfroide. Eastern philosophy intrigued him. He collected statues of the Buddha in auctions in Paris and installed them at Fontfroide. In the library where Redon's huge wall panels hung, he assembled his books, many of them rare first editions, two Buddhas, a Christ in ivory and de Monfreid's portrait of his wife. All human beliefs were represented in his collection of antique volumes.

But his greatest work of art was his restoration of the beautiful Abbey itself. The haven of peace, beauty and artistic endeavour that he, his wife and family created still inspires and delights almost a century after his death.

Maillol, Clotilde and Lucien continued to divide their time between Banyuls and Marly-le-Roi. Maillol had started working in la Métairie, three kilometres outside Banyuls in the peaceful valley of the Roume river. It was his favourite place. The small stone building stood in a grove of cypress trees, sheltered from the Tramontane wind, the vineyards sweeping up the surrounding hillsides as far as the eye could see. There he would rest from his sculpture, painting, reading and listening to Mozart and Beethoven on an old phonograph. He was a voracious reader, his tastes ranging from Shakespeare to Voltaire, from Virgil to Freud. Till the end of his days la Métairie was where he enjoyed receiving his friends.

His good friend Terrus was a keen photographer as well as a talented landscape painter. In his many self-portraits he portrayed himself leaning against olive trees, or reclining on the divan in his studio, a fierce look on his bearded face. In other photographs he appears next to Amélie Matisse at lunch, is seen wandering around Collioure with Camoin in 1912, is the centre of groups of serious looking bearded men who made up the artists of Roussillon at the time. An impressive exchange of postcards records for posterity friendships that lasted his lifetime.

Back in Paris, Fernande was forced to accept defeat. In her book of memoirs "*Picasso et ses Amis*" she says "I spent the most precious years of my life with Picasso: the years when I was happiest. The end of that era saw the end of most of my youth and all my illusions."

La Métairie, Banyuls-sur-Mer

Chapter 10

Mostly Céret, mostly 1913

Sketch of Collioure by Phil Monk

It sometimes seems curious that while the Collioure paintings of Matisse, the older, more serious, northern man, exploded with colour, freedom of expression, brightness and joy, in Céret, Picasso, man of the south, young and bohemian, was producing dark and brooding paintings full of sombre shades and straight lines.

Curious too that in a particularly fast moving decade in the history of modern art, so much of the action, by arguably the two greatest protagonists, was taking place in two small towns in the Roussillon.

Matisse returned to Collioure in 1911 and 1914. He was starting to be regarded in France as one of the foremost painters of the day. And this despite the advent of Picasso. He enjoyed the steady support of Leo, Michael and Sarah Stein, (Gertrude continued to favour Picasso). Ambroise Vollard sold every Matisse painting he could lay his hands on and the great Russian collectors, Shchukin and Morozov, were commissioning work from him with impressive enthusiasm. In all approximately fifty Matisse works went to Russia, all of which were acquired by the Russian State in 1923.

The cultural and artistic exchange between Moscow and Paris, soon to be broken by World War I and the Russian Revolution, was at its height in those early years of the twentieth century. Shchukin would swoop in from Moscow and clean out Matisse's studio. Diaghilev and the Ballet Russe were regular visitors to Paris. Shchukin ordered two murals for the grand staircase of his very grand house, the Trubetskoy Palace, in Moscow. The themes were *Dance* and *Music*. One might have thought that Matisse's wild and exuberant *Dance*, inspired by the peasants and fishermen he had first seen dancing the sardane in Collioure in 1905, could seem out of place in the opulent setting of a Tsarist Palace. In fact, within its apparent simplicity lay a boundless and primitive energy, making it both moving and very powerful.

Armory Exhibition poster.
New York, 1913

It seems that Matisse's own energy was boundless as well. He made several visits to North Africa, once, in 1913, with his close friend Albert Marquet. Between 1908 and 1912 his works were shown not only in Moscow but also in Berlin, Munich and London. In 1913 his *Luxury* was shown at the Armory Show in New York next to paintings by Marcel Duchamps and Francis Picabia. The Show was held in the 69th Regiment Armory building in New York City. Officially called the International Exhibition of Modern Art, the show was criticized by the public and the press as a circus of freaks and clowns.Nonetheless it was a circus full of life and colour, and had a great impact on American artists. Works by Picasso, Derain, Dufy and Braque, were also shown.

Meanwhile cubism was alive and well and living in Céret. Indeed, according to Picasso's friend the poet and art critic, André Salmon, Céret had become *La Mecque du Cubisme*.

In December 1912, Picasso and Eva stopped in Céret to celebrate Christmas with Manolo and Totote and Frank Burty Haviland. They were on their way to Barcelona, where Picasso planned to present Eva to his family as his potential wife. In January they returned to Paris hoping to marry in the spring if Picasso's father's health was up to it.

In March they returned to Céret. Picasso dutifully sent postcards to Kahnweiler and to Gertrude Stein. In Gertrude's a group of three costumed Catalan peasants were depicted sitting or standing and drinking from the spouted bottle much favoured by Catalan peasants.

Picasso added a beard to the seated peasant beneath whom he wrote "*Portrait of Matisse*" ...

By the end of the month his father's health was failing.

Picasso buried his worry in working. Writing to Kahnweiler he apologised for neglecting his friends and asked that Kahnweiler give Max Jacob, on his account, some money for his journey to Céret. Max Jacob was the only person capable of rousing Picasso from his gloom over his father's illness. And, although Max Jacob had been very close to Fernande, he was happy to keep Eva company while the ever jealous Picasso busied himself in his painting. Max Jacob admits in a letter to Kahnweiler that he is often a less than perfect guest. "Eva is admirably devoted to her humble household chores. She loves to write and laughs easily. She is even tempered and directs her attention toward satisfying a guest who is dirty and phlegmatic by nature when he is not ridiculously mad or idiotic."

Other hostesses have mentioned him "upsetting things on the table cloth, burning holes in sheets, leaving boot marks on bedspreads, and making such a noise going to Mass every morning at six that the whole household is aroused..."

While in Céret, Max Jacob wrote poetry, did some Cubist paintings and, to make some money, told horoscopes and read cards for the locals. He was a popular figure.

Braque was in Sorgues, teaching children to box and painting, painting, painting. Picasso wrote telling him he was worried about his father. He did not suggest Braque came to Céret. Braque remained in Sorgues with his wife Marcelle. He only occasionally saw Picasso spending more time with his old Fauve friends, Vlaminck and Derain.

Picasso's father died in May. Shortly afterwards Eva was diagnosed as having *angine*, a diagnosis that could be interpreted many ways. Picasso was ever fearful of illness. Their proposed wedding was postponed. In any case there was no way they could marry during the period of mourning for Picasso's father. Only slightly less upsetting than Eva's illness was that of his dog, Frika. Eva wrote to Gertrude Stein on May 14th explaining "Frika is done for... We have been to Perpignan to consult the best vet we could get... she will have to be put down... I hope Pablo will resume working for that's the only thing that will make him forget his woes."

Déodat and his musical entourage were very much the heart of the Céret cultural scene as a result of which musical instruments were

Frank Burty Haviland, Céret, *La vieille ville*

to play a major part in Picasso's collages and paintings. Eva was often represented by a violin or a guitar.

Picasso had always found *corridas* an inspiration. The traditional June bullfight in Céret made him hungry for more. With Max and Eva he visited Figueres and Girona. On the way back to Céret they stopped to join in dancing the sardane in a village festival. Max Jacob was enchanted by the haunting music of the *cobla* and the fluttering red and yellow Catalan flags. Nine years later he remembered the occasion in a poem he dedicated to Picasso.

Soon afterwards they returned to Paris for medical reasons. Picasso feared he had contracted typhoid. It was likely that Eva was seeking advice as well. While Picasso was recovering Eva was in constant touch with Gertrude Stein who was spending the summer in Barcelona. By July 22nd she reported that "Pablo is almost well, he gets up every afternoon. Matisse has been by frequently to find out how he is and today he brought Pablo some flowers and spent most of the afternoon with us. He's most agreeable." He also brought fruit. Oranges. Oranges were to Matisse what apples were to Cézanne. Picasso, recognizing the gesture, did not eat them but arranged them in a bowl. "Look, Matisse's oranges!" he would say, pointing them out to other visitors. Years later he bought Matisse's magnificent 1912 *Still Life with Oranges* in memory of these gifts.

By August they were back in Céret. L'Indépendant, the local newspaper, announced that " The little town of Céret is jubilant. The Cubist Master has arrived to take a well-deserved rest. ... Presently gathered around him in Céret are the painters Herbin, Braque (who was in fact in Sorgues) Kisling, Ascher, Pichot, Jean Gris and the sculptor Jo Davidson."

Picasso was less than thrilled. He had nothing against Kisling whose reputation was just beginning to take off, nor indeed Jo Davidson whom he knew through Gertrude Stein. Auguste Herbin, the most colourful and geometric of Cubists, was an old friend from Bateau Lavoir days.

Juan Gris, however, was another matter.

Les Capucins, Céret

Since 1910 Gris had aspired to be the third man of the Cubist movement. He had abandoned his career as a humorist cartoonist in order to follow his hero, Picasso, who had initially befriended him when he arrived from Madrid. Gertrude Stein had been amused that when Gris first knew Picasso, he began to refer to him as "*Cher Maître*". Picasso had been less amused but, passing on the joke, began to refer to Braque as "*Cher Maître*". A joke that backfired somewhat when some people thought Picasso really did look up to Braque as "Master."

Few of the *Bande à Picasso* had warmed to Gris. "One never had fun in Juan Gris' studio," Salmon complained. Nevertheless, doggedly, Gris learned from Picasso and Braque and became, quite quickly, a more promising painter than many other aspiring Cubists. Kahnweiler had signed him in February of 1913 and they became close friends for life. The fact that Kahnweiler liked Gris's work annoyed Picasso. Gris had also been taken up by Gertrude Stein, a further cause of irritation. In addition he was very attached to Matisse.

By the time he arrived in Céret, Gris had just begun using collage. His work was often richer in detail and had more colour than that of either Picasso's or Braque's. Fragments of newspapers, musical scores and wrapping paper were added and his painting output was prodigious. He seemed quite unaware that Picasso viewed him as his "sorcerer's apprentice", mastering his master's secrets and setting himself up as a cubist expert. As it turned out, in the autumn, when Kahnweiler showed them to him, Picasso was full of praise for Gris' Céret paintings.

The local Céretans certainly were fascinated by what was going on in their quiet country town. And not only by the art. The artists' clothes and manner of dressing attracted attention and gossip. Unlike the local women, shrouded in black, the artists' women wore bright colours. The artists themselves dressed in workmen's blues, practical clothes that identified them as belonging to their own group, an outward sign they considered themselves to be artisans, working with their hands. The local bourgeoisie were often shocked, regarding their behaviour as almost diabolic. The peasants had difficulties with a way of life apparently enjoyed without money or regular work, not ordered by the seasons in the cherry orchards or vines. Several merchants refused to accept paintings or drawings as payment. A mistake as it turned out...

Some evenings in the bar of the Grand Café or under the plane trees outside were dominated by Gris's discourses on Cubism while Picasso sat silent and fuming. Manolo, no lover of cubism, did all he could to stir up Picasso's distrust of the pupil who so threatened to outshine him.

On other evenings the atmosphere was lighter. Michel Justaffre, the *patron*, and Michel Aribaud, the wine merchant, later the town archivist, would look on, enjoying watching Picasso drawing on whatever came to hand. Sometimes Max Jacob would be present, telling his fanciful horoscopes, the young André Masson might be deep in conversation with Maillol's great friend, the poet Pierre Camo. They were often joined by Frank Burty Haviland, Déodat, and Manolo. Manolo was simply unable to understand why one might want to paint any thing in any way other than to depict reality. The talk could become tempestuous and last well into the small hours of the morning.

Auguste Herbin caused no antagonism. As a neighbour of Picasso, Gris and Braque in the Bateau Lavoir since 1909, he was well exposed to developing cubist ideas. He had been further encouraged by Picasso's German collector, William Uhde. However, where Picasso and Braque favoured increasingly sombre greys and browns, Herbin never lost his love of bright colour. He had visited Corsica in 1909 and the visual impact of the light and colour experienced there never left him. The summer of 1913 was his first visit to Céret. He was to return after the war in 1918 staying a couple of years. Three very varied paintings of Herbin's, a cubist view of the Devil's Bridge, a portrait of Michel Aribaud and a watercolour of the town, hang today in the Céret Museum of Modern Art.

However, Ramon Pichot, Picasso's longtime friend, posed a very real problem for him. They were linked not only by Ramon's family's hospitality to Picasso back in early Barcelona days but also by Ramon's wife Germaine having been Picasso's one time mistress as well as the cause of Casagemas's suicide. The previous summer it was Ramon and Germaine Pichot's arrival with Fernande that had prompted Picasso and Eva's flight to Sorgues. And now, Ramon, on his own, had come to try to persuade the increasingly prosperous Picasso to provide some financial help for the near destitute Fernande.

Any hint of criticism of his personal behaviour could throw Picasso into a rage. Add the implied criticism of Eva's treacherous treatment of her one time friend and the rage would have been more than impressive. He and Eva left immediately. By mid August they were back in Paris. "We had some disputes." Picasso wrote to Kahnweiler. "and preferred to come back to Paris to find some peace".

Picasso's third and final stay in Céret had ended.

In 1913 Frank Burty Haviland bought the beautiful old Couvent des Capucins in Céret in preparation for his marriage to Joséphine Laporta.

He and Joséphine had met at the Sunday dancing in the town. She was well educated and charming. Their wedding day in January1914 was an unforgettable, happy and impressive occasion. Frank's brother, Paul, came from New York and took photographs showing the splendour of the event. Paul and their other brother, Jean, from Limoges, were the only representatives of the Haviland family. A friend, the Count Gasparin, was witness. He brought with him two African children dressed in red and gold and bearing exotic fruit.

The Burty Havilands moved into the Couvent des Capucins. The view from its terrace overlooking Céret was painted by almost every one of the many artist friends who visited them there. The photographs taken there of *cargolades*, picnics and parties, of solitary easels and sumptuous Vallespir views would fill albums.

Above all, Picasso and the artists who lived and worked in Céret during those golden pre-war years, were a group of talented friends, some more gifted than others, some cubists, some not, all following their art in an ambiance of freedom and stimulation.

They were starting to become well known. As Braque said *"How life has changed now that we all have cooks that can make a soufflé"*.

Chapter 11
The First World War

The 1914-18 War broke the spell. Frank Burty Haviland, not yet a French citizen, spent the war in Céret as did Manolo.

Derain was mobilised and remained in the army throughout the war, fighting on the Somme, at Verdun and in the Vosges mountains. He continued to paint when he could. There was little opportunity, but his career did not come entirely to a halt. He had a one-man show with the dealer Paul Guillaume in 1916. Apollinaire wrote the catalogue preface.

Derain was forced to remain in the army until 1919, serving with the French occupation forces in Mainz. When he was finally released the French art world received him with open arms.

Braque was called up and went to war. He was badly injured in the trenches on the 11th of May in 1915.

The same year Picasso's Eva died of cancer. Picasso was heartbroken.

Picasso, like Manolo, did not take part in the war. His ties with Braque, who was fighting, were severed. He retreated to Rome with Jean Cocteau. Cocteau introduced him to Serge Diaghilev of the Ballets Russes and he painted the scenery for Cocteau's *Parade*, music by Eric Satie, in the programme notes of which Apollinaire coined the word "surrealism". Picasso met the dancer Olga Khokhlova who became his next mistress.

In January of 1918 he showed with Matisse at the gallery Guillaume. In July, when he married Olga in the Russian Church in Paris, Cocteau, Max Jacob and Apollinaire were the witnesses.

Apollinaire received a serious shrapnel wound to the head at the front in 1916 from which he would never recover. He wrote *Les Mamelles de Tirésias* while convalescing and the programme notes for the ballet *Parade*. He died in November of 1918.

Picasso had loved Apollinaire. Their early poverty days had been full of seemingly endless fun, going out to cabarets, the circus, watching puppet shows, listening to horror stories and gypsy singers. But now, of all the laughing, shouting, singing and drinking too much, all that remained were the memories.

Gris, as a deserter from the Spanish Army, had no passport and was stuck in Collioure where Matisse found him a room with his son's schoolteacher. Gris returned to Paris in 1915 where he suffered bleak poverty. In late 1916 his paintings became more stately and architectural, the forms became larger and flatter as multiple viewpoints were to an extent abandoned...

Matisse, rejected for military service in 1914, was often in Paris, trying to get into the forces despite his 45 years. He spent the war painting, in Issy, Paris and Nice. He moved to Nice in 1917, the year both his sons were drafted. Nice he considered to be "paradise". It became the place he was to spend most of the rest of his life. "In order to paint my pictures," he remarked, "I need to remain for several days in the same state of mind, and I do not find this in any atmosphere but that of the Côte d'Azur." He settled in a large apartment, in a classic white wedding cake of an Edwardian building, the wrought iron balcony and the shutters of which, plus a line of blue sky and the occasional palm tree, would appear again and again in his paintings.

Poor Herbin was rejected by the army as being too small and nearly starved in his Bateau Lavoir studio. He did, however, decorate the chapel of the military camp in Mailly-le-Camp and worked on camouflage in an aircraft factory.

Kisling joined the Foreign Legion and was so seriously wounded in the Battle of the Somme in 1915 that he was given French citizenship.

In Prades, Violet's period of great productivity was brought to an abrupt halt by the outbreak of war. Within the first couple of months, his greatest friend Louis Codet was killed. His son, Pallade, remembered, at the age of six, seeing his father's uncontrollable tears on being told of his death.

Violet himself was mobilised in 1915 and returned, totally traumatised by the horrors of war, in 1918. He weighed fifty-eight kilos. He wrote several articles and reviews on life in the trenches. He never recovered his full health.

Not all was tragedy. George Daniel de Monfreid spent the 1914-18 war at St Clément where, in 1917, the engagement of his daughter Agnès to Louis Huc was cause for great celebration. Numerous friends attended, among them Déodat de Sévérac who had composed a *Nuptial Catalan* for the occasion.

De Sévérac also served, his duties and redeployments reducing his musical output to a handful of mostly insignificant works.

The outbreak of war found Maillol in Marly-le-Roi where, near his studio, he and Kessler had established a small paper factory. Kessler had ordered illustrations for *L'Art d'Aimer* by Ovid and Maillol had created his own art paper, *le Montval*, on which to draw them. As war was declared, Kessler telegrammed him, advising Maillol to bury a statue he had commissioned. In the mad, patriotic fervour that prevailed the telegram was construed as a message to a spy and rumour spread that the paper factory concealed a reinforced concrete platform for guns with which to bombard Paris. Maillol was accused of working for the enemy and an angry crowd burnt down his paper factory. The pro-German myth from which he was to suffer in the Second World War had begun. His son Lucien was mobilised and it wasn't until he came home safe and sound at the end of the war that Maillol could regain enough peace of mind to begin working again.

Gustave Fayet – Cyprès bleus

Gustave Fayet and his wife remained at Fontfroide, overseeing the works and, in the case of Fayet, painting landscapes of the surrounding countryside. They spent three weeks of the summer of 1915 in Banyuls-sur-Mer with Maillol. Gustave Fayet's warm watercolours of the Maillol house, its ochre coloured walls and the surrounding countryside with glimpses of blue Mediterranean reflect a happy time; a profile portrait of Maillol, emphasising his sharp nose and pointed beard, captured the character of his friend to perfection.

Fayet took the cure in several Pyrenean spas.

In 1916 Redon died. Fayet had been with him the day before. Mme Redon asked him to help dig Redon's grave in the little cemetery of Brièves. In the text that appeared in the Times Literary Supplement in April 1916, Fayet described the scene: "I looked for a long while

Gustave Fayet at Abbaye de Fontfroide

Gustave Fayet – Voiles latines

into the hole into which, the next day, the remains of my friend would descend. The sandy grains of the soil were of a golden yellow. A last ray of sun caught the neighbouring tombs. And I broke down. Redon rests in this modest cemetery overlooking the valley and his little country house where he had spent so many happy days."

In 1917 Fayet bought an American tractor, an implement unseen in other vineyards of the Languedoc for a further thirty years.

Gertrude Stein was stuck in England.

Kahnweiler, who had not followed Picasso's advice to get French citizenship, was in Switzerland when war broke out. His possessions were all sequestered and he could not return to France.

German guns could be heard from Paris, no one was very interested in buying art.

Vollard shut up shop...

In a postcard Terrus sent Manguin he asked "What will become of you in this time of war when the life of each of us is so disturbed?"

The answer was that they all, with the exception of Apollinaire and Redon, survived.

Chapter 12
After the war

There was a Government sale of Kahnweiler's collection which, at the time, consisted of most of the Cubist pictures. Many of the old dealers, planning to kill off Cubism, persuaded the sales expert, also a dealer, to keep the prices artificially low. Picasso and Gris, as Spaniards, could do nothing. Braque, however, was not only French but had won the Légion d'Honneur in the war. He asked that various good clients of his be invited and, when they did not receive their catalogues, accused the expert of neglect of duty. The Steins arrived at the sale just in time to hear the expert, unwisely, calling Braque a "Norman pig". Braque was a large man, the expert was not. The expert fell, the police arrived and they were both taken to the station. Braque, the war hero, won the day. The expert was rebuked by the Magistrate but most of the buyers had been frightened off and the pictures, with the exception of those of Derain, went for very low prices.

Kahnweiler, who after all, had not fought against France, was allowed back the following year. He continued his support of the Cubist cause. Like Vollard, he was a dealer who made his money when he could, continuing to buy from artists in whose work he had faith even if there was no actual market, in the belief that by his persistence he would create a public. He had virtually lived with Picasso, Braque, Gris, Derain, and Vlaminck on a day-to-day, hour-to-hour basis. By making it possible for them to get on with their work, Kahnweiler had helped to bring into being what might now be referred to as a last great flowering of French art.

For the Armistice, Déodat de Sévérac wrote a spontaneous and memorable Te Deum. He resumed his post as organist at St. Pierre's in Céret and returned to composition. But he was ill.

In 1919 Derain designed the ballet *La Boutique Fantastique* for Diaghilev (the first of many ballet designs), which scored a major success, and in 1920 he signed another contract with Kahnweiler, replaced by a contract with Paul Guillaume in 1923.

In 1922, when his greatest friend, Terrus, died, Maillol felt he had lost a brother.

Ever popular, he had been the local artist who had forged the links between the Céret artists and those in Collioure and on the coast, the one to lead the talk from art to philosophy, from religion to social gossip. Conversations had never been dull when he was present. *"Where's old Terrus?"* Camoin would say to Matisse if he was missing. *"We need him here with a new set of his provocative ideas to get us going..."*

The town of Perpignan asked Maillol to sculpt a bust in his memory. He captured perfectly the character of the retiring, obstinate and much loved painter from Elne, founder member of the group of Roussillonais artists. At the inauguration ceremony Maillol was horrified to see it had been placed on a plinth of Villefranche marble, looking, as he remarked to Clotilde, like the "flesh of a Catalan sausage". He returned with Clotilde at dead of night, unscrewed the bust and took it home. The plinth was changed and for many years the sculpture graced the Jardin Terrus in the centre of town. It can now be seen in the Musée Rigaud while a second version looks out from the ramparts of the old town of Elne, gazing out towards the coast and Albères hills that Terrus had known and loved so well.

Rodin had died in 1917. Maillol was now recognised as the greatest living French sculptor of his generation. Commissions for municipal monuments began to trickle in. Several towns of the Roussillon invited Maillol to sculpt their War Memorials. These orders had an added benefit for the local councils in that the cost was limited to that of the materials and the hours worked... Maillol was not put off. As ever, he worked with pride and dedication to produce some of his best-known sculptures in the region.

In common with Violet and Manolo, he had no wish to glorify war. They all refused to put victorious warriors on the monuments, preferring instead to evoke the fate of the women left at home, waiting for news of husbands, brothers, friends at the front, women whose sons and lovers would never return.

Gustave Violet had been profoundly marked by the war, both physically and mentally. When the towns of Perpignan, Thuir, Prades, Claira, Collioure, Alénya, Estagel and St Laurent de Cerdans all awarded him the honour of sculpting their war memorials the monuments he created were, in reality, anti-war memorials. The women depicted are both moving and have sensual dignity. They became known as *Monuments Pacifiques.*

Gustave Violet – Monument aux Morts, Perpignan

In the enormous one in Perpignan erected outside the Palais des Congrès in 1924, his skills as an architect, a ceramicist, a sculptor and an artist are all evident. He called it *le Retable* and explained how he had used the marble of Villefranche in its natural state as to have polished it would, in his opinion, have removed the rustic nature of the monument. For the sculpture, he said, he had chosen hard and rugged stones "our race has never been aristocratic, it is the fruit of our soil, of the plain and the rocks biting into the sea. It is both harsh and elegant like our Roman bell towers... graceful French works of the XVI and XVIII centuries would not show the character of our vignerons, our shepherds and our fishermen..."

The bas-relief sculptures on the monument he designed for his birthplace of Thuir portray to a heartrending degree both the sorrow of the women and the stoicism blended with despair of the soldiers.

Gustave Violet
Monument aux Morts detail, Thuir

In 1918, Violet had won the first prize of the City of Paris for his apartment block on rue Remusat and had also built the Maison Escoffier on place Arago in Perpignan.

His monument in homage to the French Socialist leader, Jean Jaurès, in Perpignan is also a monument to his own socialist principles. Anti-militarist Jaurès had been assassinated at the outbreak of the War and remains to this day one of the main historical figures of the French Left.

Gustave Violet – Allégorie des Sports,
Piscine Alfred Nakache, Toulouse

Gustave Violet – Entente Cordiale,
Vernet-les-Bains

Violet's contacts with the local literary and musical worlds multiplied. He illustrated *Visages de mon Pays* for Ludovic Massé, wrote a play with Joseph Sébastien Pons with music by Enric Morer, *La Font de l'Albèra* that was a great success in the Arènes of Céret.

He designed the magnificent fronton dedicated to the "Glory of Sport" for the enormous Nakache Swimming Pool in Toulouse, a project he worked on with the up and coming young sculptor, Marcel Gili. Gili, Maillol's godson, studied with him for a couple of years.

He was forever involved with the local cultural and sportive life of Prades, making numerous bronze commemorative plaques. Hardly surprising the imposing Collège is today named after him.

The construction of the monument to the Entente Cordiale of 1904 in Vernet-les-Bains was delayed for a good eight years. The idea for the monument was conceived in 1912, the sculptor was to be Gustave Violet and among the patrons were Lord Roberts and General Joffre. The model Violet proposed was approved in 1913 but it was well into August 1920 before the giant granite blocks were hauled up from the valley by oxen and the heroic stone mason could begin working fourteen hour days in blazing summer sun. Local children watched, fascinated as the final iron railings were sealed in place in holes filled with molten lead.

Meanwhile there were more war memorials: in Céret, Maillol's *La Douleur,* lightly clothed, is reminiscent of his *la Méditerannée.* He was unhappy with the plinth saying it needed to be lowered by twenty centimetres to arrive at the viewing angle he intended for the figure's chin. Unfortunately and to Maillol's fury, it was actually raised by twenty centimetres. It was not altered again.

In Elne the war memorial, a sculpture, in classical tunic, is none other than his 1910 *Pomone* with clothes on. In Port-Vendres, the time weathered figure dominating the harbour, draped in soft cloth, half seated, has the look of a classical goddess, evocative of the town's origins as the Port of Venus. Once again the plinth is wrong. Maillol had wanted to see, below her raised arm, the distant line of the blue horizon. Instead one sees the dark shape of the mountain across the bay.

The star however, is the memorial of Banyuls-sur-Mer. Maillol himself said "At last I have realised something that pleases me: on a rock, in the middle of the sea, a simple sculpture; three things, the sky, the sea and a sculpted stone. I have added the sad sentiment of war as I feel it. I would have preferred a song of joy

Place Général de Gaulle,
Port-Vendres

but it is the sense of sadness I have had to leave on this Banyuls rock, that I have linked to the sun, this sea and the beautiful countryside surrounding this spot."

It takes the form of a triptych. The centre panel shows one of his rare male figures. The striking and tragic naked soldier captures the essence of a man giving his life for his country. Almost like a Christ on the Cross, it exudes a universal sadness emphasised by the female figures on the two side panels: mothers and wives, the older and younger women, mourning their lost menfolk.

Aristide and Clotilde continued to spend summers in Paris and winters in Banyuls. In Paris he worked on the large sculptures for which he was becoming famous. They saw the de Monfreids and other Roussillon friends almost daily. Sundays in Marly were as popular as ever. Gustave Violet's son remembers being taken to visit him one Sunday in 1929. He confided in Maillol that he had always admired his statue of the Little Cyclist. "Ah yes, of course, your father told me you were a great sportsman!" ... A large number of visitors began to arrive. Young Pallade Violet noted they were "well spoken men and that the women were very agreeably perfumed". They wandered around the garden, between blocks of marble and grand and naked statues. As he chatted to them, Maillol would let his hand wander over the thigh of one of his sculptures, occasionally catching Violet's eye and giving a furtive wink.

Violet's son was not the only one to remember his Sunday visits to Marly-le-Roi. Ten or so years later, just before the Second World War, a young army cadet, Florian de la Comble, was taken there on several Sundays by his friend the sculptor, Pimienta. He too admired the by then elderly Aristide Maillol. "He had a large beard and vivid blue eyes... the garden was full of many people..." Little did the young man dream then that, when he too was elderly and retired, he would live in Maillol's grandparent's house, and would be part of the team to restore Maillol's last and favourite studio in his beloved Métairie.

Le Castellas, Céret, with Canigou in the background

Chapter 13
The Roussillon between the wars

Inevitably, the war affected the painting of the period. Patriotism prevailed and there was a degree of looking back at more traditional styles of art. Typical of the work of the time was that of Pierre Brune, a painter who was invalided out of the Army to convalesce in Amélie-les-Bains in 1916. He gravitated to Céret to join his friends Manolo and Frank Burty Haviland.

Stone by stone he built a solid house on the vestiges of the town's old feudal castle. *Le Castellas*. In 1946, during a terrible thunderstorm, the house burnt down and many of his works were destroyed. Ever tenacious, he rebuilt it stone by stone, more beautiful than it had been before. It still overlooks the town below.

Sign over doorway to le Castellas, Céret

The views, over the red tiled roofs of the town, through the towering tops of the tall plane trees to a gleaming Canigou, were similar to those from the terrace of the Burty Havilands' Couvent des Capucins. Brune painted the views he loved so much, the great pottery jars on his terrace, still lifes, bouquets of flowers. He cultivated a few vines. His house became a haven for visiting artists. And artists did visit Céret in ever increasing numbers.

The first to arrive were Pinchus Krémègne and Chaim Soutine, both artists from Belarus, struggling away in La Ruche studios in Montparnasse. Their Paris neighbours had included the Polish Kisling who had visited Céret in 1913 and Chagall who was to arrive in 1927. It was in La Ruche that Soutine and Modigliani had become inseparable friends. Modigliani had also been a friend of Frank Burty Haviland and had painted some of his first canvases in Haviland's Paris studio.

Rooftops of the town viewed from le Castellas, Céret

Krémègne was a modest man, a painter of still lifes and landscape. He settled happily in Céret forgetting his expatriate past. He was a familiar figure in the streets of the town, often carrying large shopping baskets, his dog at his heels. Frank Burty Haviland even converted him to eating *cargolade*, the grilled snails with aioli of which the locals were so fond. In 1960 he built himself a house near the Capucins called the Miranda del Couvent. It was to be his home until his death at the age of ninety-one.

Soutine arrived a year later. He had known Pierre Brune in Paris and through him decided to come to Céret. However, once there, he made no secret of his dislike of the place. He had just learned of the death of Modigliani and the subsequent suicide of Modigliani's pregnant girlfriend. Soutine took to drink, nevertheless painting several hundred canvases over the next couple of years. They were wild and furious paintings, not appreciated by the local Céretans who cared neither for his art nor for the man himself. Often drunk and always dirty, he was taken for the village madman in his grubby clothes on which he cleaned his brushes, daubing them with all the colours of his palette. He would wander the countryside, rising at three in the morning to walk up to twelve kilometres, laden with his canvases and paints to find the spot he wanted to paint. His face showed no recognition of the world around him. It seemed lit by the light of interior suffering and creative strength. His turbulent, tortured pictures piled up in his studio. When his agent, Zborowski, came to collect them, Soutine attempted to burn them. Zborowski saved just over half, taking them to Paris, where he sold a hundred of them a couple of months later to Dr. Barnes, the famous American collector. In his *Recollections of a Picture Dealer*, Vollard describes Barnes' method of buying: "He gets you to show him twenty or thirty pictures. Unhesitatingly, as they pass before him, he picks out this or that one. Then he goes away. In this expeditious fashion, which only a taste as sure as his made possible, Dr. Barnes bought together the incomparable collection which is the pride of Philadelphia."

Soutine's fortunes changed, his dislike of Céret did not. Destroying his Céret canvases remained a hobby… For the rest of his life, whenever he could track one down he would buy it to burn. He left in 1922 never to return. He had been one of the most original painters to visit Céret. Dina Vierny and Picasso were two of the few mourners at his funeral in Montparnasse Cemetery in 1943. She had not known him but Picasso had asked her to accompany him. Picasso, with his horror of death, spent the day drawing…

While in Céret, Soutine's near neighbour in the Carrer de l'Hôpital, had been the 23 year old artist, André Masson. Badly wounded in the war, he could not bear violence. After a brief stay in Collioure he arrived in Céret in March 1919. He, and his friend Maurice Loutreuil were working in a pottery in nearby Palalda when they were arrested without papers on suspicion of spying. They were rescued by a "wonderful and picturesque being": Manolo…

Masson got on very well with Krémègne. Not at all well with Soutine. Soutine's insistence that painting should be "vomited out, as if from your very entrails" was not Masson's style. He painted a beautiful view of Haviland's Capucins. His work at this time was much influenced by Cézanne and Van Gogh.

When Masson married Odette Cabale on the 13th of February 1920, his witnesses were Frank Burty Haviland and Manolo. He left soon after for Paris and a very varied artistic career on both sides of the Atlantic. He never returned to Céret.

The Russian artist, Marc Chagall, was a peaceful and retiring visitor. For two years he lived with his wife, Bella in the Mas Lloret on the road to Amélie-les-Bains. Mimosa and wisteria surrounded them, the Tech river ran nearby. He liked to work in peace and solitude. Every morning he would go into Céret to do a little shopping and buy the occasional brush from the chemist Sageloli, who had wisely followed the advice of Pierre Brune and stocked a goodly selection of art materials. He had been commissioned by Ambroise Vollard to paint a series of gouaches to illustrate *Les Fables de la Fontaine*. It is probable that he was working on these at Mas Lloret. When the work was shown in 1929, Vollard had to defend his choice of artist, much criticised by the French public for not being French. He described Chagall's work as perfect, being at the same time "...dense and subtle, realistic and fantastic...". A description that sums up the fanciful dreamlike paintings of one of the greatest figurative artists of the 20th century rather well.

Meanwhile, at Fontfroide, Gustave Fayet had been working on a series of paintings on blotting paper. Dreamlike soft focus designs of flowers, leaves and underwater plants, richly coloured and fantastic. They were perfect designs for all manner of forms of interior decoration. With his friend and fellow collector, Dumas, the banker from Finestret, he opened a carpet workshop in rue la Dauphine, Paris. Their success was immediate. They were exhibited the following year at the Salon d'Automne. In fact, in 1923, when he handed the running of his wine domains on to his children, he wrote to his daughter, Yseult, telling her that he thought it might be amusing to make a living from his art, a dream he had confided to de Monfreid a couple of years previously. His dream began to come true as the carpets were collected by the State, Rothschild, the couturier Jacques Doucet and the Maharajah of Lahore.

When considering his love of literature, his collection of valuable books and the richness of the library at Fontfroide, it is easy to understand the ease with which, in the early 1920's, he took to illustration. His fantasy plants, trees and flowers, seemingly botantically accurate but, in fact, all the fruits of Fayet's imagination, began to illuminate pages of text, poetry and stories.

For his illustrations of Mistral's *Mireille* he took his sketch book to Provence returning with seventy-two exquisite drawings. He photographed and drew gnarled and ancient olive trees on Mallorca and returned from Venice with dreamlike watercolours.

In the meantime Maillol's increasing success did little to change his way of life. He spent as much time as possible at la Métairie. There he was more than happy to entertain the many artists, poets and writers who sought him out. Chagall arrived one day in 1923 with the writer and poet, Joseph Delteil. Delteil was fascinated by the attachment Maillol had for his country. For him, Maillol was so in touch with his creative energy, with the olives and waters around him that "the whole earth passed through his works. It doesn't speak, it is!"

That same summer of 1923, Henri Martin, the Post Impressonist artist, bought a house in Collioure from which, until 1939, he painted seascapes and scenes of the village. He made frequent visits to Maillol for inspiration and encouragement.

Another guest was John Rewald, the American art historian. Born Gustav Rewald in Berlin, John Rewald came from a Jewish background. He studied in several German Universities before going to the Sorbonne in Paris in 1932. On a visit to London he had fallen in love with a Maillol sculpture recently acquired by the Tate Gallery. On his return to Paris, overcoming considerable shyness, he was introduced to Maillol. He was immediately invited to la Métairie. There they worked together on an album of Catalan drawings for which John Rewald wrote the words. In Rewald's *Souvenirs de Maillol*, Maillol's quote "What I would like is that the young girl whose statue I make represents all young girls, that the woman full of maternal promise, represents all mothers ", sums up his achievements to perfection...

It wasn't till 1934 that the State finally recognised Maillol. "Better late than never" said Jean Cassou, inspector of historic monuments, and ordered *la Montagne* in 1938 for the Musée National d'Art Moderne. In the same year Maillol created *l'Air*, a hommage to the pilots of the France-South America line, ordered by the city of Toulouse.

On his 65th birthday the town of Banyuls organised a celebration. In a clearing amongst the cork oaks, a lamb was roasted, the sardane was danced, snails were grilled, speeches made and much wine drunk. At last the Town Hall had acknowledged and appreciated their town's most famous son.

Far from retiring Maillol's energy showed no sign of abating. As he said "the harder the stone, the more agreeable the work and the harder one can tap!"

Back in Céret however, Déodat de Sévérac was becoming more and more ill. He had always been a popular figure, much loved by all who knew him. In the winter of 1920/1921 George Daniel de Monfreid visited him every day.

As de Sévérac lay dying he asked only that music be played. "Music," he murmured, " is all I have lived for. It is the most beautiful thing there can be in the world." He died on March 24th, aged forty eight.

Memorial to Déodat de Séverac by Manolo, detail, Céret

Déodat de Séverac
plaque by Manolo, Céret

Much later, in 1951, under a scribbled portrait of his friend, Picasso wrote: "Yes, Déodat de Sévérac, with the admiration I have for him, will always be one of the best memories of my artistic life. I pay him homage."

The town of Céret commissioned Manolo to sculpt a monument in his memory. It stands today outside the Tourist Office.

The following year de Monfreid set off on an African voyage. Firstly to visit his daughter Agnès who was living in Oran, Algeria with her husband, then on to Djibouti where a long journey by mule brought him to the home of his son Henry de Monfreid, his wife Armgart and their three children. Almost as soon as he arrived he started to draw, working non-stop on a series of Ethiopian landscapes followed by a portrait of his nine year old granddaughter, Gisèle. Known as *La Petite Coloniale* it is a touching and rather poignant picture. When he left in December 1923, he took Gisèle with him.

Catalogue cover,
Salon d'Automne 1925

In 1925, at the Salon d'Automne, the two portraits he exhibited were *La Petite Coloniale* and *Hommage à Gauguin*.

And it was in 1925 that Gustave Fayet, in what was to be the last year of his life, wrote and illustrated *Fleurs*, dedicating it to his grandchildren. "Think that flowers are fairies and gentle genies living in palaces of grass, raising their arms to embrace the sun... it is true there is a paradise for flowers, as for all beasts. The flower paradise is the Third Door in the Air, on the right, towards the sun, just beneath the Golden Tree... Your grandfather will wait for you on the doorstep of your new home that he will have decorated to receive you. There will be all the flowers of *a dream, over* which beautiful stars will sparkle..."

His descendants adored him, remembering him years later as "more accustomed to questions than to certitudes, curious, restless, open to new ideas, full of humour, attentive to the beauty of creation, allergic to stupidity, ever sensitive to others..."

In his obituary, his contemporary, the art critic Louis Vauxcelles, listed his many and varied skills, adding that he hoped to see, soon, a retrospective exhibition to show the full talent of "*Gustave Fayet... a very rare artist.*" ...

To an extent his wish was granted in 1926 by a postumous exhibition in the sumptuous Marsan Pavillion in the Tuileries beside a retrospective exhibition of his beloved friend Odilon Redon's works. However it wasn't until 2006 that a true restrospective Fayet Exhibition took place in Terrus's home town of Elne. A hundred and fifty of his descendants gathered to pay him homage... His great-grandson, Antoine Fayet's introduction to the catalogue is illustrated by the portrait painted by George Daniel de Monfreid, sitting in a red armchair, with Gauguin's painting of *La Barque* and his sculpted *Masque de Tehura* in the background.

M. and Mme Fayet on the terrace at the Abbaye de Fontfroide

Charles Rennie Mackintosh the Glaswegian architect/designer/artist, had a close connection with Port-Vendres where he lived and worked for the last four years of his life. He and his wife Margaret were also part of the art scene in Collioure in the mid twenties and probably stayed a few months there. At any rate three of his paintings form part of the *Chemin de Charles Rennie Macintosh en Collioure*. In their distinctive metal stands, so reminiscent of the chair backs of his furniture designs, *A Southern Town* is displayed between the entrance to the parking lot and the beginning of the path along the massive walls of the Château Royal, and two others, *The Summer Palace of the Queen's of Aragon* and *Collioure* are placed appropriately along the Route de Port-Vendres. In Port-Vendres itself the *Chemin* continues and there is a small museum in his honour.

A bit like Matisse and his wife before them, the Mackintoshes arrived by train with very limited means. They too found they could live cheaply and travelled all over the Pyrenées-Orientales. Charles Rennie Mackintosh's watercolours of Collioure and Port-Vendres as well as many inland

On the Mackintosh trail, Port-Vendres

Roussillon towns were never appreciated in his lifetime. His estate, including thirty-one paintings and four of his chairs was valued at £88 16s 2d at his death in 1927.

Each summer the de Monfreids returned to Saint Clément where George Daniel would rise early to paint the countryside he knew and loved so well. They entertained and enjoyed the company of their many friends and visitors. Sometimes he stayed on into the autumn, describing his property as an "enchanted palace, surrounded by mountains…"

In November 1929, climbing a persimmon tree in the garden of his "enchanted palace" to gather some of its exotic orange fruit, George Daniel de Monfreid fell. He died the next day and was buried in the cemetery of Corneilla-de-Conflent, in a little chapel, a cast of his Mary Magdalene from his sculpture *Le Calvaire* the only ornament.

George Daniel de Monfreid le Calvaire sculpture in family tomb, Corneilla-de-Conflent

ICI REPOSENT
Caroline de MONFREID
Née BARRIERE
1823 - 1903
George Daniel de MONFREID
1856 - 1929
Armgart de MONFREID
Née FREUDENFELD
1889 - 1938
Annette de MONFREID
Née BELFILS
1887 - 1950

Plaque on de Monfreid family tomb, Corneilla-de-Conflent

Chapter 14
End of an era

So, by the end of the 19's, three out of our five local heroes were dead and gradually the band of artists, who had added so much to the life of Céret for almost twenty years, dispersed. Manolo, who had become a vital part of everyday Céret life, returned to his native Spain where the weather was better for his arthritis. He concentrated more and more on painting, mainly watercolours. His wife, Totote and their daughter, Rosa, kept up the strong friendships the family had forged with so many of the locals. In March 1953 she wrote to Joséphine Burty Haviland "Thanks to Céret I don't feel the passing of my 68 years. How could one forget the town where we were happy and where the inhabitants have remained just as we knew them; sadly many are gone but their children remain and remember us just as they do their parents."

Frank Burty Haviland sold the Capucins and bought a wine domaine near the coast that he managed with his wife's family.

Fernande Olivier noted that their once penniless artist friends now "all have cars and their present wives have fur coats. All of them have acquired needs and obligations which keep their noses to the grindstone", adding, rather poignantly, "I know some of the women who lived with those artists, companions of the good and the bad hours of their youth: and that they are growing old alone too, with only their memories as constant companions."

In 1933 Aristide Maillol was seventy-three and a model was about to enter his life who would make all his artistic dreams come true.

Dina Vierny, a schoolgirl of fifteen, was first introduced to Maillol in Marly. Her father's friend, the architect Dondel had told her she would meet many celebrated artists, writers and poets of the day if she visited Maillol's studio there. She had been told to introduce herself to the oldest man in the room. To the great amusement of the gathered company she introduced herself to Van Dongen instead of to Maillol.

In 1934 Aristide and Clotilde invited her to Banyuls. Although she was Russian she had the perfect Catalan figure he had sought all his

Dina Vierny with *Aristide Maillol*, Louis Carré 1944

life. She was passionate about art and agreed to model for him. She was to work for him for the next ten years, often encouraging him to paint as well as sculpt. She had no complexes, no inhibitions. In fact it was Maillol who was the shy one. For the first two years she kept her clothes on and, eventually, it was at her suggestion that she posed in the nude. "Since he never asked, I figured he would never have the courage," she said.

Despite the age difference she never thought of him as an old man. Her admiration for the sculptor knew no bounds and her respect for him as a man grew the more she knew him. For her he was ageless, a totally creative artist. It is said there was never anything physical between them. Nevertheless her dynamic personality inspired in Maillol a very different approach to his sculpture. In his *River*, now in the Tuileries in Paris, for example, the figure has all the classic Maillol rounded and hollowed out forms but the vivid action, the waving tumbling hair depicting flowing water, the sense of movement, all came from his new model.

Sometimes, when walking the four kilometres from Banyuls to the Métairie and modelling there, Dina would catch too much sun. This worried Maillol who liked a woman's skin to be pale. She would arrive each day from the town, their lunch in a basket on her arm. It was a wonderfully productive period for Maillol, far from the war that was then consuming the rest of his country. Louis Carré, the photographer and Parisian gallery owner, persuaded Maillol to let him have some charcoal sketches of Dina which he sold with considerable success. Journalists and cineasts came also, seeking interviews. But Maillol preferred to remain alone. Whenever Dina was absent he would work as he had always done, from his drawings.

Count Kessler, who had played such an important role in Maillol's rise to fame, died in 1937. He had always been fiercely anti-nazi, a liberal man, devoted to art and culture. When Hitler rose to power Kessler left Germany. He died in exile, in Marseille. It had been thanks to him that Maillol had had his work shown in the United States, England and, of course, Germany, where he had been well known and popular...

Picasso, at the time, was painting *Guernica*, arguably his most famous work. In 1936, at the outbreak of the Spanish Civil War, he had been appointed director of the Prado in Madrid. In January 1937, the Republican Government asked him to paint a mural for the Spanish pavilion at the International Exhibition in Paris. His monochrome picture of the German bombing of the Basque village of Guernica, the centre dominated by a grieving woman and a wounded, screaming horse embodies the inhumanity, brutality and hopelessness of war.

Legend has it that Otto Abetz, Ambassador of the Nazi regime in Paris, on seeing a photograph of Guernica asked Picasso "Did you do this?"

"No," Picasso replied, "you did."

Violet was invited to exhibit statues and statuettes at the same Paris International Exhibition of 1937, the last world exhibition to take place in Paris. Under the growing shadow of European dictatorships it was designed, optimistically, to encourage peaceful co-existence and co-operation between nations.

The Spanish Civil war brought a flood of refugees fleeing over the Pyrenees from Franco and, all too soon, Nazi Germany was causing the flight of many others escaping in the opposite direction.

In 1940, fleeing the threat of Italian invasion, after joining his wife in Nice, Raoul Dufy arrived in Céret. He suffered from crippling polyarthritis. He only managed to paint with great difficulty, using both right and left hands; whichever gave him the least pain at the time. He was in need of a safe haven in which to work in peace.

In the dark days of 1940, Dufy, Brune, Marquet and Violet would gather round the radio in the Grand Café and follow the course of the war.

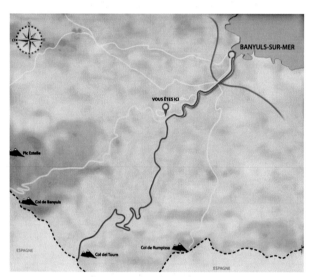

*Route of les **Chemins de la Liberté**, Banyuls-sur-Mer*

During the war, Dina began working for Varian Fry who, based in Marseille, had been funded by Eleanor Roosevelt to help Jewish artists escape German persecution and make their way to the United States. Some could not travel legally in France, even with visas, and so had to be escorted over the Pyrenees into Spain. Refugees were told to go to a certain café in Banyuls and to wait for a girl in a red dress. Dina would get up from her table in the back of the café and they would follow her. Thanks to Maillol she knew the old smuggler's route over the mountains, the *Voie Maillol* as it became known. He was horrified when she told him what she was doing but, immediately told her to use his studio at Puig del Mas for safe shelter before they made the journey over the mountains. He also told her to come to the studio the next day and to bring her red dress. His painting of Dina in 1940 is called *Dina in a red dress*.

Maillol would also send her to pose for some of his artist friends, notably Bonnard, Dufy and Matisse. "You will reduce her to one line" he said to Matisse. Matisse did, but, in that one line, it is still easy to recognise Dina's jet black hair, sparkling eyes and Rubenesque figure.

In 1943 Dina was arrested in Paris by the Gestapo. Maillol, before the war, had become a friend of Arno Breker, a very promising German sculptor. By 1940 Breker had become the official sculptor of the Third Reich. Breker had no love for Hitler, but, to have unlimited access to bronze, unlimited commissions for municipal sculptures and perfect working conditions during a World War was not a job to turn down. Maillol lost no time in contacting him and, thanks to his intervention, Dina was saved from deportation. In 1942 Maillol was invited to attend an exhibition of Brecker's work in Paris. He was given safe conduct through occupied France to get there. The event was photographed and the news item did not go unnoticed in Banyuls. His reputation as friend and lover of the occupying Germans was growing. Banyulencs chose to ignore that, as had been the case with several other French artists, the fact that Maillol's work had always been popular with many German collectors had everything to do with art, nothing to do with war.

Many bronze works of art all over France were being melted down to make arms and much of the bronze seized was used for the statues of Arno Breker... Fortunately most of Maillol's bronzes were saved thanks to the slowness of the local administration. The Roussillon region was liberated before his statues could be confiscated.

In 1943 his old time friend and fellow artist, Maurice Denis died in Paris. Maillol made the long trip to Paris to be with him at his end. It gave Maillol the opportunity to complete *River* the monumental statue for which Dina had been the model and one of his most moving and dramatic works. It captured to perfection the turbulent torment of a Europe submerged in war.

At the fall of the Vichy Government all manner of illogical revenges were taken on those accused of collaborating or being sympathetic to the Pétain regime. Maillol's son, Lucien was imprisoned in the Citadelle in Perpignan, where a distraught and aging Maillol visited him almost daily and did all he could to achieve his release.

Despite all setbacks he continued working on what was to be his last great statue, *Harmony*. Reliant to the end on the mutual support of life long friends he would turn to Matisse or Bonnard. "Have I made progress?" he would ask.

Dina was often absent, frequently in Paris. He worked on, from his many drawings and with the help of the girl who Clotilde sent with his lunch each day, grumbling to his friend Henri Frère that Dina, perhaps after all, was not so perfect a model. How could he have guessed that it would be thanks to her and her connections in the Paris art world that he would be forever immortalised in the Jardins des Tuilleries and in the Musée Maillol?

On the 16th of September 1944 he and Henri Frère took an early train into Perpignan. Frère had suggested that their mutual friend,

Dr Nicolau, might be able to help them with getting Lucien released. They spent the morning together before Henri Frère left Maillol at Nicolau's house at midday. The good doctor was late, an hour late. He had forgotten their appointment. He rustled up some lunch and tried to persuade Maillol to accompany him to Vernet-les-Bains where his patient, Raoul Dufy was taking the cure. Maillol was not fond of cars and it was with some reluctance that he agreed. He went round to Henri Frère's house and, leaving a note on the door to say he would not be returning to Banyuls with him on the train, joined Dr Nicolau in his borrowed car. In wartime Perpignan many private vehicles had been requisitioned by the Germans. Those that were in use often had bald tyres and were in a poor mechanical state. The road was wet. On a bend outside Prades the car skidded into a plane tree. Maillol was badly injured. The wait for rescue was long. From the clinic in Prades he was taken to Nicolau's clinic in Perpignan and then home to Banyuls. On September 27th he died. Most of the extended and extensive Maillol family had been evacuated before the expected Allied invasion by sea. Those locals who remained in Banyuls suspected their most famous son of collaboration with the enemy. A scant eight people attended his funeral...

Dufy apartment building, Perpignan

Pierre Brune had put Dufy in touch with his friend, Dr Pierre Nicolau in Perpignan who had always admired his painting but had never met the artist himself and Dr Nicolau introduced him into his social circle. When he moved to Perpignan, Dufy was a guest of the Nicolau's until he rented a larger apartment from the Sauvys in rue de l'Ange. It backed onto place Arago, the windows of his studio, with their small balconies encased in decorative wrought iron railings, overlooked the square, affording Dufy a perfect view of Perpignan life. It was here that Louis Carré, when visiting Maillol, made use of his journey to persuade Dufy to allow him to become his agent. Today, the local newspaper, *L'Indépendant*, has an office on the ground floor.

From his balcony he painted *le Dimanche*, *l'Orchestre*, *Le Violon Rouge*, and *l'Atelier à la Console Jaune*. His love of music features in many of his paintings. The pleasure he took in his visits to the municipal theatre with Dr Nicolau and the de Lazermes (whose family home is now part of the Perpignan Musée des

Beaux-Arts Hyacinthe Rigaud) or to hear his friend Pablo Casals at the Abbey of St Michel de Cuxa is reflected in random notes of music, the appearances of bands or musicians that characterise so much of his work. Dufy illustrated the first programme of the Pablo Casals Prades Festival.

Dufy spent the last ten years of his life in Perpignan, leaving just before his death in 1953. He worked in the San Vicens studio of Firmin Bauby, designing cartoons for carpets and making ceramics with Jean Jacques Prolongeau using the Sant Vicens oven. He painted the lively scenes unfolding beneath his window, the dancing of the sardane, scenes of carnival... In his last letter to his friend, Ludovic Masse, whose windows he could see across the square from his own, he wrote:

"the interior that you have known on place Arago, contains, for me, all Roussillon, its mountains, its vineyards, its rocks. I have, with all the work that I have done here in Perpignan, the same revelation that Matisse had in Collioure..."

By the time the war was over the Roussillon had become a bit of an artistic backwater. No major industries brought the prosperity that encouraged appreciation of art and culture. Céret concentrated on its day-to-day agricultural traditions and its official sous-prefectural tasks. The Côte d'Azur became the Mecca to which all artists in the South of France gravitated and where Matisse was to remain for most of the rest of his life. Although he did not return to Collioure his love of the vibrant, effervescent light of the south continued to shine through his paintings, the influence of Morocco and Algeria, where he had also spent time, reflected in the many interiors.

View of Collioure

His legacy to Collioure is immeasurable. Since he first stepped out of that train in 1905 a multicultural society has grown up around his legend giving inspiration to generations of artists and placing the small anchovy fishing village on the international art scene forever...

More than half a century had passed since our five local heroes had met in Paris. Only Violet remained, living in relative poverty in Perpignan and he too would die in 1952.

Picasso, like Matisse, was on the Côte d'Azur.

Joséphine Matamoros, until 2011 director of Céret's Museum of Modern Art, surrounded by the richness of the canvases, drawings, sculptures and ceramics that form the legacy donated by Céret's itinerant and local artists, said "Picasso, Braque as well as other artists of the twentieth century such as Masson, Gris, Herbin, Picabia, Chagall – to name just the best known – found in Céret a ideal haven of peace and quiet in which to work."

Newer, younger artists were moving in. Céret and Collioure had lost none of their power to attract new painters keen to follow in the footsteps of the super stars whose time in Roussillon had created a revolution in Modern Art in the twentieth century.

Place des Neuf Jets, Céret

Part 2

The Museums

The
Museums

General view of la Métairie, Banyuls-sur-Mer

Le Musée
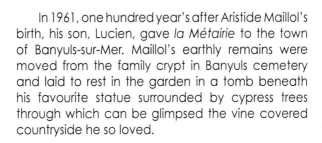
Maillol

In 1961, one hundred year's after Aristide Maillol's birth, his son, Lucien, gave *la Métairie* to the town of Banyuls-sur-Mer. Maillol's earthly remains were moved from the family crypt in Banyuls cemetery and laid to rest in the garden in a tomb beneath his favourite statue surrounded by cypress trees through which can be glimpsed the vine covered countryside he so loved.

Dina Vierny, following the advice of Matisse and Bonnard, opened her own gallery in Paris in 1947, increasing her collection with the years. In 1963, with Lucien Maillol's agreement, she was able to make Maillol's dream of having his monumental statues in a garden in Paris come true. Through her influence, in 1964 André Malraux, the then Minister of Culture, installed eighteen of Maillol's monumental statues in the gardens of the Tuileries. In 1983 Dina Vierny began creating the Musée Maillol in Paris, the *Fondation Dina Vierny* was formed and, finally, in 1995, the Musée Maillol opened its doors to the public. It has become one of the most visited museums in Paris, a true "cathedral" to Maillol of which the "chapel" was to be in his precious Métairie in Banyuls.

Françoise Gilot, before she became Picasso's partner, met Dina Vierny in Picasso's Paris Studio in 1945, describing her as "More than a muse, she was a priestess of art." She noted with amusement that Picasso was "deferential and attentive...as if beguiled by her charm and mastery. If he had not been afraid of Maillol's ghost (Picasso was notoriously superstitious) he might have expressed his admiration more openly." Of herself Gilot said "I would have loved to befriend Dina, but her triumphant femininity made me shy."

Yvon Berta-Maillol at home near Banyuls-sur-Mer

Musée
Aristide
MAILLOL

4 km →

Fortunately for us, Aristide Maillol's great nephew, Yvon Berta-Maillol, overcame any such reservations while working with Dina Vierny to preserve and protect his great uncle Aristide's statues in the Pyrenees Orientales. He does, however, describe her as a formidable woman, dedicated to Maillol and determined to ensure his work should receive the admiration and respect it deserves. Dina Vierny in her introduction to her son Bertrand Lourquin's book on Maillol, describes Maillol as a "true revolutionary... nothing in him was ordinary... in sculpture his simplification of form made him, with the cubists, one of those who lead art towards abstraction and modernism..."

From 1979 onwards Dina Vierny and Yvon Berta-Maillol were determined to save many of the stone statues that had been allowed to deteriorate. They started with the war memorial of Elne.

In 1984, with the blessing of Banyuls Town Hall, they also started work on La Métairie. Florian de la Comble, who as a young cadet had met Maillol before the war, was now living in Maillol's grandparents' house nearby. He, with his wife, Claude, volunteered his help with the reconstruction. He remembers Dina's visits, remembers her as a woman to be reckoned with, but a woman who ensured the name of Maillol would never be forgotten.

Florian de la Comble at the Musée Maillol, Banyuls-sur-Mer

In the course of these projects, on one of the many visits to inspect the restoration work on the war memorial in Elne, Yvon Berta-Maillol collected Dina from Perpignan Airport. En route for Elne, she was snoozing in the car, as she often did. Waking suddenly, she looked at him and asked him what he was thinking of. He had been thinking of the sensuality of his great uncle's statues of a much younger Dina Vierny.

"Of you." he said.

"What about me?" She asked.

Feeling unable to describe his exact thoughts, "Of how you resemble Aunt Clotilde," he said.

Silence. A black silence.

When Dina knew Clotilde Maillol she was no longer the beautiful young girl who had modelled for her husband in the early years of their marriage. She wore thick spectacles, her figure had become heavy, her beauty faded.

Yvon Berta-Maillol and Dina Vierny inspected Elne war memorial in silence, drove back to Perpignan in silence. The following month it was with trepidation that Yvon drove to the airport to meet her. She got into the car in silence. Then, turning to him she said *"You're right. I have become like Aunt Clotilde!"*

From then onwards, each time she rang, each time they met *"Hello!"* she would say, *"It's your aunt!"*

Maillol plaque at la Métairie, Banyuls-sur-Mer

They remained friends till her death in 2009.

During his twelve years on the Council of Banyuls-sur-Mer, Yvon Berta Maillol fought hard and won protection for the valley of the Roume, ensuring that la Métairie would remain the haven of peace and calm it had been during Maillol's lifetime. It is easy to find. From Banyuls-sur-Mer, a narrow twisty road leads to the Col de Banyuls. Prickly pears sprout from the rocky cliffs on one side, on the other, small vineyards stretch upwards towards the mountains that separate France from Spain, the mountains through which the girl in the red dress had led her escapees. There is a path from the car park to the Métairie, passing Florian de la Comble's house on the other side of the river.

And, at La Métairie, where, as Dina said, "... he loved to be alone in one of the most beautiful landscapes of the world, in the clearing where he worked in the open air with his model, and where he now rests, crowned by his favourite work "La Méditerannée", is a modest museum, telling of his work and his participation in the art of the twentieth century."

The museum is often manned by young members of the Maillol family, charming, knowledgeable and helpful.

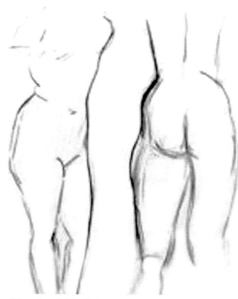

Sketch of Maillol statuettes in the Musée Maillol by Jenny Hill Norton, 2006

The forty statues in bronze and terracotta on show, as well as drawings and paintings, photographs of Maillol, his contemporaries and the youthful and beautiful Dina Vierny, all give an insight into his work and the influence he had on sculpture in the twentieth century. His tomb is beneath La Méditerannée, the sculpture he was working on when Matisse first visited him with Terrus in 1905. As he always did, Maillol had worked the idea in many forms. His wife Clotilde had modelled for him. The finished figure seems to rest, in perfect harmony, proclaiming the beauty of a woman eternally young.

Aristide Maillol's great-great neice and great-great nephew at the Musée Maillol

His *Jeune Fille Allongée* relaxes on the walkway by the Marina in Banyuls-sur-Mer and, as well as the superb war memorial perched on the end of the jetty, two other large bronzes can be found in the garden of the Town Hall beneath a large jacaranda tree and on the seafront next to the Tourist Office.

Musée Maillol

Vallée de la Roume
66650 Banyuls-sur-Mer

Tel. 04 68 88 57 11

www.musee-maillol.com

Opening hours:

10:00 - 12:00 and 14:00 - 17:00 October 1st - April 30th
10:00 - 12:00 - 16:00 - 19:00 May 2nd - September 30th

Closed on Mondays and on public holidays.

Bust of Hyacinthe Rigaud, Musée Rigaud, Perpignan

Musée des Beaux-Arts
Hyacinthe Rigaud
Perpignan

Hôtel de Lazerme, 16 rue de l'Ange, is a large grey house in the heart of Perpignan. Grey walls, grey shutters, a grey cobbled courtyard in which a bust of Hyacinthe Rigaud, in his flamboyant 17th century wig, looks slightly out of place. The only inhabitant at present is Paule de Lazerme, an old lady of some hundred years. In 1979, her house had been bought by the town of Perpignan and Perpignan's art collection moved from the Ancienne Université into a wing of the Hôtel de Lazerme, becoming the new Musée des Beaux-Arts Hyacinthe Rigaud.

Originally the property of the Marquis de Blanes, it became the family home of the de Lazerme family in 1827. They were a cultured family, Carlos de Lazerme, father of Jacques, was a good friend of Max Jacob and Apollinaire at the start of their careers. The family enjoyed the company of artists, and would often visit Manolo and Pierre Brune in Céret. As Pierre Brune could not drive it was Jacques de Lazerme who drove him to stay with Picasso on the Côte d'Azur, a visit that was to be reciprocated several times in the 1950's.

Very much part of the Perpignan bourgeoisie, the de Lazermes were close friends of Doctor Nicolau, with whom Maillol made his ill fated journey to Prades in 1944. Other family friends included Dr Puig and the Baubys of Sant Vincens. From 1936 onwards Firmin Bauby had been restoring an old Mas on the outskirts of Perpignan. In it he had created a ceramic workshop that was fast becoming one of the most original art centres of the region. Picasso was one of the many artists who dreamed of working there, planning with Firmin Bauby the ceramics with which to decorate his *Temple de la Paix* outside Céret at Fontfrède, a project never realised.

The de Lazermes knew the senator Gaston Pams whose Collioure villa now houses the Modern Art Museum of Collioure, and the Sauvy family of Château d'Esparrou who, towards the end of the war, entertained Chagall, Dufy and Cocteau.

In the fifties Picasso visited Jacques and Paule de Lazerme several times. He used the rooms put at his disposal as a studio, often working in the sumptuous library of Carlos de Lazerme as well. It was from the Hôtel de Lazerme that he sallied forth to visit his old friends Totote and Rosa Manolo in Céret, giving Pierre Brune, the first curator, the series of decorated bowls that take pride of place in Céret's Museum of Modern Art. He painted a charming portrait of Jacques' wife, Paule de Lazerme, dressed in Catalan costume, hanging it with portraits he had drawn of Totote and Rosa Manolo on the walls of the winter dining room.

In all his time in Céret, Picasso had never visited Collioure, perhaps he regarded it as too much Matisse territory. However, during his visit to the de Lazermes in 1953 he was taken to the bullfight that precedes the magnificent firework display on August 16th. He left immediately afterwards but was back in September. He stayed with the Pous family in their Café des Sports (now the Templiers Hotel), he ate Pauline Pous's wonderful *soupe de poissons*, he lay in the sun, he bathed in the sea. He signed the Livre d'Or. He considered buying the Château Royal across the way but decided it was not spacious enough for his needs and returned to the Côte d'Azur...

The Museum's considerable collection, started in 1820 by the Préfet Villeneuve de Bargemont, was first placed on public view in the Ancienne Université in 1833 by the artist M de Capdebos. An academic painter and traditional portraitist, Capdebos was a great admirer of Hyacinthe Rigaud. As well as donating most of his personal

George Daniel de Monfreid - Hommage à Gauguin

collection, he also lent works of art and encouraged others to do the same. At the turn of the century many rich and successful businessmen, prosperous industrialists and patrons of the arts living in Perpignan invested in painting and sculpture to decorate their mansions and improve their social standing. Many of the loans were converted into gifts and, with works bought by the town, the collection grew. Jules Pams, a successful politician married to the wealthy Jeanne Bardou of the Bardou Job cigarette paper dynasty, was a great patron of the arts. He filled his houses with treasures commissioned from leading artists of the day. He would visit the Paris Salons to judge the quality of the works the State proposed giving to Perpignan's Museum.

It was Jules Pams who, in 1908, founded the Association of Friends of the Museum, open to men "qualified by their situation, education, taste and fortune". So great was its success that the Museum was soon far too small to display the works of art that flooded in.

Martin Vivès, curator of the museum from 1944-68 was a skilled Roussillon artist. His paintings, full of colour and light, were strongly influenced by Cézanne. At the end of the Spanish Civil War, he had been largely responsible for the escape of Republican artists from the tragic refugee camps on the beach of Argelès-sur-Mer and in Perpignan in which they had been interned after the *Retirada*, the retreat of the republican forces in the Spanish Civil War in February 1939. Having seen their drawings in an exhibition of refugees' work in Perpignan, he went to the camps to meet the artists and used his connections in the Town Hall to achieve their release.

Raoul Dufy was a good friend of his as were many well-known Catalan artists. He was one of the few Roussillonais to be at the funeral of Maillol in 1944.

Vivès, rather like Etienne Terrus, never lost sight his strong Catalan roots. Painting the countryside he knew and loved, the scenes of daily life, he never sought a Paris career.

In 1959, to celebrate the tercentenery of Hyacinthe Rigaud's birth, the Museum, still housed in the Ancienne Université, was renamed Musée des Beaux-Arts Hyacinthe Rigaud. Martin Vivès began its reorganisation. He put on several exhibitions with the twofold aim of emphasising the importance of Catalan artistic creativity and re-placing the Roussillon in its rightful position in the history of art. In a photograph of the opening of an exhibition put on at the Casa Parail in Collioure, dedicated to "*Paul Gauguin, Daniel de Monfreid and their friends*" he is seen leaning over a showcase with Pablo Casals. He toiled ceaselessly to obtain the canvases of Clave, Flores, Descossy, the sculptures of Gili... So much of the wonderful art created in the Roussillon in the first half of the twentieth century had slipped away, unrecognised at the time. Vivès did all he could to reverse the trend. The State helped. The collection of Dufy's in the Museum were a gift from the Centre Georges Pompidou as were several of the Hyacinthe Rigaud's.

In 1979 the collection was rehoused in Hotel de Lazerme. Farail's *Girl with a Snail* that so inspired Maillol is one of the first sculptures on view in the museum. Rooms of gothic masterpieces from the fifteenth century give way to Hyacinthe Rigaud and his contemporaries, followed by, thanks to the incredible generosity of Martha Daura, daughter of the Catalan artist, Pierre Daura, rooms renovated and filled with fifty-six of her father's paintings. Pedro Francisco Daura y Garcia was born in Minorca in1896. Pablo Casals was his godfather and Picasso's father his art teacher in Barcelona in 1914. A staunch Republican, his two paintings of the post Spanish Civil War refugee camps at Argelès are an emotive reminder of a black period in Perpignan's history.

Picasso's portraits of Madame de Lazerme still hang in the room in which they were painted, a young woman in Catalan costume, looking demure and pretty. Strange to know that the old lady that young woman has become lives just across the courtyard in the opposite wing of the mansion. There are a few Maillol sketches and statues, and his beautiful 1891 painting of Farail's niece. Paintings by George Daniel de Monfreid, Terrus, Bausil, Brune hang nearby.

The Dufy's given by the Pompidou Centre can be seen in the same room as the Picasso's.

A room not to be missed is that of the *Collection Maître Rey*. In 1991, on his death, Maître Rey, a well known Perpignan solicitor, left the Museum two hundred and ten very small paintings he had collected and hung in his bureau between 1950-1991. He had asked all the artists he knew to paint him a tiny picture. The result is a fun collection of framed postcard sized paintings, some by the famous (Derain, Miró, Giacometti for example), some by unknown artists, some are signed, some not.

Only one wing of the Hotel Lazerme was turned into Perpignan's Musée des Beaux-Arts. It lacked space to show the entire collection. Fortunately, the town owns the neighbouring Hotel Mailly so that the two mansions, amalgamated, now form a Museum divided into three parts: the Golden Age of the Kingdom of Mallorca, followed by the period of the Treaty of the Pyrenees in 1659 and Hyacinthe Rigaud and finally the era of the rich industrial families at the turn of the century to that of the twentieth century artists who lived and worked here.

Claire Muchir, the current director/curator explains that the new improved Musée des Beaux-Arts Hyacinthe Rigaud de Perpignan complements the Modern Art Museums of Céret and Collioure, grounded as they are in the twentieth century. In Perpignan, artistic life stretches from the thirteenth century to the present day. There is space for it to be shown in its entirety including, for example, a recently received collection of photographs of Picasso's visits to the de Lazerme family.

Musée des Beaux-Arts

Hyacinthe Rigaud

16 rue de l'Ange
66931 Perpignan

Tels. 04 68 35 43 40
& 04 68 34 73 47

Opening hours:
10:30 -18:00 every day except for Mondays, May 1st, December 25th and January 1st.

musee-rigaud@mairie-perpignan.com

Le Musée d'Art Moderne
de Céret

The poet, Pierre Camo had been a popular member of the *Bande à Picasso* both in Paris and in Céret. Ever since the exciting early days and the long evenings in the Grand Café he had dreamed of asking all the visiting artists to each leave one of their paintings in order to start a museum in the town of his birth.

When he left for Madagascar the idea was taken up by Michel Aribaud. He had been the local wine merchant back in the early days and had befriended many of the artists. He was much loved and had a good collection of the works of Gris, Kisling, Manolo, Masson and Herbin. When he died in 1932, his widow bequeathed the whole collection to the town as well as his considerable library and a sum of money for the creation of the museum. The artist Pierre Brune was invited to be the first curator. This turned out to be a frustrating role as there was no actual building and the town hall had insufficient funds with which to buy and support the dreamed of museum. Pierre Brune was curator of a Museum that didn't exist. In addition there was a world war going on. The idea was put on hold.

However Pierre Brune, with the encouragement of Frank Burty Haviland, continued to dream his long time dream of opening a museum to safeguard the traces left by the many artists who had lived and worked in Céret.

In 1948 Brune went to Paris. There he got in touch with both Picasso and Matisse and told them the story of the phantom museum. Both artists promised him their support and encouraged him to keep working on the Town Hall. He returned to Céret and visited the Mayor. He contacted anyone he knew for further donations: Kahnweiler, other artists, sculptors, their widows or families…

Picasso and Matisse kept their word. Matisse gave fourteen drawings, sketches he had made in 1905 in preparation for his paintings of Collioure. Picasso gave posters, paintings and some remarkable ceramics, a total of fifty-three works. The old Couvent des Carmes, used since the 19th century as a prison, was transformed into a museum: *le Musée d'Art*

Pierre Brune's house, le Castellas, Céret

Moderne de Céret, Céret's Museum of Modern Art. It was inaugurated on the 18th of June in 1950. On the walls the works of Desnoyer, Marchand, Pignon, Brune, Krémègne, Maragall, Haviland, Maillol, Gargallo, Gris, Manolo, Herbin, Kisling, Masson, Picasso, Braque, Matisse, Chagall, Marquet, Osouf, Fenosa, Carvillain, Lhote were hung. Pierre Brune's dream had come true.

In the summer of 1953, Picasso, who was staying in Perpignan with his friend the Comte de Lazerme, returned to visit Pierre Brune. He did not arrive empty handed. In his large car, driven by his son Pablo, was a series of ceramic bowls decorated with bull fighting scenes that are, to this day, the star of the Museum's collection. It was at this time that Picasso proposed erecting a monument to the Matadors of the World. The idea then changed into a Monument to Peace on the heights of Céret. It was never built.

However, later that year, after presiding over the *corrida*, in a few moments in the Grand Café, he dashed off *La Sardane à la Colombe*, a splendid drawing of the local dance of friendship and joy combined with a dove of peace.

When Pierre Brune died in 1956 he was given a hero's funeral by the town. He was succeeded as director of the museum by Frank Burty Haviland whose first exhibition was for his good friend Manolo. Picasso designed the poster.

In 1965, Dalí, who, despite being a mere hour or so's journey away in

Exterior of Musée d'Art Moderne, Ceret

Spain had never visited Céret, made his entrance. It was not a modest one. Ever the showman, he and his wife, Gala, accompanied by an ocelot, arrived in a horse drawn coach. Behind them strode the Mayor, the town counsellors, a *cobla* band and a fanfare. Speeches were made, overseen by a sizeable rhinoceros, before the party adjourned to the bullring where Dalí and Gala dined beneath a large parasol. They left on a 1914 goods train bound for Perpignan station, *le Centre du Monde*. Dalí is said to have claimed Perpignan Railway Station to be the "centre of the world" as it was in its waiting room that he got all his best ideas.

Joséphine Matamoros became the chief curator of the Modern Art Museum of Céret in its new building. She oversaw its modernisation and expansion. The resulting Museum was opened by François Mitterand in 1993. The annual exhibitions are always exciting. Retrospectives of artists who have worked in Céret are often featured as well as current works. In the Museum's permanent exhibition are the works of many of the artists who have starred in this book. Many more are stored in the Museum archives. Walking around the town it is easy to find the houses in which they lived and to imagine the lives they led. The Grand Café's clientele is composed more of tourists than artists now but the décor and the ambiance have not changed so very much.

On the Chemin Faisant, Céret

Pierre Brune, could he return, would be proud to see his paintings hanging with those of his friends Picasso, Braque, Gris, Matisse, Masson, Manolo, Herbin, Soutine, Haviland and Chagall half a century after his death. Pleased to see that his dreamed of museum is in good hands and the ever growing collection of art of the twentieth and twenty first centuries is enjoyed by visitors from all over the world.

Musée d'Art Moderne de Céret

8 bd. Maréchal Joffre
66400 Céret

Tel. 04 68 87 27 76

www.musee-ceret.com

Opening hours:
10:00 – 19:00 July 1st – September 15th
10:00 – 18:00 September 16th – June 30th
Closed Tuesdays, January 1st, May 1st, November 1st and December 25th

Musée d'Art Moderne
Collioure

Old postcard of le Faubourg, Collioure

The Museum is housed in the beautiful Villa Pams. The house has been remodelled since the days of Senator Gaston Pams who used to own both the house and the park that surrounds it. The two strange pointy towers, *ses deux clochetons*, so visible on all the old postcards of the Faubourg are no more, replaced by a single tower in the style of the famous *Clocher* or that of the Dominican Convent next door. Now paintings cover the walls of the luminous rooms, there is a bookshop and a tranquil feeling to the whole place.

The Cloisters of the Convent were bought by the town in 1992 and installed in the gardens of the museum, adding to their peace and beauty.

*View of Collioure with **Museum** and Couvent de Dominicains*

The Museum is known as the Musée Peské after the artist Jean Peské. Just as Pierre Brune had done in Céret, Peské dreamed of starting a Museum by collecting the works of the artists who had lived and worked in Collioure at the same time as he did.

Born in the Ukraine in 1870, he studied at the Kiev Beaux-Arts, the Odessa Beaux-Arts and the Warsaw Beaux-Arts. There he took evening classes with Wojciech Gerson who was a great admirer of Delacroix and advised young Peské to go to Paris. This, in 1891, Jean Peské did. Arriving at the Gare de l'Est in his fur-lined Russian coat and fur hat he found himself surrounded by a gang of urchins crying "It's a bear, it's a bear... No it isn't, it's a wolf!"

He made contact with Polish society in Paris and was introduced to the art critic, Fenéon and to the artists, Signac and Luce. Particularly influenced by Signac, Pissaro and Bonnard and a great admirer of Monet, by 1900 he had found his place amongst the Post-Impressionists. Peské is perhaps best remembered for his landscapes both of the

Forest of Fontainebleau and, of course, the Mediterranean. He worked with Signac in St Tropez and became a good friend of Maximilien Luce. Luce's portrait of Peské now hangs in the Collioure Museum.

He met his wife, the Russian sculptor, Ekatarina Alexieff Louchnikoff, in 1901 while she was working with Rodin in Paris. They married and had four children resulting in her sculpture career being put on hold. However, her evident pleasure in her maternal role delighted Peské who made many moving pastel portraits of his wife and their young children. Peské had first visited Collioure in 1894 and, in 1903, returned with Ekatarina and their family. As he remarked in his memoirs, "for anyone who loves light and colour, it was the open air school of dreams!"

His path in Collioure failed to cross that of Matisse or Derain. While they were there in Collioure in 1905, Peské was painting trees and landscapes near Fontainebleau. His paintings were shown in the famous Salon d'Automne of 1905 but went unnoticed in the uproar over the fauves of room seven...

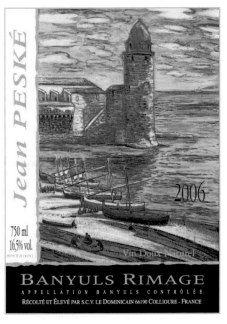

Couvent des Dominicains wine label by Jean Peské

From 1910 onwards Peské and his family holidayed on the Mediterranean at Bormes, his drawings in Indian ink, his pastels and oils all expressing his love of the sea, the villages, the people and the trees of the Midi.

During the 14-18 war he was wrongly accused of being a spy. Upset, deeply hurt, feeling he would always be a suspect foreigner to the French, he found he could no longer work. Fortunately he decided the only way forward was actually to work. The drawings and paintings he produced affirmed his position in Paris as an artist of repute. He visited Foix, Collioure, Sorède and Argelès-sur-Mer. Many of his drawings and paintings had been collected by Llinas, a friend and patron of more that thirty years, from Argelès-sur-Mer. When Llinas died in 1932, his collection was dispersed. It was probably at this point that Peské decided he would like to create a small local museum, similar to the one he knew in Bormes. His aim was to gather the works of the many artists who, like himself, had enjoyed working in the area.

Couvent des Dominicains wine label by Augustin Hanicotte

Collioure had already become a village of artists. Peské, Hanicotte, Terrus, Signac, Matisse, Derain, Marquet, Camoin, Luce, Marre, Gris, Valtat, Foujita, Henri Martin, Survage and the poet Max Jacob had, since the end of the 1880's, all fallen under its spell. It was in Collioure that Peské decided the Museum should be located and, thanks to him, the initial foundation of the Museum of Modern Art in Collioure took place in 1934. It was Peské who collected the works of his fellow artists, including Augustin Hanicotte, and convinced the municipality that they should be displayed. Altogether he managed to show a hundred and ninety canvases, drawings and lithographs.

Couvent des Dominicains wine label by Camille Descossy

After his death in 1949 and again during the sixties the Mairie was reorganised and, sadly, the Collection halted. Finally, in the 1980's, the Museum's Friends Association came into being and persuaded the town to reopen the Museum in the Gaston Pams' Villa.

The collection contains works by many famous twentieth century and contemporary artists, including those of Balbino Giner, Descossy, Perrot, and Cocteau.

It is a shame there are no fauve images from the famous summer of 1905. However both Derain's and Matisse's legacy to Collioure remains in the form of the *Chemin de Fauvisme*, a guided walk around the town, viewing reproductions of twenty of their paintings from the positions in which they were painted. It is a *Chemin* very well worthwhile taking. (Guided visits in July and August, every Thursday at 10:00h. Espace Fauve-Quai de L'Amirauté Tel: 04 68 98 07 16).

The Museum's Collection continues to grow, helped and encouraged by a European project that, every two years, allows the winner of the Collioure Art Prize to work in the Museum's studio for a year. The artist's work is exhibited at the end of that time and there is an obligation to leave the Museum one of the works when leaving.

From time to time the permanent collection makes way for exhibitions of a single artist, often shared with Céret's Museum of Modern Art.

And, of course, following in the footsteps of Matisse, Derain, Dufy, Chagall, Marquet and the many other famous artists who set up their easels in Collioure, are the thirty or so artists who today will welcome you in galleries scattered throughout the flower filled alleys and winding streets of the old town.

The rue René Pous by the Couvent des Dominicains leads to the gate of the Musée Peské. A proximity borne out on the vintage wine labels of the Couvent des Dominicains cellars.

*On the Chemin de Fauvisme,
ancienne rue de la Gare, Collioure*

Musée d'Art Moderne de Collioure

Villa Pams
Route de Port-Vendres
66190 Collioure

Tel. 04 68 82 10 19

Opening hours:
Normally July and August: 10:00-12:00 and 14:00-18:00
September 1ˢᵗ-June 30ᵗʰ: 10:00-12:00 and 14:00-18:00
but closed on Tuesdays.
Closed January 1ˢᵗ, May 1ˢᵗ, November 1ˢᵗ and December 25ˢᵗ.

Photo of Etienne Terrus painting in the Roussillon countryside

Elne

Musée Terrus

High up on the ramparts of the Roman city of Elne, Musée Terrus is to be found in a house once belonging to Terrus's old friend, Jacques Carrère, the mayor of Elne at the time.

Narcisse Planas, Mayor of Elne from 1965-1995, was responsible for creating the Museum in the town of the artist's birth. Wanting to pay tribute to Etienne Terrus, he collected as many of the artist's works as he could. By 1994 he had enough to open the Musée Terrus, well

Elne town plaque

placed near the cathedral and not far from where Maillol's bust of his old friend gazes out towards the le Racou beach he so loved.

Although he studied art in the capital, Paris life did not appeal to Etienne Terrus, and, as soon as he could, he returned to the city of his birth. His deep love of Elne, the Roussillon countryside and the rocky coast of the Côte Vermeille shines through all his landscapes. Almost a Fauve before Fauvism was born, his *"Plage au Racou"* shows a sea of blue virtually invaded by the red roof of a small hut built on a dune. He loved to work on the Côte Vermeille, indeed the hut was probably his. He would climb the tower of Violet's house in Prades to paint the far Pyrenean horizon shimmering in the heat. De Monfreid noted the "intimate emotion of the artist, an emotion that seemed to leave the canvas and evoke emotion in the viewer just as music does in the ears of the listener..." With easel and paint box he would set out on his ancient bicycle, pedalling the byways he knew so well until he found the scene he wanted. There he would paint till the sun became too hot at which point he would take a siesta, closing his eyes and snoozing under his hat, resting, as his friends said "in the undergrowth of his beard."

Far from Paris, Terrus preferred to be in Banyuls, Collioure, le Racou, the Vallespir and the Aspres. He would travel to Prades to stay with Gustave Violet and to Corneilla-de-Conflent to visit de Monfreid. He

*Bust of **Etienne Terrus** gazing out over
the ramparts of Elne towards le Racou*

went once a year to Paris to show at the Salon des Indépendants and to see his friends there. But he did not stay long. He would return to Elne where he was securely rooted in his native Catalan soil.

He was always generous with his local knowledge, would show the Paris crowd his favourite spots. Matisse came to rely on his encouragement and welcomed his visits. Over the years, Matisse and his fellow artist friends became regular visitors to Terrus's light filled whitewashed studio. The garden, a table shaded by awnings, surrounded by fruit trees, flowers and birdsong, formed the perfect setting for long, convivial lunches. The view from the studio high up in the Roman ramparts of Elne extended to the sea in one direction and to the snow capped peak of Canigou in the other.

Maillol, his greatest friend and mentor, was a constant admirer of his painting. "He had an extraordinary eye, a sensitivity in all he did, all his tones are felt, every touch alive." Two of Terrus's landscapes were the only canvases by another artist Maillol ever hung in his own studio.

He painted exactly as he wanted to, never seeking fame or fortune, often to the exasperation of his friends who recognised in him a talent that would sink into near obscurity after his death. "You will be famous!" Maillol would tell him and Terrus, panicking, would race back to Elne.

He was proud and pleased to collaborate with Maillol, Louis Bausil, Gustave Violet and George Daniel de Monfreid to develop the annual *Salon des Artistes Roussillonais* in Perpignan. They all wished to maintain a lively art scene on their home ground. Maillol mostly presented his tapestries, Terrus, despite from time to time trying to "do a Gauguin", remained a traditional landscape painter and always showed his Roussillon landscapes in oil or watercolour.

He was a keen photographer and many of his self -portraits adorn the walls of the museum. On the ground floor his old cameras and photographic eqipment takes pride of place among the works of his fellow Roussillon artists, Luce, Maillol, Violet, de Monfreid, Petitjean and Bausil.

Extracts from his lengthy correspondence with Matisse with addresses such as "*Matisse, Artiste Peintre, Collioure*" ... make fascinating reading. Sadly the correspondence is rather one sided as Matisse's replies have been lost.

His watercolours and oils hang on the walls, mostly landscapes of the countryside he knew and loved and from which he refused to be parted. Actually he didn't much care for being parted with his paintings either. He showed Maillol a dozen watercolours Maillol described as "Marvels! A dozen small masterpieces!" and took them to a dealer who accepted them for an exhibition. A few days before the exhibition was to open Terrus arrived crying "My watercolours, I want my watercolours! I don't want them to be shown!"

Thanks to Narcisse Planas many of them can be seen now in the museum that bears his name.

Musée Etienne Terrus

3 rue de la Porte Balague
66200 Elne

Tel. 04 68 22 88 88

Opening hours:

April-May 09:30-17:45 / June-September 09:30-18:45
November-March 09:30-11:45 and 14:00-16:45

LA PREDICATION AUX POISSON

Stained glass window
by Richard Burgsthal, Abbaye de Fontfroide

Abbaye de
Fontfroide

From the moment Gustave Fayet bought the Cistercian Abbey of Fontfroide in 1908, his creative genius stimulated all who worked on its restoration and renovation, artisans and artists alike. Under his direction and that of his wife Madeleine Fayet d'Andoque, the once great, but by then ruined Abbey, set in the harsh landscape of the Corbières massif, became a source of artistic endeavour and a font of creativity. It is still the private home of their descendants.

Abbaye de Fontfroide cloisters

Nevertheless, over a hundred thousand visitors a year flock there to enjoy the concerts, the master classes or to join the guided tours of the abbey, the gardens and the Fayet Museum.

Nine centuries of history impregnate the ancient stones of the church, the cloisters, the monks' dormitories and refectory. The restoration undertaken by the Fayets, the skills of the artists they commissioned, the inspiration of the musicians who made up the *Fontfroidiens* in those early days, the gift of friendship the Fayets possessed so abundantly and in which the entire endeavour was conducted, are all reflected in the harmony of the Abbey and its grounds. The guided tours are fascinating and informative and in French. Audio guides in other languages are available.

In the Fayet Museum there are many photographs of the restoration work and of the family and friends as well as an assortment of Gustave Fayet's watercolours of the landscape surrounding the Abbey, his beautiful pen and ink book illustrations and the *buvards*, the watercolours on blotting paper he also used for his carpet designs. They glow with the rich colours he so loved. The entire collection allows an insight into the many talents of a multi talented man.

*Collection of plates from Manises,
Spain at Abbaye de Fontfroide*

In summer, night visits are possible. A sound and light show allows visitors to imagine the long summer evenings before the First World War when Gustave Fayet and his family, surrounded by Redon, de Monfreid, Violet, de Sévérac, Maillol, Burgsthal, Viñes would relax and discuss the occult, philosophy, literature and art, when music would be played, poetry recited...

In winter, visits to the Abbey take in the private rooms decorated by Richard Burgsthal, the kitchen and pantry with its dresser full of the pottery Gustave Fayet bought in 1910 in Manises, a Spanish village near Valencia. Copies of the pottery can be bought in the Abbey boutique.

In the old Bergerie is a restaurant, *La Table de Fontfroide*, where fresh local produce is used in simple dishes for the lunches and snacks served from midday till 5pm. Tel: 04 68 41 02 26 for reservations and to check opening times for dinner.

The wine is the Abbey's own prize winning Corbière, tastings of which are available as are visits to the vineyards. Tel: 04 68 45 50 72 www.caveau@fontfroide.com

The Boutique is an Aladdin's Cave of books, gifts and wine and locally produced gourmet delights open from 9:30-12:00h and from 13:30-17:00h.

The Abbaye de Fontfroide is open every day except the 25th of December and January 1st. For times of guided visits and information on group reservations, concerts and workshops check details.

Abbaye de
Fontfroide

RD 613
11100 Narbonne

Tel. 04 68 45 11 08

Closed December 25th,
May 1st and January 1st

info@fontfroide.com

*Gustave Fayet
Les allées Paul Ricquet la nuit (Béziers)* ▶

Gustave Fayet – Mer et rochers

Gustave Fayet – Crépuscule

Sculpture Tours

Sculpture
Tours

The Roussillon of de Monfreid, Maillol, Terrus, Violet and Fayet a hundred years ago was a remote, little known corner of France. Matisse and Derain in 1905 and Picasso and Braque in 1911 may have ensured it a place on the world map of art history but it is still a remote, rather magic place, definitely one of the lesser-known French holiday destinations. On the border with Spain, with the Mediterranean Sea to the east and the Pyrenees to the south, the Roussillon is a land rich in history, fought over for centuries, a land of mountains, rivers and lakes, ancient cities, towns, villages, thermal springs, abbeys, cathedrals and châteaux.

Tracking down the sculptures of Maillol, Violet and Manolo, exploring the towns and villages where the Paris *Bande à Picasso* practised their cubist theories, where Matisse and Derain created the first Fauvist paintings and visiting the local art museums provides an ideal opportunity to explore and enjoy some of the riches with which the Roussillon is blessed.

Tour 1

Perpignan

We will start in Perpignan, at the Palais des Congrès.

Violet's magnificent War Memorial shows off the full panoply of his artistic skills as an architect, a ceramicist, a sculptor and an artist. His monumental sculpture combines wrought iron, mosaics, bas-reliefs and sculpted stone to create his own very personal and moving reaction to war.

From the massive monument, a wander down the Allée Maillol passes two of Maillol's statues. Cross the boulevard Wilson, pass the Castillet Cinema, through the Porte de Notre Dame Gate by the Castillet, originally built in 1368 as the gate to the city, and on to the place de la Loge where Maillol's Venus stands facing the old Café de la Loge where Manolo made his headquarters back in 1910. In the nearby courtyard of the Hotel de Ville is Maillol's bronze of *La Méditerannée* and, if you are allowed into the Salle des Mariages, you will find Violet's *L'Avia*.

Gustave Violet – Monument *des Morts, detail, Perpignan*

From the place de la Loge walk along under the overhanging medieval houses and enter the impressive place de la République by rue Mirabeau. The small rue Voltaire leads to the even smaller but very charming rue Paratilla and into the place des Poilus. To see Violet's impressive fronton of the Collège Jean Moulin on the Place des Esplanades it is best to walk up rue Grande La Réal. You could at this point visit the Palais des Rois de Majorque, or, following our chosen artists, go back down the rue Grande la Réal, rue Paratilla and turn left into rue Voltaire, which becomes rue de l'Ange. At no 16

Summer view of Allée Maillol, Perpignan

Place de la Loge, Perpignan

is the Musée des Beaux-Arts Hyacinthe Rigaud. The rue d l'Ange will bring you into place Arago where Dufy lived above what is now the office of L'Indépendant. Violet's Maison Escoffier is now the Café Vienne and his Maison Sully is to be found housing a branch of the Crédit Agricole Bank on the corner of place Jean Payra/ rue Maximilien de Sully.

Maison Sully, Perpignan

His statue to Jean Jaurès dominates the small garden near the FNAC in the beautiful Belle Époque building Les Dames de France. A wander along the Quai Vauban will bring you back to the Castillet and the Parking Wilson.

From Perpignan it is a small drive out towards Canet via Bompas to Claira. There, at the entrance to the cemetery, is a typical Violet war memorial.

Gustave Violet – *Monument à Jean Jaurès, Perpignan*

Framed by a rectangular marble arch, one sad woman wrapped in a shawl, holds some leaves in her hand and mourns her loss for eternity.

Gustave Violet
Monument des Morts, Claira.

View from cemetery, Ortaffa

Tour 2

From Perpignan
to Banyuls-sur-Mer

Take the N914 out of Perpignan following the signs to Argelès and Port-Vendres. At the second Elne sign, Elne sud, exit 7, branch off to Alénya. An avenue of oleanders leads to the old wine village and in the centre, impressive buildings for which Simon Violet, uncle of Gustave is responsible. They were to have been the birthplace of the Byrrh distillery but, for lack of nearby rail transport in Alénya at the time, the Violets set up their enterprise in remarkably similar buildings in Thuir.

Opposite the Tourist Office, through a small gateway is the war memorial, Gustave Violet's last, built in 1948, four years before his death. With the memorial in Perpignan it is the one of the only two he signed. Thirty years after the war ended *La Douleur* depicts a veiled woman still mourning her dead soldier.

From Alénya, St Cyprien is a well signposted 3 kms. In the centre of the old village is the Desnoyer Collection, the star of which is Maillol's *Baigneuse*. Interesting contemporary exhibitions are often held both here and at the nearby Gallery of Contemporary Art.

Desnoyer mural, Saint-Cyprien village

View of Elne ramparts with monument by Gustave Violet

Gustave Violet monument detail, Elne

From St Cyprien, the road to Elne, again well sign posted, leads directly to the town centre. Park up on the high ramparts near Elne cathedral, consecrated in 1069. Maillol's bust of his friend Terrus gazes out towards the Albères hills and, following the rambla around, beneath some plane trees is the Maillol's *Pomone* modified and clothed, the war memorial whose restoration was overseen by Dina Vierny and Yvon Berta-Maillol. The cathedral and cloisters are well worth visiting as, of course, is the Terrus Museum. Walk through the old town to the Tourist Office from whence an easy descent leads to the Cami de la Réal. Set into the old ramparts is a large terracotta bas-relief by Violet depicting many of the scenes of everyday agricultural Catalan life he so enjoyed sculpting. Easy to imagine him appreciating the local market that takes place just below his sculpture on Wednesday mornings.

Leaving Elne in the direction of Bages, take the road to the left beneath the railway bridge towards Ortaffa, a small village dominated by a huge clock tower in the shape of the Eiffel Tower. Violet's war memorial is high up in the cemetery behind the small village church. A tragic couple, grief stricken at the loss of their young soldier son who failed to return from the 1914-18 war stands above the list of all the sons of Ortaffa who never returned. The neighbouring graves bear out the extent of the tragedy.

After Ortaffa, via Brouilla, it is easy to get onto the expressway to the coast, turning right in the direction of Port-Vendres just before Argelès.

Come off at exit 13. The coast road passes the Plage de l'Ouille where Matisse and his family used to bathe and descends into Collioure. Park where you can, possibly up by the station, little changed since Matisse stepped off the train in 1905. Dame Rosette's Hôtel de la Gare no longer exists and the avenue leading from the station is now known as rue Aristide Maillol. Walk down it to the place de Général Leclerc where the market is held on Wednesdays and Sundays and Violet's war memorial, adorned by one sad girl, a flower in her hand, standing over the list of the Colliourencs who fell, is in the market place.

Following the riverbed, walking towards the sea, it is impossible to miss the Hôtel des Templiers and, a little further on, the office of the Chemin de Fauvism. If you follow it, with or without a guide (guide highly recommended), it is easy to see why Matisse, Derain and every artist since has fallen in love with Collioure.

Gustave Violet Monument des Morts, Collioure

On the opposite side of the bay, Collioure's Peské Museum of Modern Art is just visible beneath the ancient windmill next door to the Dominican Convent. The church of Notre Dame des Anges juts out into the bay facing the Château des Rois de Majorque, small shops, bars and restaurants abound as do artists' studios.

Three of Charles Rennie Mackintosh's paintings form part of the *Chemin de Charles Rennie Mackintosh* which continues to Port-Vendres where he and his wife Margaret lived for the last four years of his life. His watercolours of Port-Vendres, Collioure and many inland Roussillon towns were never appreciated in his lifetime.

Port-Vendres, just 4 km further along the coast, with its natural deep-water harbour, has been a port since Roman times. Maillol's war memorial, based on his *Monument à Cézanne*, surveys the Port. Draped in soft cloth, she has the look of a classical goddess, evocative of the town's origins as the Port of Venus. Sadly, she is not surviving the sea breezes, her arm is broken and she badly needs some loving care and restoration.

Behind her is the place de l'Obélisque with the obelisk the Comte de Mailly had erected in honour of his King Louis XVI and, behind place de l'Obélisque, is the Dôme, now an art gallery. Beneath the Dôme Gardens is a small but permanent Charles Rennie Mackintosh Exhibition.

Fishing port, Port-Vendres

The last stop on this tour is Maillol's birthplace of Banyuls-sur-Mer. With its palm fringed, horseshoe shaped bay, safe swimming, cafés and restaurants, it has become a popular family seaside holiday town. Nevertheless its wine industry is every bit as important now as it was in Maillol's day, indeed the Maillol family continue to produce excellent wines. Fishing, however, is reduced to a couple of small boats, the port now more used by private yachts and pleasure boats, divers, kayaks and a sailing school. Maillol's masterpiece war memorial, on the *"presqu'ille"* beyond the Aquarium and Laboratoire Arago, is much visited. The view from it of the bay of Banyuls and the vine covered hills is magnificent. It is easy to imagine the by then aged sculptor, content with his work, admiring the landscape he so loved and into which he fitted so perfectly.

Three more of his works are in the town. His *Jeune Fille Allongée* relaxes by the Port de Plaisance, a further young girl, *l'Ile de France* this time without arms, stands by the Tourist Office and a third young girl in bronze is shaded by a large jacaranda tree behind the Town Hall.

Watercolour of Maillol's tomb at la Métairie by Jenny Hil Norton, 2006

The Musée Maillol, is a well indicated 4 kms from the town hall in the direction of the Col de Banyuls.

Sign to Musée Maillol, Banyuls-sur-Mer

Boulevard in summer, Céret

Tour 3
The Vallespir,
mainly Céret

The centre of Céret has changed little over the last hundred years. The plane trees lining the boulevards that replaced the old town ramparts about a century and a half ago have grown into gracious giants. The shops and cafés may be different, but the church, the place des Neuf Jets, the old city gates, and the surrounding countryside are much the same.

A walk around old Céret is a good way to get the feel of the town and to imagine the people who lived and worked there a century ago. The Grand Café, on boulevard Maréchal Joffre, where Picasso and his *bande* used to hang out, is a good starting point. Céret's Museum of Modern Art is close by. On the same street is the Town Hall in the entrance

Musée d'Art Moderne, Ceret

Monument to Déodat de Severac by Manolo, detail, Céret

hall of which is a bas-relief by Gustave Violet depicting peasants at work thanks to the newly opened irrigation canal. The Tourist Office on avenue Georges Clemenceau, with Manolo's statue *La Catalane* in homage to Déodat de Sévérac is just around to the left. There you can pick up a map of the *Chemin Faisant* and wander around looking at reproductions of the artists' paintings with useful information on the painters and their time in Céret.

With the Tourist Office behind you, walk up to the corner and turn left into av. Michel Aribaud. As the road passes La Capelleta where contemporary exhibitions are often held, bear right into the rue des Capucins. The road climbs and, soon, on the right is the 16th century Couvent des Capucins, the house Frank Burty Haviland bought when he married Joséphine Laporte in 1913. So easy to imagine the gatherings on the terraces, the number of picturess painted there, the hospitality of the Burty Havilands and the fun enjoyed by both the visiting Parisians and the locals. A little further on is Krémègne's house, the Miranda del Couvent. A footpath runs behind it leading to a walk around the *Balcon de Céret* or a longer one up to Fontfrède.

Retracing your steps to La Capelleta, take the rue Rameil to Place Picasso. A lively market is held here every Saturday beneath the ancient plane trees. In place Picasso is the 13th century gate of Spain with an archaeological museum in the West Tower. Continue left up the Boulevard Lafayette, and, as it curves to the right into boulevard Arago, soon, on your left, you will see the rue Pierre Brune. It is very straight and very narrow and ends in steps leading to Pierre Brune's

Couvent des Capucins, Céret

Rooftops of town viewed *from le Castellas, Céret*

Rue Pierre Brune, Céret

Castellas and the remains of the old castle of Céret. If you climb the steps you get a beautiful view of the rooftops of Céret and, on the left, easily visible, the Maison Delcros, home to Braque and Picasso in 1911.

An interesting detour can be had by returning to the corner of boulevard Arago and boulevard Lafayette, pushing open the metal gate marked *Impasse Forne* and walking up the pathway between a mass of vegetable gardens to the irrigation canal all overlooked by Pierre Brune's Castellas. A sharp left turn, no choice, leads along the canal and back to the rue des Capucins.

Either way, retrace your steps to the boulevard Arago and turn left into the place de la Liberté. Under the magnificent plane trees is Maillol's war memorial, with its statue *La Douleur* of a beautiful, sad woman grieving over the missing sons of Céret.

Place de la Liberté, Céret

On the far side of the square turn left into the rue des Evadés de France. No 3 is the Maison Delcros. Picasso lived and worked there in the summers of 1911, 12 and 13. His name and Braque's are still on the doorbells.

Turn around. The rue des Evadés becomes the rue de la Fusterie and ends at the Italian Renaissance style Porte de France.

The place de la République by the Porte de France was the old market place, the scene of many a local festival and doubled as a bullring until the new Arènes were built. Picasso, ever a great bullfighting aficionado, would have known it well.

Back to the Grand Café and opposite, beneath an arch, the rue de l'Eglise leads to the church where Déodat de Sévérac played the organ.

Gustave Violet Irrigation Monument, Céret

From the Grand Café, turn left and walk down rue St Ferréol. No 72 used to be the Hôtel de Canigou and opposite it is Violet's grand monument to the Irrigation Canal. Although the monument was erected in 1934, the canal itself had opened in 1866 at much the same time as the ramparts were replaced. The town was growing fast and needed air to breathe and water both to irrigate and, equally important when pigs and poultry were kept within the city walls and all transport was by horse, mule or donkey drawn vehicles, to cleanse the town centre. The gutters running with sparkling water add greatly to Céret's charm today.

From the monument it is possible to walk on and eventually come to the 14th century Devil's Bridge, one of the three bridges spanning the Têt. Unfortunately Frank Burty Haviland's Maison Alcouffe is no longer there and it is probably easier to take to your car to visit the Devil's Bridge before leaving Céret for the 40 minute drive up the Vallespir to St-Laurent de Cerdans.

The N115 passes the old station near where Manolo's house would have been, past where Chagall would have lived, continues through

Chapelle de Notre Dame, St-Laurent de Cerdans

Amélie-les-Bains (where Frank Burty Haviland, Manolo and Déodat de Sévérac chose not to settle), and runs on through Arles-sur-Tech until, after a few more kilometres, you turn left onto the D3 to St-Laurens de Cerdans (and Figueres). As you enter the town, take the road to the left marked to the church and then left again to the Chapelle N.D. de la Sort. Violet's monument is perfectly designed to merge with the design of the chapel, indeed, from a distance is seems to be integrated into the wall of the Chapel. The Chapel itself was used as an infirmary during the Retirada when the Republicans escaping Franco poured over the border at Coustouges into St Laurent de Cerdans. The town's museum, in the old *espadrille* factory, is well worth a visit and tells the story.

Publicity poster advertising Byrrh

Tour 4
The Têt Valley

The tour starts in Thuir, Gustave Violet's birthplace and home of his family's Byrrh enterprise. A suitably dramatic and moving Violet memorial dominates the gateway to the cemetery. The bas relief sculptures portray to a heartrending degree both the sorrow of the women and the stoicism blended with despair of the soldiers.

While in Thuir you might like to visit the Byrrh factory and admire the Gustave Eiffel station roof and the largest oak barrel in the world...

It is a pleasant drive through peach and nectarine orchards from Thuir to Prades via Corbère, Bouleternère and Marquixanes. Gustave Violet's war memorial dominates Prades' cemetery. Built in imposing red marble and flanked by two palm trees it has one grieving widow as the central figure.

Driving round the *rocade* en route to Villefranche-de-Conflent, after passing the Super U roundabout, on the left hand side, after the small lake you can just make out the white crenellations of Gustave Violet's mansion and the bell tower of the little chapel of St Martí. Easy to imagine Terrus in the room he considered "his" and all the artistic and social activity centred round the house, workshops and kilns. Unfortunately it is privately owned and no-one can visit to admire Violet's ceramic decorations, the balconies, fountains, tiles, chimney pieces and chandeliers he made for the mansion he had designed for his new bride in 1903.

Gustave Violet
Detail war memorial, Thuir

Gustave Violet
War memorial, Prades

The next town is Villefranche-de-Conflent, the railway station for Corneilla-de-Conflent, Vernet-les-Bains and the Yellow Train. It is a perfect medieval town, fortified since 1090, almost a mini Carcassonne, with Vauban's Fort Libéria towering over it, guarding the meeting of the Cady valley with that of the Têt.

A permanent Charles Rennie Mackintosh Exhibition opened in the Fort in 2012.

It was at Villefranche station that George Daniel de Monfreid met Terrus and Matisse on June 12th 1905 and walked them to Château St Clément near Corneilla-de-Conflent. One cannot visit Château St Clément although it can be glimpsed across the meadows and through the trees on a winter's day. The cemetery of Corneilla-de-Conflent can be visited and, in a small tomb chapel, a cast of de Monfreid's sculpture of Mary Magdelene is the only ornament.

Continue on to Vernet-les-Bains, the popular spa town that drew de Monfreid's mother, Caroline, to the region in the first place. Canigou towers over it, snow capped most of the year, the little town nestling in its shadow. It was a popular Belle Époque spa resort when Ibrahim Pasha, son of the Pasha of Egypt and Constantinople, took the waters there, not to mention Rudyard Kipling, the Princess of Battenberg (Queen Victoria's daughter), and many other well known members of European high society.

At the very top of the town, near the Town Hall, is Gustave Violet's monument to the Entente Cordiale of 1904. The pedestal is of Canigou

Gustave Violet Entente Cordiale monument, Vernet-les-Bains

granite, standing on it the two immense white marble statues represent France and England. The whole monument takes up about a thousand square metres and was commissioned in 1912. By the time it was built in August 1920, the 1914-18 war had finished and the purpose of the monument was enlarged to commemorate both the Entente Cordiale and those who fell in the war. The work building it was long and hard, involving blazing August sun and fourteen hour days of hauling the great bocks of granite up from the valley in a cart pulled by oxen. Eventually it was completed:

To the Entente Cordiale.
To the glory of the Allied Nations.
To the memory of soldiers from Vernet who died for their country.

De Monfreid's *Calvaire* statue is in the new church of Vernet-les-Bains near the Tourist Office.

Back in Villefranche-de-Conflent one can take a trip on the Yellow Train, sixty-three kilometres up to the Cerdagne and Latour de Carol, passing through Bolquerre Eyne, the highest SNCF station in France at 1,593 metres and continuing to Bourg Madame where Frank Burty Haviland and Manolo spent such a happy summer in 1909.

The line passes the Violet monument to Jules Lax, the highways inspector who, in 1902, proposed electric traction as opposed to steam engines to reduce the cost of the enterprise. Violet's monument stands above the train line next to the road on a small hill with a fantastic

Le Petit Train Jaune
crossing le Pont Séjourné

view, like a gateway to the high plateau of the Cerdagne's rolling farmland. Horses and cattle are raised there and the whole scene is ringed by mountains and the ski stations of the Pyrenees.

In 1902, when line was first proposed, it took two days by stagecoach from Perpignan to reach the high Cerdagne. (De Monfreid, Bausil and co. could, and indeed did, cycle up on their bikes in a very few hours.) The line was completed in 1910, reducing the journey time to three hours. Initially a vital commercial lifeline, the Yellow Train is now one of the most popular tourist attractions in the Pyrenées-Orientales.

Old postcard of Gustave Violet
Lax monument, Saillagousse

Gustave Violet – Monument des Morts, Tautavel

Tour 5
Estagel & Tautavel

One alternative to racing along the A9 towards Narbonne and the Abbey of Fontfroide is to take the rural route via Paziols, Durban and Tuchan. Not only is it an absolutely beautiful drive but it could take in the two remaining Violet war memorials, one in Estagel, birthplace of François Arago, (1786-1853), mathematician, physicist, astronomer and politician, and the other in Tautavel, birthplace 450,000 years ago of Tautavel man.

Both villages are pretty and well worth visiting. Both chose Gustave Violet to sculpt their war memorials. In Estagel, the monument is by the gate to the cemetery. Surrounded by cypress trees, it shows an elderly couple: the old man has his arm around the old woman who lays her head on his shoulder. He is rugged, she looks frail, both are sad, both grieving. The marble surround lists the sons of Estagel who fell in two world wars.

Turn right in central Estagel and continue up the Agly valley, over the river, and take the well-signed road on the right to Tuchan, Durban and Tautavel. Take the Tautavel fork (you will have to return and take the Paziols fork later if Fontfroide is your destination). The village is backed by impressive limestone cliffs topped by a ruined castle. Cross the bridge over the river Verdouble and a left turn brings you to the allée de la Légion d'Honneur, l'Espace de la Mémoire et des Arts and a car park. There you

Gustave Violet Monument des Morts, detail, Estagel

will find Violet's war memorial flanked, somewhat incongruously, by a sculpture depicting Tautavel man and a bunch of grapes *d'Erectus à Bacchus* and two dancing figures named *Tramontane* and *Marinade*. Behind it, equally bizarrely, is a bright blue metal enclosure containing a sports ground. Violet's sculpture is of an old, inevitably sad but resigned woman pondering the follies of war.

The town has a brilliant museum of Prehistory, part of the European Centre of Prehistory. The limestone cliffs of the surrounding Corbières hills are popular with lovers of *escalades*, the wine industry flourishes and produces many good local wines. There is an excellent raku pottery and several restaurants, cafés and bars.

Brief notes on people

• Guillaume **APOLLINAIRE** 1880-1918

Wilhelm Albert Włodzimierz Apolinary Kostrowicki, known as Guillaume Apollinaire, French poet, playwright, short story writer, novelist and art critic was born in Italy to a Polish mother. Apollinaire eventually moved from Rome to Paris and became one of the most popular members of the artistic community of Montparnasse in Paris.

On the 7th September 1911, police arrested and jailed him on suspicion of aiding and abetting the theft of the Mona Lisa and a number of statuettes from the Louvre, but released him a week later. These thefts were committed by a Russian friend to whom Apollinaire gave shelter. Apollinaire implicated his close friend Pablo Picasso, who was also brought in for questioning regarding the theft of Mona Lisa, but he was also exonerated.

Apollinaire fought in the first World War and, in 1916, received a serious shrapnel wound to the temple from which he would never fully recover. He was one of the foremost poets of the early 20th century.

• Michel **ARIBAUD**

Aribaud was the town archivist of Céret. A friend of the artists who frequented Céret, Aribaud collected their works. His collection was left to the Musée d'Art Moderne of Céret.

• François **BALOFFI** 1888-1979

A fisherman from Collioure who started painting when he retired.

• George Grey **BARNARD** 1863-1938

Barnard was an American sculptor. He collected Romanesque sculptures that would, after the First World War, form the basis of the Cloisters Museum in New York. Amongst others he acquired the cloisters of St Guilhem le Désert in the Hérault and Saint Michel de Cuxa near Prades in the Roussillon.

• Le **BATEAU LAVOIR**

Le Bateau Lavoir is the name given to a building in the Montmartre district of Paris. It became famous in art history as the residence and meeting place for a group of outstanding early twentieth century artists, men of letters, actors and art dealers. It was located at No. 13 rue Ravignan, just below the place du Tertre.

A fire destroyed most of the building in May 1970 leaving only the façade but it was completely rebuilt in cement in 1978.

The name Le Bateau Lavoir was coined by Max Jacob. The building was dark and dirty. On stormy days it swayed and creaked, reminding people of washing-boats on the nearby River Seine – hence the name.

Kees van Dongen and Pablo Picasso took up residence between 1900 and 1904. After 1904 more artists and writers moved in, including Juan Gris, André Salmon, Pablo Gargallo, Max Jacob and Pierre Reverdy. It became an unofficial club that included artists such as Matisse, Braque, Derain, Dufy, Laurencin, Modigliani and Utrillo, writers such as Apollinaire and Gertrude Stein and art dealers such as Vollard, Kahnweiler and Berthe Weil.

• Louis **BAUSIL** 1876-1945

Bausil was a painter from the Roussillon who was well known for his pictures of flowering fruit trees. He figured in the Roussillonais group that included de Monfreid, Fernand Dumas, Maillol, de Sévérac, Violet and Terrus. He was a keen cyclist and made many long excursions with de Monfreid. His portrait was painted by de Monfreid and is in the collection of the Narbonne Museum.

• François **BERNADI** b.1922

An artist and writer from Collioure, the son of a fisherman.

• Pierre **BONNARD** 1867-1947

French painter associated with the Nabis, a Post Impressionist avant garde group of artists in France in the 1890's.

• William Adolphe **BOUGUEREAU** 1825-1905

Bouguereau was a French academic painter. He was very much a traditionalist who used mythological themes in his realistic genre paintings. These were modern interpretations of classical subjects, both pagan and Christian, with a marked concentration on the naked female body. The idealised world of his paintings brought to life goddesses, nymphs, bathers, shepherdesses, and madonnas in a way that appealed to wealthy art patrons of the era.

• Georges **BRAQUE** 1882-1963

Major 20th-century French painter and sculptor who, along with Pablo Picasso, developed the art style known as Cubism. His earliest works were impressionistic, but after seeing the work exhibited by the Fauves in 1905, Braque adopted a Fauvist style. In May 1907, Braque successfully exhibited works in the Fauve style in the Salon des Indépendants.

Braque studied at the Beaux-Arts Académie Humbert where he met Marie Laurencin and François Picabia. His paintings between 1908 and 1913 reflected his new interest in geometric shapes and simultaneous perspectives. Starting in 1909 Braque began to work closely with Pablo Picasso who had been developing a similar style of painting. At the time, Pablo Picasso was influenced by Gauguin, Cézanne, African tribal masks and Iberian sculpture, while Braque was interested mainly in developing Cézanne's ideas of multiple perspectives. The invention of Cubism was a joint effort between Picasso and Braque, then residents of Montmartre. Between them they were the style's main innovators of the ground breaking new artistic movement.

A decisive time in the development of Cubism occurred during the summer of 1911. Braque and Picasso painted side by side in Céret, each artist producing paintings that are often so similar in approach that it is difficult to distinguish from those of the other. In 1912, they began to experiment with collage and *papier collé*. The French art critic Louis Vauxcelles first used the term Cubism in 1908 after seeing a picture by Braque. He described it as 'full of little cubes', after which the term quickly gained wide use.

• Marcelle **BRAQUE**

Georges Braque's wife. She was a professional model and Braque was introduced to her by Picasso. They were married in 1912. She is not to be confused with Marcelle Humbert.

• Constantin **BRANCUSI** 1876-1957

Romanian born sculptor who made his career in France.

• Pierre **BRUNE** 1887-1956

Brune was a painter who was invalided out of the French Army to convalesce in Amélie les Bains in 1916. He gravitated to Céret to join his friends Manolo and Haviland. His home was le Castellas overlooking the town.

Brune was later largely instrumental in the creation of the Musée d'Art Moderne at Céret.

• Richard **BURGSTHAL** 1884-1934

Burgsthal's real was name René Billa. Originally a musician, he met Gustave Fayet in Paris in 1910 and was engaged by him to decorate his newly acquired Abbaye de Fontfroide. When in 1912 Fayet bought a glassmaking factory Burgsthal started producing stained glass and rediscovered the techniques to produce stained glass in the famed reds and blues of Chartres. Later Burgsthal became a restorer of ancient stained glass windows.

• Alexandre **CABANEL** 1823-1889

Painter and professor at the École des Beaux-Arts in Paris. Cabanel won the Grande Médaille d'Honneur at the Salons of 1865, 1867, and 1878. He was closely connected to the Paris Salons: "He was elected regularly to the Salon jury and his pupils could be counted by the hundred at the Salons. Through them, Cabanel did more than any other artist of his generation to form the character of belle époque French painting". His refusal together with William-Adolphe Bouguereau to allow the impressionist painter Édouard Manet and many others to exhibit their work in the Salon of 1863 led to the establishment of the Salon des Refusés.

Amongst his many pupils were Maillol and Terrus.

• Amédée **CALMEL**

Known familiarly as 'the dentist from Béziers', this art collector was a friend of Fayet and de Monfreid. He was present on the famous evening of Matisse's visit to Château St Clément where the latter encountered Gauguin's sculptures for the first time. His portrait was painted by de Monfreid and is in the collection of the Musée des Beaux-Arts at Quimper.

• Pierre **CAMO** 1877-1974

Poet from the Roussillon and a friend of Maillol's. Camo also wrote biographies of both Maillol and Dufy.

• Charles **CAMOIN** 1879-1965

French Fauvist painter. Camoin met Matisse in Gustave Moreau's class at the Ecole des Beaux-Arts in Paris. Matisse and his friends (including Camoin, Manguin, Marquet, Rouault, Derain and de Vlaminck), formed the original group of artists labelled the Fauves for their wild expressionist use of colour. Camoin always remained close to Matisse.

• Carlos **CASAGEMAS** 1881-1901

Spanish painter, now best known for his friendship with Picasso. They first met at the Barcelona café Els IV Gats. In 1901 the two friends moved from Barcelona to Paris.

The first people that the two friends befriended in Paris were Louise Lenoir (known as Odette) and Germaine Florentin (later Germaine Pichot). Picasso began having an affair with Odette while Casagemas fell in love with Germaine. During this time Casagemas found out he was impotent which threw him into a deep depression from which he never recovered.

Early in 1901,Casagemas gave a party for seven people at a restaurant. One of the guests was Germaine. During dinner, Casagemas stood up, delivered a speech, then pulled a gun out of his pocket and aimed it at Germaine. She was able to dodge the bullet's full impact by diving under the table and suffered only a flesh wound. Casagemas, on the other hand, angry at his failure to shoot Germaine, turned the gun on himself. He died of the bullet wound to his head almost immediately.

Picasso, shocked at his friend's tragic demise, seemed to blame himself for the suicide. He began painting the death of Casagemas even though he had neither witnessed the death nor the burial. Casagemas's suicide triggered Picasso's Blue Period.

• Pau CASALS 1876–1973

Known during his professional career as Pablo Casals, the Spanish cellist and conductor was born in the region of Catalonia. Casals was an ardent supporter of the Spanish Republican government and after its defeat vowed not to return to Spain until democracy was restored. He settled in the French Catalan town of Prades in the Roussillon following the *Retirada* (the huge influx into France of Republican refugees from the Spanish Civil War).

Between 1939 and 1942 he made sporadic appearances as a cellist in the unoccupied zone of southern France and in Switzerland. So fierce was his opposition to the dictatorial regime of Francisco Franco in Spain that he refused to appear in countries that recognized the authoritarian Spanish government.

He is generally regarded as the pre-eminent cellist of the first half of the 20th century, and one of the greatest cellists of all time. He founded the summer Casals Festival in Prades in the Roussillon in 1950 which remains an annual event attracting musicians from all over the world.

• Enric CASANOVAS 1882–1948

Spanish sculptor and friend of Picasso and Maillol.

• Marc CHAGALL 1887–1985

Russian French artist who moved from Russia in 1910 to Paris where he developed friendships with Apollinaire and other avant garde figures. His connection with the Roussillon came in 1927 when he lived just outside Céret in a secluded villa off the road to Amélie-les-Bains working on the illustrations for *Les Fables de La Fontaine* to be published as a *beau livre* by the art dealer Vollard.

• Académie COLAROSSI

Famous art school in Paris founded by the Italian sculptor Filippo Colarossi in 1815. First located on the Île de la Cité, it moved in the 1870s to the VIᵉ arrondissement. The Académie was established as an alternative to the government sanctioned École des Beaux-Arts that had, in the eyes of many promising young artists at the time, become far too conservative. Along with its equivalent Académie Julian, and unlike the official École, the Colarossi school accepted female students and allowed them to draw from the nude male model.

De Monfreid and his friend Schuffenecker attended the studio of Ernest Colarossi in the 1880's.

• Louis CODET 1876-1914

Poet, novelist, art critic and landscape painter in the Roussillon and a great friend of Gustave Violet. A Parisian dandy, he was friendly with many artists and had a close relationship with Apollinaire and Marie Laurencin. He died of his wounds in the First World War.

• Henri-Edmond CROSS 1856-1910

Born Henri-Edmond-Joseph Delacroix, he was a French painter and printmaker. He is most acclaimed as a master of Neo-Impressionism. Henri Matisse and many other artists were influenced by his work thereby contributing to the development of fauvism.

His first residence in southern France was in Cabasson, near Le Lavandou. He then settled a short distance away in the small hamlet of Saint-Clair where he spent the remainder of his life, leaving only for visits to Italy and for the annual Indépendants exhibitions in Paris. In 1892 Cross's friend Paul Signac moved to nearby Saint-Tropez. Cross and Signac frequently hosted gatherings in Cross's garden, attended by such artists as Matisse, André Derain, and Albert Marquet.

• Maurice DENIS 1870–1943

French painter and writer, Denis was a member of the Symbolist and Nabi movements whose theories contributed to the foundations of cubism, fauvism, and abstract art.

• André DERAIN 1880-1954

French painter. He attended painting classes under Eugène Carrière, and there encountered Matisse. In 1900 he met and shared a studio with Maurice de Vlaminck and began to paint his first landscapes. His studies were interrupted from 1901 to 1904 when he was conscripted into the French army. Following his release from service, Matisse persuaded Derain's parents to allow him to abandon his engineering career and devote himself solely to painting; subsequently Derain attended the Académie Julian.

Derain and Matisse worked together through the summer of 1905 in Collioure and later that year displayed their highly innovative paintings at the Salon d'Automne. The vivid, unnatural colours led the critic Louis Vauxcelles to derisively dub their works as les Fauves, marking the start of the Fauvist movement.

In 1907 the art dealer Daniel-Henry Kahnweiler purchased Derain's entire studio, providing Derain with financial stability. He experimented with stone sculpture and moved to Montmartre to be near his friend Picasso and other artists. In Montmartre, Derain began to shift from the brilliant Fauvist palette to more muted tones, showing the influence of Cubism and Paul Cézanne.

• François DESNOYER 1894–1972

French figurative painter. He left his collection of modern art to the town of Saint Cyprien.

• Kees van DONGEN 1877-1968

Dutch painter who participated in the controversial 1905 exhibition Salon d'Automne, in a room also featuring Henri Matisse. The bright colours of this group of artists led to them being called Fauves.

In these years he was part of an avant-garde wave of painters – Maurice de Vlaminck, Othon Friesz, Henri Rousseau, Robert Delaunay, Albert Marquet, Édouard Vuillard – who aspired to a renewal of painting that was stuck in Neo-Impressionism. In 1906 he moved to the Bateau Lavoir at 13 rue Ravignan, where he was friends with the circle surrounding Pablo Picasso and his mistress, Fernande Olivier.

• Eugène DRUET 1867-1916

French photographer and Parisian Gallery owner.

• Raoul DUFY 1877–1953

French painter. Dufy studied at the Ecole des Beaux-Arts in Paris where he met George Braque. In 1902 he had an exhibition at Berthe Weil's gallery. In 1905 he was greatly influenced by seeing Matisse's Luxe, Calme et Volupté at the Salon des Indépendants and this directed his interests towards Fauvism. He later flirted with cubism before developing his own distinctive style.

In 1940 Dufy spent time in the Roussillon at the spa town of Vernet-les-Bains being treated in the waters for his severe rheumatoid arthritis. In 1944 Maillol, whom Dufy had regularly visited in Banyuls-sur-Mer, was on his way to visit Dufy who was taking the cure at Vernet-les-Bains when the car

Maillol was travelling in crashed and he was badly hurt. Maillol died shortly afterwards.

Dufy then lived in Perpignan until 1950.

• Fernand DUMAS

A banker from Perpignan, he was a close friend of de Monfreid. Dumas was one of the first car owners in the Roussillon and served as guide and chauffeur to Mette, Gauguin's widow, in her travels in the Roussillon. He was a patron of the Roussillonais painters.

Dumas owned a house in the village of Finestret not far from Prades.

• Gabriel FARAIL 1839-1892

A Roussillonais sculptor who started life as a joiner and became well known for his sculptures. He was later curator of the Musée Hyacinthe Rigaud in Perpignan where Maillol studied drawing. He was a considerable influence on the young Maillol who painted *Mademoiselle Farail au Chapeau* in 1890.

• Othon FRIESZ 1879-1949

French artist of the Fauvist movement. Friesz was born in Le Havre. It was while he was at the Lycée in Le Havre that he met his lifelong friend Raoul Dufy. He and Dufy studied at the Le Havre School of Fine Arts in 1895-96 and then went to Paris together for further study. In Paris, Friesz met Matisse, Marquet, and Rouault. Like them, he rebelled against the academic teaching of Bonnat and became a member of the Fauves, exhibiting with them in 1907. The following year, Friesz returned to Normandy and to a much more traditional style of painting,

• Varian Mackey FRY 1907-1967

An American journalist. Fry ran a rescue network in Vichy France that helped approximately 2,000 to 4,000 anti-Nazi and Jewish refugees to escape Nazi Germany and the Holocaust.

• Paul GAUGUIN 1848-1903

The leading French Post-Impressionist artist who was not well appreciated until after his death. In 1891 Gauguin sailed to French Polynesia to escape European civilization and "everything that is artificial and conventional".

Gauguin left France finally again in July 1895, never to return. His friend, George Daniel de Monfreid, acted as his unofficial agent in France in his absence and did much to promote his work to wealthy collectors such as Gustave Fayet as well as to fellow artists who were greatly influenced by him.

Gauguin was later recognised for his experimental use of colours and his synthetist style that was distinguishably different from Impressionism. Gauguin's posthumous retrospective exhibitions at the Salon d'Automne in Paris in 1903 and an even larger one in 1906 had a stunning and powerful influence on French avant-garde artists.

• Mette GAUGUIN 1850-1920

Paul Gauguin's Danish wife to whom he remained officially married even after he had abandoned her and his children in Europe.

• GIL BLAS

Parisian literary periodical founded by Augustin-Alexandre Dumont in 1879. It ceased publication in 1914.

• Marcel GILI 1914-1993

Roussillonais sculptor, painter and professor at the Ecole de Beaux-Arts in Paris. Many of his works can still be viewed at Mas Génégals near Vingrau in the Roussillon.

• Balbino GINER 1910-1976

Catalan artist who lived in Collioure and is buried there. A staunch republican and vehemently anti-Franco, he left Spain during the Spanish Civil War. His son, also an artist and also called Balbino Giner, died in Collioure in 2012.

• Eva GOUEL 1885-1915

When Picasso's mistress Fernande Olivier took up with a minor Italian artist in 1912 in an attempt to pique his jealousy, Picasso began seeing her close friend, Eva Gouel (Marcelle Humbert). Picasso's time with her coincided with the development of synthetic cubism. While Picasso never painted Eva, he paid homage to her, by including the words *Ma Jolie* in his paintings. He was devastated by her early death from cancer.

• Paul GUILLAUME 1891–1934

One of the leading cultural players and art dealer-collectors of Paris in the early twentieth century.

- Juan **GRIS** 1887-1927

José Victoriano González-Pérez better known as Juan Gris. He was a Spanish painter and sculptor who lived and worked in France most of his life. His works, which are closely connected to the emergence of Cubism are among the movement's most distinctive.

In 1906 he moved to Paris from Spain and became friends with Matisse, Braque and Léger. In Paris, Gris followed the lead of another friend and fellow countryman, Pablo Picasso. Although he submitted darkly humorous illustrations to journals he had developed a personal Cubist style. His portrait of Picasso in 1912 is a significant early Cubist painting done by a painter other than Picasso or Braque. Although Gris regarded Picasso as a teacher, Gertrude Stein wrote in *The Autobiography of Alice B. Toklas* that "Juan Gris was the only person whom Picasso wished away".

After 1913 he began his conversion to synthetic Cubism, of which he became a steadfast interpreter, with extensive use of *papier collé* or, collage. Unlike Picasso and Braque, whose Cubist works were monochromatic, Gris painted with bright harmonious colours in daring, novel combinations in the manner of his friend Matisse.

- Augustin **HANICOTTE** 1870-1957

French artist, born in Béthune on the Belgian border. He spent the first part of his life in Holland. He suffered from polyarthritis and settled in Collioure after the First World War because of its milder climate. He encouraged local children to paint and formed a group of budding artists known as *Les Gosses de Collioure*.

- Frank Burty **HAVILAND** 1886-1971

Frank Burty Haviland was born in Limoges in 1886. He studied music at school with Ricardo Viñes, who introduced him to Déodat de Sévérac, who in turn introduced him to the Spanish artist, Manolo Hugué. The three became friends, and through Manolo, Burty Haviland came into close contact with the Cubist painters in Paris.

In 1910, Burty Haviland travelled to southern France with Manolo and de Sévérac, and he subsequently bought an old convent in Céret, Le Couvent des Capucins. Haviland married Joséphine Laporta, a girl from Céret, in 1913.

He lived most of his life in Céret and was one of the driving forces behind the creation the Musée d'Art Moderne de Céret in 1950, helping it to acquire 14 works by Henri Matisse and over 50 works by Picasso.

- Auguste **HERBIN** 1882-1960

French painter. In 1901 he settled in Paris. The initial influence of Impressionism and Post-Impressionism visible in paintings that he sent to the

Salon des Indépendants in 1906 gradually gave way to an involvement with Cubism after his move in 1909 to the Bateau Lavoir studios, where he met Picasso, Braque and Gris; he was also encouraged by his friendship with Wilhelm Uhde.

• Marcelle HUMBERT

See Gouel, Eva.

• Max JACOB 1876 -1944

French poet, painter, writer, and critic. After spending his childhood in Brittany, Jacob enrolled in the Paris Colonial School, which he left in 1897 for an artistic career. On the Boulevard Voltaire, he shared a room with Pablo Picasso with whom he became great friends. Picasso introduced him to Apollinaire, who in turn introduced him to Braque. Jacob stayed with Picasso in Céret.

• Académie JULIAN

The Académie Julian was an art school in Paris established in 1868 as a private studio school for art students. It not only prepared students for the exams at the prestigious École des Beaux-Arts, but offered independent training in arts. At that time, women were not allowed to enrol for study to the École des Beaux-Arts but the new Académie Julian accepted them, providing an alternative education and training.

Men and women were taught separately but women participated in the same studies as men, including the basis of art training – the drawing and painting of nude models.

Like its counterpart, the Académie Colarossi, it was popular with French and foreign students from all over the world, particularly Americans.

• Daniel-Henry KAHNWEILER 1884–1979

German-born art historian, art collector, and one of the premier French art dealers of the 20th century. He opened his first small art gallery in Paris in 1907 at 28 rue Vignon and was among the first to champion Picasso, Braque and cubism.

Kahnweiler is considered the major dealer in, champion of, and spokesman for Cubism. He was among the first people to recognize the importance and beauty of Picasso's *Les Demoiselles d'Avignon*, immediately expressing a wish to buy it and all of Picasso's works. Picasso once wrote of Kahnweiler "What would have become of us if Kahnweiler hadn't had a business sense?" – a compelling statement because, at the time that he was creating some of his most famous works, Picasso was largely unknown as an artist and virtually destitute.

Kahnweiler supported in his gallery many of the great artists of the time who then had no audience or collectors. Initial purchases included works by Van Dongen, Derain, Léger, Braque, Gris, de Vlaminck and several others of the same generation. Kahnweiler wanted, as he said, to defend artists whom he believed in and who had no dealers to promote them.

As a businessman Kahnweiler innovated many new ways of working with artists and art dealing which have subsequently become established practice with art dealers. In 1907 when there were only half a dozen good galleries in Paris, he made contracts with artists to buy all of their work thus freeing them from the financial worry. He saw his artists daily to discuss their work, he photographed each work because he felt it imperative to keep a record, he held exhibitions of their work and he promoted their work internationally.

He also acted as a publisher of fine books in which contemporary artists illustrated works by contemporary authors.

• Harry Clément Ulrich **KESSLER** 1868–1937

Half German, half Scottish, Count Kessler was an immensely rich patron of the arts. He had grown up in France, England and Germany, was educated first in Paris and then, from 1880, at a boarding school in England. He studied law and art history in Bonn and Leipzig, was familiar with many cultures, travelled widely, was active as a German diplomat, and became known as a man of the world and patron of the arts. In 1908 he journeyed to Greece with Maillol.

• Moïse **KISLING** 1891–1953

Polish born French painter who studied at the School of Fine Arts in Kraków. In 1910 Kisling moved to Montmartre and a few years later to Montparnasse where he was part of the renowned artistic community gathered there at the time. For a short time he lived in the Bateau Lavoir and in 1911-12 spent nearly a year in Céret. In 1913 he took a studio in Montparnasse, where he lived for the next 27 years. He became close friends with many of his contemporaries, including Modigliani, who painted a portrait of him in 1916.

• Pinchus **KRÉMÈGNE** 1890-1981

A Litvak French artist, primarily known as a sculptor, painter and lithographer, he came to Paris in 1912. There he joined the group of painters of Montparnasse and soon became one of the respected residents of La Ruche. In 1915, he gave up sculpture in order to dedicate himself to painting.

It was he who encouraged Soutine to come to Paris. Krémègne left Paris to live in Céret and this move in turn attracted other painters such as Soutine. Although Soutine did not like the town very much, he completed many paintings there over a couple of years. He never settled but his compatriot Krémègne had a house built there around 1960. This small unassuming house, a reflection of the man himself, is nestled into the mountain and overlooks the town.

Underestimated as an artist today, he is overshadowed by Soutine and Chagall.

• Le LAPIN AGILE

The Lapin Agile was a famous Montmartre cabaret. It was originally called Cabaret des Assassins. Tradition relates that it received this name because a band of assassins broke in and killed the owner's son. The cabaret was more than twenty years old when, in 1875, the artist André Gill painted the sign that was to suggest its permanent name. It was a picture of a rabbit jumping out of a saucepan, and residents began calling their neighbourhood night club Le Lapin à Gill, meaning Gill's rabbit.

Over time the name evolved into Cabaret Au Lapin Agile, or, the Nimble Rabbit Cabaret. At the turn of the twentieth century, the Lapin Agile was a favourite spot for struggling artists and writers, including Picasso, Modigliani, Apollinaire, and Utrillo.

• Marie LAURENCIN 1883-1956

Marie Laurencin was French painter and print maker. During the early years of the 20th century she was an important figure in the Parisian avant-garde and a member of *La bande à Picasso*. She became romantically involved with Picasso's friend, the poet Guillaume Apollinaire, and has often been identified as his muse.

• Maximilien LUCE 1858-1941

French artist, print maker, and anarchist.

• Charles Rennie MACKINTOSH 1868-1928

Scottish architect, designer, watercolourist and artist. He was a designer in the Arts and Crafts movement and also the main representative of Art Nouveau in the United Kingdom. He had a considerable influence on European design. He spent the last four years of his life in the Roussillon, mainly in Port-Vendres.

• Henri MANGUIN 1874 -1949

French painter. He studied with Marquet and Matisse in Gustave Moreau's atelier in 1894. His best work was achieved working on the Mediterranean Coast, notably featuring light filled landscapes and portraits of his wife and family.

• MANOLO 1872-1945

Pseudonym of Spanish sculptor and painter, Manuel Martínez i Hugué.

He was a pupil at the École des Beaux-Arts in Barcelona and frequented the artistic café Els IV Gats where he met Picasso. At the age of twenty he deserted from the Spanish army and visited Paris where he settled between 1901 and 1909. He later moved to Céret where he lived with his wife Totote until 1917.

• Albert MARQUET 1875-1947

French painter. In 1890 Marquet moved to Paris to attend the Ecole des Arts Décoratifs where he met Henri Matisse. They shared a room for a time and influenced each other's work. Marquet began his studies in 1892 at the École des Beaux-Arts under Gustave Moreau, the symbolist artist.

During this period Marquet exhibited paintings at the Salon des Indépendants. Although he did not sell many paintings, the artistic community of Paris became aware of his work. His early compositions were characterised by a Fauvist approach.

In 1905 he exhibited at the Salon d'Automne where his paintings were put together with those of Matisse, de Vlaminck, Derain, Rouault, Dufy, Manguin and Braque. Although Marquet painted with the Fauves for years, he tended to use less bright and violent colours than the others. He favoured greyish yellow and greyish violets or blues.

At the end of 1907 he remained in Paris and dedicated himself, together with Matisse, to a series of city views.

• Ludovic MASSE 1900-1982

Catalan novelist, born in Evol in the Roussillon.

• Amedeo MODIGLIANI 1884-1920

Italian figurative painter and sculptor who worked mainly in France. Primarily a figurative artist, he became known for paintings and sculptures in a modern style characterised by mask-like faces and elongation of form. He died in Paris of tubercular meningitis, exacerbated by poverty, overwork and addiction to alcohol and narcotics.

• Adolphe Joseph Thomas MONTICELLI 1824-1886

French painter. Monticelli was born in Marseille. He studied at the École des Beaux-Arts in Paris, made copies after the old masters in the Louvre and was an admirer of the oil sketches of Eugène Delacroix. He developed a highly individual Romantic style of painting, in which richly coloured, dappled, textured and glazed surfaces produced a scintillating effect. He painted courtly subjects inspired by Antoine Watteau; he also painted still lifes, portraits, and Orientalist subjects that owe much to the example of Delacroix.

After 1870, Monticelli returned to Marseille, where he would live in poverty despite a prolific output. An unworldly man, he dedicated himself single mindedly to his art. The young Paul Cézanne had befriended Monticelli in the 1860s, and the influence of the older painter's work can be seen in Cézanne's work of that decade. Between 1878 and 1884 the two artists often painted landscapes together, once spending a month roaming the Aix countryside.

• Gustave MOREAU 1826-1898

French symbolist artist. He became a professor at the Paris École des Beaux-Arts in 1891 and among his many students were the fauvist painters, Henri Matisse and Georges Rouault.

During his lifetime, Moreau produced more than 8,000 paintings, watercolours and drawings, many of which are on display in Paris at the Musée National Gustave Moreau. The museum is in his former workshop, and opened in 1903. André Breton famously used to "haunt" the museum and regarded Moreau as a precursor of Surrealism.

• Ivan MOROZOV 1871-1921

Russian art collector. He was a wealthy Moscow businessman, owner of a complex of textile mills, and a passionate lover of French Impressionist and Post-Impressionist painting on which he spent huge sums. Many of the pictures in his collection were bought from Durand-Ruel's gallery, but Morozov also employed a representative in Paris to buy from other sources. He also regularly visited Paris himself.

In 1907 he acquired a group of pictures from Ambroise Vollard and later bought from this dealer a Cubist portrait by Picasso even though – unlike the other great Russian collector of the time, Sergei Shchukin – he was not particularly sympathetic to Cubism. Morozov corresponded regularly not only with dealers, but also with many French artists direct, including Bonnard, Matisse, and Vuillard, from whom he also commissioned works.

• Henry de MONFREID 1879-1975

French adventurer and author. He was the son of the artist George Daniel de Monfreid and knew Paul Gauguin as a child.

• Willy MUCHA 1905-1995

French painter of Polish origin. He lived in Collioure.

• Musée MAILLOL

61 rue de Grenelle VIIe Paris. Maillol's drawings, engravings, pastels, tapestry panels, ceramics and early Nabis-related paintings, as well as his sculptures and terracottas can all be seen here.

• Les NABIS

Nabi means prophet in Hebrew and in Arabic. Les Nabis originated as a rebellious group of young student artists who banded together at the Académie Julian. Possibly the nickname arose because "most of them wore beards, some were Jews and all were desperately earnest". They paved the way for the early 20th century development of abstract and non-representational art.

Considered to be on the cutting edge of modern art during their early period, their subject matter was representational (though often symbolist in inspiration), but was design oriented along the lines of the Japanese prints they so admired, and art nouveau. Pierre Bonnard, Edouard Vuillard and Maurice Denis became the best known of the group.

• Patrick O'BRIAN 1924-2000

Born Richard Patrick Russ, he was an English novelist and translator, best known for his Aubrey–Maturin series of novels set in the Royal Navy during the Napoleonic Wars. He was a biographer of Picasso and lived for many years in Collioure.

• Fernande OLIVIER 1881-1966

Born Amélie Lang, she was a French artist and model known primarily for having been a model and mistress of Picasso's and for her written accounts of her relationship with him. Picasso painted over 60 portraits of Fernande.

Fernande was born of an out of wedlock relationship between her mother and a married man. She was brought up by an aunt who attempted to arrange a marriage for her. Instead Fernande ran away and married a man who abused her. In 1900, when she was 19 years old, she left her husband without a formal divorce and moved to Paris. She changed her name so that her husband could not find her. Fernande quickly found work modelling for artists and figured in the circle of friends of writer Guillaume Apollinaire.

She met Picasso at the Bateau Lavoir in 1904 and by the next year they were living together. Their relationship lasted seven years and was characterized by its tempestuousness. Both Fernande and Picasso were jealous lovers, and their passions sometimes exploded into violence.

When Picasso finally achieved success as an artist, he began to lose interest in Fernande as she reminded him of more difficult times. Eventually they separated in 1912, leaving Fernande with no means to carry on living in the style to which she had become accustomed. She had no legal right to expect anything from the painter, since she was still technically married to her first husband. To survive, she took various odd jobs, from a cashier at a butcher's to an antiques saleswoman. She also supplemented her income by giving drawing lessons.

• Walter PACH 1883-1958

Artist, critic, lecturer, art adviser, and art historian who wrote extensively about modern art. He became a good friend of Matisse whom he had met in Fiesole near Florence with the Steins.

• Jules PAMS 1852-1930

French politician. He was married to Jeanne Bardou of the wealthy cigarette paper family and became Agriculture Minister in 1911. Their summer residence was Château de Valmy, a wedding present from her father. Their Perpignan residence was the Hotel Pams, part of which was originally the cigarette paper factory and their residence in Port-Vendres is the current Town Hall.

• Jean PESKÉ 1870-1949

French painter and engraver of Russo-Polish origin. He studied at the Académie Julien. He was friends with Apollinaire, Signac, Pisarro and Bonnard.

• Germaine PICHOT

Germaine Pichot's original name was Laure Gargallo; she was a relative of a sculptor named Pablo Gargallo, who was a friend of Pablo Picasso. She married while she was still in her teens and took her husband's last name of Florentin. Germaine was an artist's model in Paris but also worked as a laundress and seamstress.

When Picasso and his friend Casagemas moved to Paris in 1900, the first people that the two friends befriended were Louise Lenoir (known as Odette) and Germaine. Picasso began having an affair with Odette while Casagemas fell in love with Germaine. During this time Casagemas found out he was impotent which threw him into a deep depression from which he never recovered from. Picasso hoped to revive Casagemas and erase all thoughts of Germaine from his head so he took his friend on a tour through Spain.

Early in 1901, Casagemas returned to Paris without Picasso. He threw a party for seven people at the restaurant L'Hippodrome, which was located in the building he lived in. One of the guests was Germaine. During dinner, Casagemas stood up, delivered a speech in French, then pulled a gun out of his pocket and aimed it at Germaine. She was able to dodge the bullet's full impact by diving under the table and suffered only a flesh wound to her upper body. Casagemas, on the other hand, angry at his failure to shoot Germaine, turned the gun on himself. He died of the bullet wound to his head almost immediately.

Picasso, shocked at his friend's tragic demise, seemed to blame himself for Casagemas's death. He began painting the death of Casagemas (even though he had not witnessed it) and his burial. Casagemas's suicide triggered Picasso's Blue Period.

After a while, Germaine and Picasso split up and Germaine married Ramon Pichot, a friend of Picasso's. Germaine was not faithful to her new husband and had many affairs.

• Ramon PICHOT 1872-1925

Spanish artist friend of Picasso from Els IV Gats days in Barcelona. He was to become a major influence on Salvador Dali's early work.

• Jojo POUS b 1927-2013

Late owner of the hotel and restaurant, Les Templiers, in Collioure. Les Templiers is home to an extensive and varied collection of paintings donated by artists or bought by the Pous family over the years. over the years.

• Jean-Jacques PROLENGEAU 1917-1994

French ceramicist. He established himself in Perpignan in 1940 and from 1944 to 1960 reorganised and then became director of the school of design in the city. It was with Prolongeau that Dufy produced his celebrated blue pottery. He created the tiled ceiling of the terrace of the Templiers Hotel in Collioure.

• Hans Marsilius PURMANN 1880-1966

German painter, collector and writer. He became a pupil and friend of Matisse with whom he set up a painting school in Paris. He was photographed with the Matisses on Terrus's terrace in Elne. Matisse and Purmann visited Germany together several times between 1908 and 1910.

• Els IV GATS

A renowned café bar in Barcelona which opened in 1897. It was a popular meeting place for writers and artists including Picasso and Manolo.

It still operates as a bar and restaurant.

• Odilon REDON 1840-1916

Bertrand-Jean Redon, better known as Odilon Redon, French symbolist painter, printmaker, draughtsman and pastellist. A friend of Gustave Fayet, his dramatic painted murals decorate the walls of the library at Gustave Fayet's Abbaye de Fontfroide near Narbonne.

- Hyacinthe **RIGAUD** 1659-1743

French baroque painter of Catalan origin whose career was based in Paris. He was the most important painter during the reign of King Louis XIV.

In 1820, the Musée des Beaux-Arts Hyacinthe Rigaud in Perpignan was dedicated to him and shows some of his work

- Henri **ROUSSEAU** 1844-1910

French Post-Impressionist painter in the Naïve or Primitive manner. He was also known as *Le Douanier* (the customs officer), a humorous description of his occupation as a toll collector. Ridiculed during his life, he came to be recognised as a self-taught genius whose works are of high artistic quality.

When Picasso chanced upon a painting of Rousseau's being sold on the street in Paris as a canvas to be painted over, the younger artist instantly recognised Rousseau's genius and went to meet him. In 1908 Picasso held a half serious, half burlesque banquet in his studio in Le Bateau Lavoir in Rousseau's honour.

- La **RUCHE**

La Ruche (The Hive) was the name given to the building in Montparnasse that part took over from the Bateau Lavoir after the first world war. Alfred Boucher, the sculptor who was a founder member, chose the name believing that the artists it housed would be overflowing with creativity and busy as bees. Originally the structure was of metal, designed by Gustave Eiffel. Created to help young artists of limited means, La Ruche became one of the most important artistic centres of the twentieth century. The octagonal, three-story building was divided into numerous small studios of around thirty square metres. Modigliani, Soutine, Brancusi, Marie Laurencin, and Chagall, were among the artists who lived and worked there. Today there are sixty studios of varying sizes, still used by artists. It is not open to the public.

- John Peter **RUSSELL** 1858-1930

Australian born artist John Peter Russell was a man of means. Having married a beautiful Italian, he settled and established an artist's colony on Belle Île off the coast of Brittany. In 1897 and 1898 Henri Matisse visited Belle Île. Russell introduced him to Impressionism and to the then relatively unknown work of Van Gogh. Matisse's style changed radically, and he would later say "Russell was my teacher, he explained colour theory to me."

- Clovis **SAGOT** d .1913

The story goes that Sagot was originally a circus clown. Later he worked with his brother who dealt in prints. Around 1903 he opened his own gallery in an old pharmacy very near Vollard's. He was a tough negotiator who bought his paintings cheaply and sold them on expensively. Fernande Olivier related that once Clovis presented Picasso with a bunch of flowers in the expectation that Picasso would paint them and give the ensuing picture to Sagot.

Leo Stein bought his first Picasso from Sagot. Picasso painted a portrait of Sagot in 1909.

• André SALMON 1881-1969

French poet, art critic and writer. He was one of the defenders of cubism together with Guillaume Apollinaire.

• Claude-Emile SCHUFFENECKER 1851-1934

French Post-Impressionist artist, painter, art teacher and art collector, nicknamed "Schuff".

In 1872, Schuffenecker joined the stockbroker Bertin, where he met Paul Gauguin. They became close friends. Both used to study old masters at the Louvre and worked at the Académie Colarossi. By 1880 both painters evidently had earned enough money to leave Bertin – just in time before the French Panama canal project began to turn into a disaster. Both opted for a career in the arts and earned additional income at the stock exchange. Then in January 1882 the Paris Bourse crashed, and while Gauguin chose to remain independent, Schuffenecker decided to apply for a diploma to teach. Two years later, he was appointed to teach drawing at the Lycée Michelet in Vanves. Schuffenecker was instrumental in establishing the Volpini exhibition in 1889.

• Victor SEGALEN 1878-1919

French naval doctor, ethnographer, archaeologist, writer, poet, explorer, art theorist, linguist and literary critic. He brought back Gauguin's effects from the Pacific after the latter's death.

• Déodat de SÉVÉRAC 1872-1921

Of aristocratic background, Déodat de Sévérac was profoundly influenced by the musical tradition of his native Languedoc. He is noted for his vocal and choral music, which include settings of verse in Provençal and Catalan.

He left his native Toulouse to study in Paris. He worked as an assistant to Isaac Albéniz and returned to the south of France, where he spent the rest of his rather short life. His opera *Héliogabale* was produced at Béziers in 1910. The last years of his short life were spent in Céret where he was a close friend of Picasso, Manolo, de Haviland and other artists.

• Sergei SHCHUKIN 1854-1936

A Russian businessman who became an art collector, mainly of French Impressionist and Post-Impressionist art following a trip to Paris in 1897 when he bought his first Monet. He later bought numerous works totalling 258 paintings with which he decorated the walls of his palatial home in Moscow. By 1914 Shchukin owned thirteen Monets, four Van Goghs, sixteen Gauguins, seven Douanier Rousseaus, eight Marquets and sixteen Derains.

Shchukin was particularly noted for his long association with Matisse who decorated his mansion and created one of his iconic paintings, La Danse, specially for him. The collection also featured fifty choice works by Pablo Picasso, including most of his earliest Cubist works.

• Paul SIGNAC 1863-1935

French Neo-Impressionist painter who, working with Georges Seurat, helped develop the pointillist style.

Many of Signac's paintings are of the French coast. He loved to paint the water. He left the capital each summer to stay in southern France. He was the first notable painter to feature views of Collioure in his work. He later bought a house in St Tropez to which he invited his artist friends.

• Chaïm SOUTINE 1893-1943

Abstract impressionist painter. He was born near Minsk in Belarus. He studied in Vilnius at the Vilna Academy of Fine Arts. In 1913, with his friend Pinchus Krémègne, he emigrated to Paris and studied at the École des Beaux-Arts. He soon developed a highly personal vision and painting technique. For a time he and his friends lived at La Ruche, a residence for artists in Montparnasse where he became friends with Amedeo Modigliani. Modigliani painted Soutine's portrait several times, most famously in 1917, on the door of an apartment.

In 1919 he was invited by Pierre Brune to come and live in Céret where he painted extensively, later destroying many of the paintings of this period.

• Gertrude STEIN 1874-1946

American writer, poet, art patron and collector who spent most of her life in France.

Much of Gertrude Stein's fame derives from the collection of modern art which she assembled from 1904 to 1913 with her brother Leo Stein. Their joint collection began in late 1904 when their brother Michael Stein announced that the family trust account had accumulated a balance of 8,000 francs. They spent this at Vollard's Gallery, buying two Gauguins, a Cézanne, and two Renoirs. The art collection grew and the walls at rue de Fleurus, their Paris home, were rearranged continually to make way for new acquisitions. Shortly after the opening of the Paris Autumn Salon of 1905, the

Steins acquired Matisse's *Woman with a Hat and Picasso's Young Girl with Basket of Flowers*.

By early 1906, Leo and Gertrude Stein's apartment displayed paintings by Manguin, Bonnard, Picasso, Cézanne, Renoir, Honoré Daumier, Matisse, and Toulouse Lautrec. The Steins' elder brother, Michael, and sister-in-law Sarah acquired a large number of Matisse paintings.

Contemporaries of Leo and Gertrude, Matisse and Picasso became part of their social circle and were a part of the early Saturday evenings at 27 rue de Fleurus. Gertrude attributed the beginnings of the Saturday evening salons to Matisse "Matisse brought people, everybody brought somebody, and they came at any time and it began to be a nuisance, and it was in this way that Saturday evenings began."

• Leo **STEIN** 1872-1947

American art collector and critic and the older brother of Gertrude Stein. He became an influential promoter of 20th-century paintings.

• Sarah **STEIN** 1870-1953

Sarah Stein was the wife of Michael Stein, elder brother of Gertrude Stein.

Sarah and Michael lived in conventional bourgeois comfort as they accumulated paintings and other objects with as much enthusiasm as Leo and Gertrude Stein. The couple concentrated almost exclusively on the work of Henri Matisse. She was one of Matisse's staunchest friend and supporters from 1905 until she and her husband left Paris in the 1930s.

• Leopold **SURVAGE** 1879-1968

One of Jojo Pous' favourite artists, born in Moscow and died in Paris, he was the son of a piano maker and the first to give a painting to Jojo's father, René Pous, thus beginning the art collection of the Templiers hotel and restaurant in Collioure. He had studied with Matisse in Paris in 1908, knew Picasso and Braque, dabbled in cubism, worked with Diaghilev and the Ballets Russes, knew Auguste Herbin and had a house in Collioure. Two of his paintings hang in the Céret Museum, both executed in Collioure.

• Louis **VAUXCELLES** 1870-1945

He was one of the most influential art critics at the start of the twentieth century and wrote for the weekly review Gil Blas.

• Claude **VIALLAT** b. 1936

French contemporary painter born in Nîmes. He painted the walls of the dining room of Les Templiers in Collioure.

- Dina VIERNY 1919-2009

Art dealer, collector, museum director and former artists' model.

Vierny was a 15 year old lycée student in Paris when she met Aristide Maillol, almost 60 years her senior, in the mid-1930s. The architect Jean-Claude Dondel, a friend of her father decided that she would make the perfect model for the artist who was then 73 years old, and reportedly in the professional doldrums. She became Maillol's muse for the last ten years of his life. Both Matisse and Bonnard, artists for whom she also posed, attributed a renewed inspiration for painting and sculpture to Vierny.

In the early 1970s, Dina Vierny decided to start a Maillol museum. She began buying up apartments on the rue de Grenelle in Paris, selling off her collection of 654 dolls along the way. In 1995 she opened the Fondation Dina Vierny-Musée Maillol, whose permanent collection also includes work by Degas, Kandinsky, Picasso, Duchamp and other artists.

- Ricardo VIÑES 1875-1943

Spanish pianist born in Lleida, Catalonia. He studied at the Conservatoire in Paris and later became known for presenting new music, especially of French and Spanish origin. He was friends with Ravel, de Falla, Debussy and de Sévérac.

He was a frequent visitor to Fayet's country estate at the Abbaye de Fontfroide where Redon included portraits of him and de Sévérac in his great mural *La Nuit* which can be seen in the library.

- Martin VIVÈS 1905-1991

Roussillonais artist and curator of the Musée Rigaud in Perpignan. He spent his early childhood in Figueres and was in the same class at school as Salvador Dalí .

- Maurice de VLAMINCK 1876-1965

French painter. Along with André Derain and Henri Matisse he is considered one of the principal figures in the Fauvist movement.

The turning point in his life came through a chance meeting in 1900 on the train to Paris towards the end of his army service. Vlaminck, then 23, met an aspiring artist, André Derain, with whom he struck up a lifelong friendship. The two rented a studio together for a year before Derain left to do his own military service. In 1902 and 1903 Vlaminck wrote several mildly pornographic novels illustrated by Derain. He painted during the day and earned his livelihood by giving violin lessons and performing with musical bands at night.

• Ambroise **VOLLARD** 1866-1939

One of the most important dealers in French contemporary art at the beginning of the twentieth century. He is credited with providing exposure and emotional support to numerous notable and at the time unknown artists, including Cézanne, Maillol, Renoir, Picasso, Derain, Rouault, Gauguin and Van Gogh. He is also well known as an avid art collector and publisher.

In 1893, he established his own art gallery in rue Laffitte, then the centre of the Parisian market for contemporary art. He was a shrewd businessman who made a fortune with the "buy low, sell high" policy. His clients included Albert C. Barnes, Henry Osborne Havemeyer, Gertrude Stein and her brother, Leo Stein.

Vollard died in July 1939 at the age of 73 on his way to Paris when his chauffeur-driven car skidded off the road. He was dozing when the car crashed. The impact of the crash caused a small bronze by Maillol to shoot forward hitting Vollard in the side of the neck, fracturing his cervical vertebrae.

Vollard died without direct heirs. Much of the art was left to extended family and close friends, although a significant number of works apparently were sold, dispersed, or disappeared during World War II.

Several hundred works were given by Vollard to a protégé, Erich Slomovich, who deposited many in a French bank and hid other's behind a false wall in a farmhouse for safety during the war. Slomovich was gassed shortly afterwards. When the French bank put them up for auction in the early eighties fifteen parties stepped forward to claim the art. The sale was cancelled and the works were auctioned twenty nine year's later in 2012. Among them was *Arbres à Collioure* by Derain in 1905.

• Jean-Edouard **VUILLARD** 1868-1940

French painter associated with the Nabis.

• Berthe **WEILL** 1865-1951

French art dealer who played a vital role in the creation of the market for twentieth century art. Although she is much less known than her well-established competitors such as Vollard, Kahnweiler and Rosenberg, she may be credited with producing the first sales in Paris for Picasso and Matisse and with providing Amedeo Modigliani with the only solo exhibition in his lifetime .

The impressive list of artists who made their way through her gallery and into the canon of modern art continues with names such as Dufy, Derain, Vlaminck, Diego Rivera, Braque, van Dongen, and Utrillo.

Select
bibliography

BALDASSARI Anne & others – *l'ABCdaire de Picasso* – Flammarion – 1996

BAROU Jean-Pierre – *Matisse fauve* – Edition Payot et Rivages – 2005

BAROU Jean-Pierre – *Matisse ou le miracle de Collioure* – Indigène Editions – 1997

BASSERES Docteur – *Maillol mon ami* – 1979

BONNEL Jean-Pierre – *Dina Vierny: une grande dame au pays de Maillol* – Editions Frontières – 2000

BONNEL Jean-Pierre – *Moi, Matisse à Collioure* – Balzac – 2003

CAHN Isabelle & others – *l'ABCdaire de Maillol* – Flammarion – 1996

CANTALOUBRE Pierre & LAUVERNIER Pierre – *La côte vermeille* – Presses Littéraires – 2007

CATALOGUE EXPOSITION – *Augustin Hanicotte Collioure 1905-1945* – Musée Art Moderne et Château Royal de Collioure – 2005

CATALOGUE EXPOSITION – *Céret un siècle de paysages sublimes 1909-2009* – Gallimard – 2009

CATALOGUE EXPOSITION – *Dufy en Méditerannée* – Editions Au Fil du Temps – 2010

CATALOGUE EXPOSITION – *Gauguin Maker of Myth* – Tate Publishing – 2010

CATALOGUE EXPOSITION – *George-Daniel de Monfreid 1856-1929* – Somogy Editions d'Art – 2003

CATALOGUE EXPOSITION – *Gustave Fayet, "Vous, peintre"* – Musée Terrus – 2006

CATALOGUE EXPOSITION – *Herbin 1882-1960* – Musée d'Art Moderne de Céret

CATALOGUE EXPOSITION – *Hommage à Frank Burty Haviland 1886 – 1971* – Musée d'Art Moderne de Céret – 2010

CATALOGUE EXPOSITION – *Matisse Derain Collioure 1905, un été fauve* – Gallimard – 2005

CATALOGUE EXPOSITION – *Matisse et ses amis Collioure 1905-1906* – l'Association des Amis du Musée de Collioure – 2005

CATALOGUE EXPOSITION – *Matisse Terrus, histoire d'une amitié 1905-1907* – Musée Terrus – 2002

CATALOGUE EXPOSITION - *Picasso: Dessins et papiers collés Céret 1911-1913* – Musée d'Art Moderne de Céret – 1997

CATALOGUE EXPOSITION – *Soutine: Céret 1919-1922* – Musée d'Art Moderne de Céret – 2000

CATALOGUE EXPOSITION – *The Steins Collect: Matisse Picasso and the Avant-Garde* – San Francisco Museum of Modern Art – 2011

CRICHTON Robin – *Monsieur Mackintosh* – Luarth Press – 2006

De la FUENTE Véronique Richard – *Picasso à Céret 1911-1914* – Editions Mare Nostrum – 2002

DUCHÂTEAU – *La mecque du cubisme 1900-1950* – Alter Ego Editions 2011

FONTBONA Francesc – *Manolo Hugué* – Museo de Arte Contemporaneo Esteban Vicente

FREEMAN Judi – *The Fauve Landscape* – Abbeville – 1990

GAUGUIN Paul – *The Letters of Paul Gauguin to Georges-Daniel de Monfreid* – translated by Ruth Pielkoyo – Dodds Mead – 1922

GRANDCLEMENT Daniel – *L'incroyable Henry de Monfreid* – Grasset 1998

GUIDE DU MUSÉE D'ART MODERNE de *Céret* – 1999

LAUVERNIER Pierre – *Les Villages des Pyrénées Orientales par l'éditeur Fau* - Les Presses Littéraires – 2011

LORQUIN Bertrand – *Maillol peintre* – Réunion des Musées Nationaux – 2001

MAILLOL *Témoignages de ses amis* – Musée Rigaud – 1994

MILLET Laurence – *l'ABCdaire de Matisse* – Flammarion – 2005

O'BRIAN Patrick – *Picasso* – Collins - 2003

OLIVIER Fernande – *Picasso and his friends* – translated by Jane Miller – Appleton Century – 1965

REWALD Jean – *Les ateliers de Maillol* – Le Point – 1938

RICHARDSON John – *A Life of Picasso* – Volume I: 1881-1906 – Jonathan Cape – 1991

RICHARDSON John – *A Life of Picasso* – Volume II: *1907-1917* – Jonathan Cape – 1996

SAINT RAMON – 1905-1954 *Les pionniers de l'art moderne en pays Catalan* – Alter Ego Editions – 2005

SPURLING Hilary – *Matisse the Master: Volume One: 1869-1908* – Hamish Hamilton – 1998

SPURLING Hilary – *Matisse the Master: Volume Two: 1909-1954* – Hamish Hamilton – 2005

STEIN Gertrude – *The Autobiography of Alice B Toklas* – 1933

VIERNY Dina – *Histoire de ma vie raconté à Alain Joubert* – Gallimard – Témoins de l'Art – 2009

Acknowledgements

Acknowledgements

The researching, writing and illustrating of this book has been made immensely easier and more enjoyable by the help and encouragement we have received from all the people who have given their time, shared their knowledge and advised us on numerous details.

So thank you...

Jojo Pous, for being the initial inspiration and for sharing so many memories with us and, Joséphine Matamoros, for your advice and corrections.

Peggy Merchez and Etienne Sabench at Céret's Museum of Modern Art for suggesting the Juan Gris painting for the front cover and for giving invaluable practical advice on illustrations as well as lending rare books for the initial research.

Claire Muchir at the Musée Rigaud, Perpignan for being a source of wisdom and help, ever patient, ever positive.

Our thanks to Yvon Berta-Maillol for his memories of Dina Vierny and of the creation of the Musée Maillol at Banyuls-sur-Mer and to his son and daughter Jean-Marie and Claire at the museum itself during our many visits there.

Thank you Olivier Lourquin, director of the Musée Maillol in Paris and President of the Foundation Dina Vierny for permission to use the evocative photograph of your mother, Dina Vierny, with Maillol taken by Louis Carré in 1943. We are grateful to Galerie Louis Carré et Cie in Paris for agreeing to its use in this book.

Thanks also to the Cellier des Dominicains, place Orphila, 66190 Collioure for the use of their wine labels and Pernod Ricard for the use of the classic Byrrh posters.

Thank you Nicolas d'Andoque for permission to use the photographs of the Abbaye de Fontfroide and to the Association du Musée d'Art Gustave Fayet for the use of further pictures.

Thanks also to Phil Monk for his sketches of Collioure and to Jenny Hill Norton for sketches inspired by her visit to the Musée Maillol in 2006.

Once again Jérôme Fricker of Les Presses Littéraires has been a constant source of enthusiasm for the entire project and our thanks go to Emilie Noguera for her design skills and patience in arranging our words and pictures on the page.

And, lastly, and far from least, thank you Sarah Cotton and Phil Monk for your encouragement, tolerance and patience over the last few years while we have been researching, discussing, writing and often enjoying the whole process of putting this book together for the Les Presses Littéraires to publish.

Sunset over the Pyrenees

278

Permissions

The authors are grateful to the following for permission to use photographs and artwork in this publication:

Cover
Juan Gris – Landscape of Céret
Courtesy Moderna Museet, Stockholm

Page 4
DUFY Raoul Œuvre © Adagp, Paris 1913
Courtesy Jojo Pous et Joséphine Matamoros

Pages 4, 11, 13, 14, 15, 16, 17, 18, 19, 20, 21, 22, 250, 251, 257, 263
Courtesy Jojo Pous et Joséphine Matamoros

Pages 6, 23, 66, 75, 97, 151
Courtesy Phil Monk

Pages 25, 163, 164, 225
Courtesy Association du Musée d'Art Gustave Fayet à Fontfroide, collection particulière. Ces documents proviennent du site internet www.gustavefayet.fr. Photographe Henri Gaud: www.editionsgaud.com

Pages 28, 36, 49, 101, 104, 203, 206
Courtesy Collection Musée des Beaux-Arts Hyacinthe Rigaud / Ville de Perpignan © Pascale Marchesan: service photo ville de Perpignan

Pages 30
Courtesy Ville de Thuir

Pages 30, 242
Courtesy Pernod Ricard

Pages 114, 122, 129, 139, 148, 164, 179, 222
Courtesy Abbaye de Fontfroide, Espace presse

Page 155
Courtesy Collection Musée d'Art Moderne de Céret, © Robert Townsend, Espagne

Page 182
1941 Louis Carré, Courtesy Louis Carré & Cie. Courtesy Bernard Lourquin.

Pages 198, 236
Courtesy Jenny Hill Norton

Pages 215, 216
Courtesy Cellier le Dominicain, Place Orphila, 66190 Collioure

Page 217
Collection Terrus – Ville d'Elne

Author
biographies

Jane Mann

Jane Mann, ex-restaurateur, photographer, seaside landlady, journalist and writer, first fell in love with Collioure in the late 80's and spent many happy holidays there. With her companion, the artist Phil Monk, she moved to the Pyrenées Orientales in 2000 and has been writing books and articles about the region ever since.

Brian Cotton

Brian Cotton worked in book publishing as international sales director before settling with his wife Sarah in the Roussillon in 2002. For some years they ran a business distributing English books to shops in the Languedoc and Provence. Now retired, he has turned author in this collaboration.

ACHEVÉ D'IMPRIMER
EN MAI 2013
DANS LES ATELIERS
DES PRESSES LITTÉRAIRES
À SAINT-ESTÈVE – 66240

D.L. : 2e TRIMESTRE 2013
N° D'IMPRIMEUR : 22186
Imprimé en France